Myth-M
Religious
and Their Roots
in Crises

ARTHUR G. NEAL *and*
HELEN YOUNGELSON-NEAL

McFarland & Company, Inc., Publishers
Jefferson, North Carolina

ISBN 978-0-7864-9858-1 (softcover : acid free paper) ∞
ISBN 978-1-4766-2131-9 (ebook)

LIBRARY OF CONGRESS CATALOGUING DATA ARE AVAILABLE

BRITISH LIBRARY CATALOGUING DATA ARE AVAILABLE

Front cover image © 2015 iStock/Thinkstock

Printed in the United States of America

*McFarland & Company, Inc., Publishers
Box 611, Jefferson, North Carolina 28640
www.mcfarlandpub.com*

Myth-Making and Religious
Extremism and Their Roots in Crises

To the graduate students in
the senior author's seminars on
Myth and Myth-Making and
The Sociology of Violence

Table of Contents

Preface

C. Wright Mills (1963) once observed that "we do not live in a world of solid fact. No such world is available." Instead, the world we live in is one that has been constructed by humans through their communication with each other. Without human interaction and some degree of consensus on the meanings derived from those interactions, there is no social reality that is known or knowable. The illusions that persist for very long periods of time are those deeply embedded in the social heritage of any given people and stem from social conventions shaped by symbols, language, norms, and other aspects of culture (Shils, 1988).

From the hominids that emerged on the plains of Africa a few million years ago, an evolutionary process resulted in the modern species of *Homo sapiens*. It was perhaps the capacity to develop a language, to create cultures, and to form social groups for engaging in problem solving that accelerated the dominance of humans within the animal kingdom. Through evolving verbal symbols that are necessary for stable systems of culture, it became possible to share experiences and to elaborate on problem-solving techniques. The emergence of a complex brain permitted knowledge to be stored in collective memories for transmission to future generations. As a result, the understandings of our time and place are comprised of images received from dead men and women we have never known and never shall meet.

It is through symbolic communication that we create a social order comprised of models and perspectives that we impose on the physical world. We may understand symbolic communication as systems of meaning by which people, objects, and events are defined, clarified, and evaluated. The created order is always fragile because both the physical and social environments fail to conform to what men and women expect of them. People must do a great deal of repair work as they respond to

1

the changes that are occurring within themselves and within their physical environments.

Peter Berger (1969) has described the cognitive and perceptual processes of the human condition as involving the dual tasks of world construction and world maintenance. Berger did not mean that humans literally construct or maintain the world, but that they face the problem of making sense out of their experience and out of the conditions of their existence.

The concept of *world construction* refers to the realities created by humans through inventing language, tools, social norms, and other aspects of culture. The realities are constructed out of the activities in which humans are engaged. But once created, these realities become endowed with factual qualities, they are experienced as objective, they are defined as the natural state of affairs. As social influences impinge on the myth-making process, thought and action, the world constructed at the individual level becomes two steps removed from the physical world. The first step involves constructing the realities at the collective level, while the second step consists of efforts of individuals to make sense out of their personal experiences.

Within any given society, *world construction* is evident in the process of developing plausible explanations about the unfolding of events. We tend to form images about the causes of illness, the changes in climate, the value of money, the existence of God, what happens after we die, the value of children, and other topics that are of concern to us. Through modern means of communication we are aware of many more events than we could experience directly and the assessments we make of these occurrences reflect the qualities of our personal lives and our relationships with others. When we regard the news as incomplete or untrustworthy, we tend to fill in the gaps with our own constructions of social reality through discussion with friends, relatives, and neighbors. Through filling in the gaps of missing information, we in effect, are constructing events by forming opinions about those happenings that enter into our awareness (Shibutani, 1966).

World maintenance consists of the social influences, controls, and supports by which people uphold definitions of reality in any given social context. A great deal of repair work is required because both societies and individuals always remain unfinished products; people frequently pursue self-interests at the expense of the group's well-being; human efforts frequently lead to frustration and failure; people make mistakes and do stupid things. In efforts at world maintenance, the social definitions of reality come to be defined as the ultimate realities of the universe and as the basis for order in human affairs (Berger, 1969).

Language is the primary vehicle humans draw upon to create and maintain their social worlds. Our uses of language shape our reality perceptions, permit us to identify and classify events in our environment, give meaning to our experiences, structure our social acts, and enable us to communicate with each other. In these processes we notice only a small portion of environmental events; most of them we ignore or give only slight notice in passing. Through naming and labeling, we create a symbolic universe and the symbols we use become the central aspects of reality as we know and understand it. In the conduct of human affairs, the symbols that are used and the objects they represent become blended inseparably in reality perceptions, in communication, and in social action.

According to the Vedantic version of Hindu philosophy, the world of apparent reality that we perceive through our senses is a world of illusions (Stevenson, 2000). Things as they appear are misleading, unreliable, and not what they seem. From this view, the problem of illusions account for everything that goes wrong with life; when things go wrong, when committed lines of action fail to work out as planned, the reason is the shifting world of illusions that cannot be depended upon. Accordingly, for many Hindu, achieving enlightenment is the highest challenge of existence and may require many lifetimes.

While humans program the world mentally in order to act meaningfully in relationship to it, there is an objective, factual world out there that exists independently of human perceptions. But obviously, humans must have accurate knowledge in order to build bridges, skyscrapers, airplanes, and atomic bombs. The limits of our empirical knowledge, however, become evident when bridges collapse, ships sink, planes crash, volcanoes erupt, and hurricanes strike. A basic feature of the human condition is that our knowledge is always partial, incomplete and not at all free from contradictions. Perhaps the best we can hope for is that the illusions we create work in our favor, rather than against us.

The myth-making aspect of religion is apparent in explanations of how the universe was created, the relationship of humans to other animals, and how men differ from women. The myth-making aspects of religion are inherent in the human condition and in the variety of attempts to deal with them. These include, for example, coping with the death crisis, the treatment of illness, and the problem of evil. Emotional involvement in these events preclude remaining indifferent.

In life we observe that there are certain events that have occurred in the past, still occur today, and will occur again in the future. Such events include illness, death, and acts of evil that have origins as varied as mental illness and religious extremism. The tragedy of these events is of such a magnitude that individuals cannot remain emotionally indifferent to them. Instead, collective myths emerge as explanations, some plausible, some less so, for explaining and dealing with such events. These myths are deeply embedded in the social heritage of any given group of people, and they stem from social conventions and are shaped by symbols, language, norms and other aspects of a given culture.

At all times and places, universal concerns are elaborated in the myth-making process, such as the relationship of humans to their physical environment and to other animals; the qualities of men and women and their relationships with each other; the desire for stability and coherence in contrast to encounters with social change and chaos. Recognizing that few things last forever, many religions come to focus their myth-making on the end of the world, personal escape from the apocalypse, and a planet without people.

Collective tragedies become endowed with sacred meanings as they are drawn upon to embellish perceptions of society as moral community. Among Americans, there are three major events that stand out above all others in shaping a national identity. These are the epic struggles of the American Revolution, the trauma of the Civil War, and the heroic undertakings in winning World War II. These events are commemorated on anniversaries and holidays. Monuments and memorials are designated to remind younger generations of the heroic sacrifices that were made for the nation.

Beliefs and practices are considered "extremist" when they are held to be infallibly correct. Through extremist mythology the complexity of the world is simplified, charismatic qualities are imputed to religious leaders, and a sharp separation is made between believers and nonbelievers. The willingness to die for a cause is perhaps the most extreme characteristic of religious extremism and has been demonstrated dramatically at Jonestown, among the Branch Davidians at Waco, and among the members of the Heaven's Gate cult. Recent examples include the hijackers of September 11, 2001, and the suicide bombers recruited by extremist Islamic cult leaders.

The chapter on terrorism can be regarded as an extension of the topic of religious extremism. Extreme forms of evil in modern consciousness include the witch trials of Western Europe, the Nazi Holocaust, war crimes, serial killers, and sex offenders. The master symbol of evil in the modern world consists of the atrocities of the Nazi Holocaust. Other examples include national policies of genocide and state terrorism.

In being "born again," a sudden transformation of the self is interpreted by religious congregations as deriving from divine intervention. However, there is no learning theory in psychology that would account for such sudden and dramatic change in self-identity. The self is the product of a long developmental process involving family, peer group, and many significant others. The developmental variables in the conversion process include finding a meaning in life, and developing a sense of membership and belonging. Religious groups socialize new members to produce dedication and commitment. The emphasis on continuity makes it difficult for members to disaffiliate once disenchantment occurs.

In contrast to the animism of primitive cultures, modern culture holds that the gap between humans and other animals is very wide. The sharp separation between humans and animals is reflected in animal insults and in other negative typifications of animals. Yet, counter expressions can be seen in the uses of animal logos among intercollegiate athletic teams and in tattooing. Drawing upon increased awareness of the many forms of cruelty to animals, activists seek to put an end to the rigid conceptual distinction between humans and other animals. Opposition is expressed toward factory farming of animals, the hunting of endangered species, and the cruel use of animals in scientific research. As an increasing number of endangered species vanish, the mythology about the relationship of humans to other animals will continue to evolve.

The Genesis account of Adam and Eve provided justifications for the rule of patrimony, and supported notions about the inferiority of women. The enduring effects of classical gender myths are reflected in the creation of modern celebrities. Modern mythology in advertising and mass entertainment has led to the commodification of the body and to the popular view that the body in its natural form is ugly. The expanding emphases on sexual pleasure and desire have generated expectations that exceed the possibility of fulfillment. The traditional definitions of male and female roles have crumbled under the weight of modern emphasis upon freedom and the liberation of women.

One of the great mysteries of the human condition is how it all got started and how it will end. Many monotheistic religions hold that creation was a product of one God who was self-created, all-powerful, all-knowing, and all-present. The creation of order out of chaos occupies a prominent place in the creation mythology of many of the world's religions. The edifices that humans create cannot endure for very long. The doomsday myth holds that the gods who were the creators of all that exists became disenchanted with the objects of their creation and decided to destroy them. Reasoning by analogy from the life cycle, our experiences with birth and death provide a miniature model of the creation and destruction of the world.

In contrast to the religious and cultural myths of the beginning and the end, many scientists hold that human life will not end from an angry god or divine intervention, but from some decidedly secular event, such as a huge asteroid colliding with the Earth, a nuclear holocaust, or a catastrophic pandemic. The scientific evidence fails to support the conclusion that the Earth is now, or ever has been, a self-evident entity. It has always been undergoing change and modification. If there are drastic changes in the world's climate, or if the natural environment becomes overly toxic, or if we are unable to develop immunity fast enough to some deadly microorganism, we may be destined to travel the route of the dinosaurs.

The book potentially includes the readership of those who followed with interest Bill Moyers's interviews with Joseph Campbell on *The Power of Myth*. The potential audience also includes those who have read with interest Peter Berger's more recent one on *In Praise of Doubt*.

The book will be especially appropriate as a text or a supplemental text on religion in sociology, psychology, anthropology, and philosophy. The organization and analysis of the book is oriented toward elaborating the imperative of myth making in contemporary social thought as well as in those cultures of historical concern to anthropologists. Thus the focus is both sociological and multicultural.

1

Why Myth-Making
Is Necessary

Myths are created to make sense out of a senseless world. It is through myth that significance is given to meaningless and chaotic events. According to the narrow view of myth, it is a story about a sacred event that is handed down from one generation to another. Indeed, some such accounts are central to the collective identity of a particular group of people. As myths are transmitted from the past, the stories become elaborated and embellished to meet the needs of the present time and place. They are indeed a part of the social heritage of any given group of people.

But the social and cultural contexts of myth involve much more than that. Myths are also the realities that are constructed anew for each generation as attempts are made to make sense out of the human condition. From the vast changes that have occurred with the developments in science and technology, the need for myth has not diminished. Instead, new myths are created to give coherence to the events that are transpiring in our time and place. The predictions from the Enlightenment were that the needs for religion, superstition, and myth would diminish as the basis for knowledge came to be grounded in the scientific method. This prediction did not come to pass. Instead, the uncertainties, the sense of incompleteness, and the chaos of the modern world has generated an even greater need for myth than before.

Within any given society, the myth-making process is evident in the development of plausible explanations about the unfolding of events about which there is a major concern. We make assumptions about cause and effect because we must if we are to live in a world that is understandable. Without the assumption of causality, events would appear to be random, haphazard, and chaotic. In this respect, we construct the world through our perceptions of it. Especially important in construct-ing a predictable world are notions about how human intentions, deci-sions, and actions are linked in shaping the course of events. Causal explanations promote an understanding, even if erroneous, of the social world and reinforce a sense of management both in the social realm and in personal lives.

The process of reality construction never ends. It is always ongoing, always developmental, always being modified and refined. New realities are created in response to changing environmental circumstances. The process is guided not so much by a concern for defining what is actually out there as it is for extracting relevant elements from the environment and elaborating on their meaning. Humans may endow rivers, moun-tains, and stones with extraordinary qualities and sacred meanings, as they have at many times and places, or they may regard them as prime examples of mundane and uninteresting things. It is for this reason that having sacred qualities is not so much an inherent attribute of anything, as that the qualities that are imputed to them along with the reverence and respect accorded to them.

Because of the social consequences of myth, it is important that the myths we live by work in our favor. Some of the prevailing myths of the modern world are dangerous and promote the interest of one seg-ment of the population at the expense of another. For example, Ashley Montagu (1998) described the race myth as *Man's Most Dangerous Myth*. Racism constitutes one of the major contradictions of the modern world. The many forms of racial discrimination and racial violence significantly qualify the pride of modern nations in the creation of civil society.

From the pluralism of the modern world, there is no longer a set of specific myths that are believed to hold vitality for all of the popula-tion. The competitions among modern mythologies play a central part in modern cultural wars and in rancorous political campaigns. Many are not at home in the modern world. The past is dead and the future is uncertain. It is the uneasiness of our times that makes myth-making necessary. We grope for something firm to hold on to from the mythical narratives and legends from the past.

Through myth-making, explanations are provided for the creation of the universe, for the emergence of human beings, for the establish-ment of relationships between human and other animals, and for how women were created to be different from men. The importance of myth is based not so much on whether it is true or false, but on whether or not it is believed, and with what intensity (Campbell, 1986). We do not really know whether most of the beliefs we hold are true or not. Instead, we assume, as we must, that our own beliefs are a valid basis for personal action.

The popular notion that myths are false beliefs is prominent in the modern world (Eliade, 1963). By this view, the myth is a false belief held by someone else. We do not recognize our own beliefs, particularly those that are central to our self-identities, as mythical. The truth of the matter is that we do not know whether most of the ideas we carry around in our heads are true or not. We act on the basis of our understanding of the world and the realities we construct as viable for reducing chaos and making coherent the unfolding of events.

Purpose, Meaning, Coherence

According to Viktor Frankl (1965), the search for meaning is the primary sustaining force in human affairs. Finding a purpose for living and sorting out those things that are important from those that are not are basic human concerns. The ingredients of the quest for meaning include determining the options available, setting priorities, and striving to attain the goals that are worthwhile. In Frankl's view there is futility in the search for an overriding sense of unity and coherence to either one's personal life or the events in one's surroundings. The basic human endeavor should be to find a more limited sense of purpose by striving for specific goals that are attainable.

The pursuit of meaning is complicated by conditions of uncertainty. Perceptions of social life as chaotic and unpredictable are evident in the lack of confidence to select and pursue social goals. Joachim Israel (1971) observed that the condition of meaninglessness is the most serious form of alienation in modern social life. In this form of alienation, the individual feels that his or her minimal standards for clarity in decision-making and understanding are not met (Seeman, 1975). Conditions of uncertainty are promoted by the increasing complexity of social life, by the rapid rates of social change, and by the perception of unpredictable futures.

In the final analysis, a sense of meaning, coherence, and purpose derives from the cultural apparatus. Individuals are born into an ongoing set of social arrangements, and their basic challenge is to find a place for themselves in the broader scheme of human affairs. Following the cultural blueprints on how to live one's life is perhaps the path of least resistance for most people. Under these conditions, the individual's behavior is predictable and understandable to others, and there is a sense of comfort with living in one's society.

Humans are doubly cursed: They know that there is a future, but they are required to live out their lives without knowing what that future has in store for them. In response to this curse, there is a universal desire to know the unknowable and to control the uncontrollable. It is for this reason that humans everywhere draw on divination to foresee future events or to discover hidden knowledge. They do so by drawing upon extraordinary, mysterious, or supernatural means.

In some cases, knowledge from divination is sought through changing the physiological or emotional state of the individual. The many religious practices for seeking assistance in the decision-making process or for obtaining information about the future include the vision quest of the Plains Indians, consulting the oracle at Delphi, or going into the wilderness for communion with God.

In other cases, divination is more fortuitous in that meanings are read into the unfolding of events that are interpreted as advanced indicators of future occurrences. These include for example, finding meaning in the appearance of a comet, seeing a black cat cross the road, sneezing, walking under a ladder, breaking a mirror, or countless other conditions that are believed to be indicators of future events. Among the Apache, the appearance of an owl in camp was taken as a sign of impending death. Less fortuitous forms of divination are found through deliberately seeking hidden information by consulting astrology columns in a newspaper, going to a palm reader, or attending a séance.

Those uncomfortable with the complexity and chaos of the modern world are susceptible to the persuasive appeals of a religious movement. As several observers have noted, those seeking a simplified answer system are among the ready converts to proselytizing movements (Neal, 1970). The pursuit of meaning from this standpoint reflects an inadequate frame of reference and derives from latent fears that one's life will fall into fragments and become meaningless. Proselytizing movements not only provide seemingly more adequate understanding of the apparent chaos, but also provide programs of action for improving on the social world, while at the same time offering an avenue to personal salvation.

Tragic Events

Regardless of how well social life is organized, it is subjected to disruption at the least expected time and in the least expected ways. Acute traumas are implicit in the human condition and can never be eliminated. When serious illness, death, or some other personal tragedy occurs, it must be dealt with in some way or another. Tragic events unfold with such a dramatic and emotional impact that ignoring them is not a relevant option. It is for this reason that coping mechanisms are called into play and it becomes imperative to link the tragic event with one's general understanding of social life.

According to Talcott Parsons (1954), the myth-making aspects of religion grow out of crisis events in which men and women are "hit" by tragic occurrences that could not have been foreseen nor circumvented. For example, this occurs with the premature death of a college student who is killed in an automobile accident. It is easy enough to understand how an automobile accident could cause the death of an individual, but not why it happened to that individual at that particular time.

Survivors must confront the emotional attachments that are altered by the death of a close friend or relative. Religious ideologies come into play in attempts to deal with this type of crisis. No major religion has been able to directly "beat death": the dead are dead and nothing can be done about that. Religions are designed to somehow help the bereaved adjust to what has occurred. Mythical interpretations of death and a denial of its finality are universal to all societies.

Premature death is but a single case of the many ways in which tragedy and unexpected outcomes grow out of the human condition. Uncertainty and a frustration of emotional investments are implicit in many fields ranging from health care to long-distance travel, from love affairs to warfare, from crop production to earthquakes and hurricanes. Through the search for meaning in tragic events, individuals do not merely "take it" when things do not go as expected. Instead, explanations are sought in attempts to understand how and why an unfortunate event occurred.

Enduring narratives from classical mythology provide modern men and women with dramatic examples of how hard things can get among humans and among the gods. From the Old Testament, we are provided with accounts from the book of Job of an extreme case of grief, suffering, and divine injustice. According to the Biblical narrative, Job was a man who had been exceptionally successful in building a life for himself and his family. He possessed much livestock and many servants. He had seven sons and three daughters and was respected by all of his neighbors. Job was a righteous man, but his virtues were put to extreme tests when his riches, his livestock, his house, and his servants were all taken away from him. His children all perished in a variety of disasters. After continuing to assert his faith in God, Job was smitten with boils and other personal calamities. Job endured these calamities without reproaching God or Divine Providence.

Over the centuries, hundreds of theologians have attempted to develop adequate explanations of the question posed by Rabbi Harold S. Kushner (1983) in his book *When Bad Things Happen to Good People*. In May 2007, there were more than 12 million entries concerning the book of Job on the Internet. Attempts to explain the tragic life of Job in view of beliefs in a just world generally lack credibility. Any conception of divine justice should lead to positive rewards for good and righteous people and punishments for those who do not follow Biblical prescriptions on what must or must not be done.

In response to the tragic death of his twelve-year-old son, Harold S. Kushner examined the narrative about Job in order to make sense out of it. His conclusions maintain that God is not all-powerful and all-knowing. In his view, God does not intervene to save good people from hurricanes and disease and does not send misfortunes to punish the wicked. Some things are circumstantial, random developments and there is no reason to look for an explanation of them. This view is consistent with the modern view that unfortunate events are chance occurrences that have nothing to do with the actual behavior of individuals.

From India, the doctrine of karma provides an alternative explanation of unfortunate events. This doctrine rejects the notion that the outcome of events could be due to blind chance. According to the Buddhist concept of karma, nothing happens to a person that is not deserved for some reason or another. The outcomes of both positive and unfortunate events stem from both past actions and present behavior. Accordingly, it is the differential karma that determines such forms of inequality as being beautiful or being ugly, being rich or being poor, being healthy or being diseased. The concept of karma does not imply fatalism or predestination, but only the view of causation that is due to present and previous lives (Casland, Cairns, and Yu, 1969).

In many traditional societies throughout the world, unfortunate events were attributed to the practice of witchcraft. Witchcraft provides a ready-made explanation of the relationship between human beings and unfortunate events. It can be applied to those outcomes that cannot be explained as due to carelessness or normal causes. Beliefs in witchcraft become convenient stereotypes to account for failures and frustrations in human endeavors. Since the evil operates through the medium of living men and women, it can potentially be brought under control so as to reinforce the normative order. In this sense, witchcraft provides convenient scapegoats for venting the frustrations of failure (Lessa and Vogt, 1979).

The Prometheus episode from Greek mythology provides a narrative about extraordinary tragedy, suffering, and punishment. Prometheus stole fire from Mt. Olympus and gave it as a gift to human beings. Zeus was furious over the unauthorized gifting of this highly valued resource that until then had only been available to the gods. In anger, Zeus had Prometheus captured and chained to a rock. By day, an eagle came, pecked out his eyes and tore at his liver. But since Prometheus was a god, he would become rejuvenated during the night. The next day the eagle would return and start over again. The myth serves as a referent for extraordinary tragedy and may be drawn upon for making our own personal problems look small by comparison. Regardless of our personal problems, it's hard to imagine anything that would match the tragedy of Prometheus.

Mechanisms of coping with stress, contradictions, and conflict are required for reducing the potentially harmful effects of social living (Pearlin and Schooler, 1978). Coping is a cognitive process of making adaptations to those situations in which conflicts cannot be directly confronted and eliminated. The individual feels that he or she is vulnerable, psychological damage can occur, and problems exist that cannot be solved through practical lines of action. Under these circumstances, coping mechanisms can be understood as subjective meanings individuals give to events in the mobilization of social and psychological resources.

The tragic events of the past provide reference points for assessing the quality of life in the present. While the emotional impact of the traumas of the past can only be experienced vicariously by the more recent generations (Landsberg, 2004), they do provide cognitive frameworks in stereotypic form for shaping what is perceived as the dangers and opportunities of the human condition. A sense of comfort may develop through recognizing that present troubles may be small ones when compared to the difficulties people faced in the past. In this respect, the collective representations in movies and television provide individuals with frameworks for locating their present lifestyles somewhere along a continuum between "the best possible" and the "worst possible" of all social worlds.

Moral Community

In his classical writings, Emile Durkheim (1961) maintained that sharing a common mythology serves a cohesive function for any particular group of people. In totemic societies, for example, it was the creation myth that provided the foundation for kinship and bound men and women together. In Durkheim's view, totemism embodied the earliest and basic ingredients of what is essential to religion and to moral community. In primitive societies, totemism provided the sacred grounds for kinship among the members of a particular clan. There were strong taboos regulating the rules of marriage and prohibiting killing, touching, or eating the totemic animal. While totemism took varied forms in many parts of the world, it provided a basic source of membership, belonging, and identity.

It is through myth-making that a moral basis is provided for keeping a society orderly. Rules are created that are binding on human conduct. Sigmund Freud (1918) maintained that the taboos against incest and in-group murder were basic to all other forms of morality. The sacred underpinnings of the normative order are such that basic norms are given supernatural sanction. Among the Inuit, the violation of a taboo was regarded as one of the major causes of illness. The violation automatically carried a supernatural sanction, whether detected by another human being or not. Taboo violation was regarded as a threat not only to the individual but also to the entire community. Through the sharing of a common framework of mythology, reinforcements were provided for cohesive social relationships.

All human beings are faced with the problem of creating and living in a moral universe. Such a cultural edifice was created by generations of men and women whom we have never met and will never meet. Yet, it was the cumulative effects of their efforts to deal with the problems of human living that led to the emergence of a normative order. It was this rule-based system that specifies what must be done and what must not be done under given circumstances. It is this moral order that provides a sense of community and a primary sense of personal identity. It is the means by which a given group of people minimizes internal conflict and obtains a basic orientation toward the world.

Collective memories of tragic events and heroic accomplishments provide the raw material for a great deal of myth making in any society. Severe crises are remembered and so deeply etched in the memories of any given group that they are embellished and elaborated as attention-getting devices for passing on the heritage of any social system. It is through the elaboration process that legendary heroes are elevated to supernatural status, and gods and demons are postulated to account for extraordinary events. Thus, myth-making provides the ingredients for the creation of a moral universe.

Collective morality enters into the awareness of individuals as attributes of communal living that they must confront as a basic reality of group living. Creating social norms is not an option available to most people; instead, norms and morality are a part of the social givens that individuals must accept as basic realities of social living. The suggestion would seem strange to us that we sit down and attempt to work out a policy statement on whether cannibalism, in-group murder, or incest should be permitted in our society. These are among the issues that have been settled in advance, and the moral solutions are transmitted through the social heritage we have received from our remote ancestors.

Since social norms and morality are created and enforced through group living, the matter of choice for the individual primarily centers on the decision of whether to comply with norms or to disregard them in the pursuit of personal goals and objectives.

The social norms that have the highest level of support within the community are those to which sacred qualities are assigned, and they are viewed as being related to the ultimate conditions of human existence. The sacred qualities of social norms are to be found in the attitudes that the community holds toward the rules of conduct. Norms become sacred in character if they are treated with a high degree of respect, if they are regarded as having supernatural support, and if they are deeply embedded in what is necessary for sustaining order and stability in one's personal life. If norms are held to be sacred, their violation has a belittling effect, and self-punishment is likely to occur even if others do not detect the violation or bring it forward for any kind of official action.

Sacred norms are internalized in the sense that they are fundamental to notions about reality and the manner in which serious mistakes can be made. Such norms often take the form of taboos, which consists of rules prohibiting us from engaging in certain lines of action. For example, the norm prohibiting the eating of human flesh is universally understood as binding on conduct. Cannibalism is so severely condemned that we can understand a violation only in terms of survival needs or mental derangement. Consuming the flesh of a deceased relative or friend is unthinkable, and if it did occur we would automatically associate it with abnormality. No sane or reasonable person would commit such an act unless the alternative was starvation, and even in a survival situation the eating of human flesh would have serious emotional consequences for most people.

Because the norm prohibiting cannibalism is so firmly held in notions about morality, the enactment of formal laws making such behavior illegal is not necessary. On the other hand, most norms are mundane in character and mainly reflect standardized operating procedures for promoting the coherence and stability of social relationships. In contrast to cannibalism, many regard the law that sets the speed limit at 55 miles per hour as so arbitrary and secular that it may be violated with impunity. Nevertheless, the laws regulating the speed of automobiles do constitute social norms since they are enforceable and are oriented toward the standardization of behavior. The final sources of authority on what constitutes a social norm do not reside with the individual but with group sanctions that regulate the rules of conduct.

By growing up in a given society, we become aware of the many norms that specify what we should or should not do in given situations. We are clearly aware of the norms prohibiting murder, kidnapping, armed robbery, having sex with genetic relations, and excessive drinking of alcoholic beverages. But there are numerous norms that lack such clarity as guidelines for conduct. The complexity of modern society includes such a diversity of experiences with group living that there are often serious disagreements on what the norms actually are and on what kinds of punishment are appropriate if norms are violated. From the pluralism of modern life, we often find ourselves in situations in which we cannot assume that others share our own understanding of norms, values, and morality. We frequently enter into social relations with some degree of suspicion and distrust of the motives and behavior of others.

New Beginnings

Myths become modified and altered through their transmission from one generation to another. Each new generation is required to take the social heritage from the past and rework it in order to fit the circumstances of their own time and place. It is for this reason that the communities humans create do not endure. There may be a desire for permanence and stability, but the basic realities are those of social change. With the passing of time the edifices that we have created crumble as though they rested on a foundation of sand. The challenge is that of creating new mythologies that work in our favor.

There are certain periods of intellectual fervor when efforts are directed toward making a new world (Glendon, 2001). Such periods give rise to innovative forms of mythology. New styles of mythology serve as the intellectual background for moving social systems in innovative directions and for the mobilization of collective efforts. The 17th and 18th centuries in Western Europe provided the context for setting into motion the historical forces that produced the modern world. The ideas emanating from the Enlightenment were foremost among the historical developments of modernity (Neal, 2007). The new mythologies included the Protestant Reformation, the industrial revolution, the growth and development of science, and the creation of civil society. In combination, these new ways of looking at the world contributed to breaking the dominance of society by feudal landlords and corrupt church officials.

The voyage of Columbus and the discovery of the Americas galvanized an emerging new mythology in Western Europe (May, 1991). Attention was directed outwardly to a broader world as a potential source of wealth and new opportunities for adventure and discovery. The voyage of Columbus was seen by some clerics as part of God's plan to give the people of Europe an opportunity for a new beginning. The events set in motion by the discovery of the Americas was so dramatic that it would have seemed implausible if it hadn't really happened (Aronson and Glenn, 2007).

Following the conquest of the Aztecs and the Incas, the conquistadors brought back to Spain ships loaded with plundered gold. The mythology of vast riches in the New World became widespread, and serious expeditions were organized to find them. For example, the Spanish explorer Coronado led an expedition well into the interior of North America looking for the "lost cities of gold." While he failed to find the

elusive cities of gold, he did carve out a vast territory for Spanish domination (Rutter, 2005).

The search for "the fountain of youth" undergirded the expedition
of Juan Ponce de Leon in 1513 to what is present-day Florida. The myth
of the "water of life" was widespread in human history, from ancient
societies up to the Age of Discovery. Ponce de Leon had heard of the
fountain from the people of Puerto Rico when he conquered the island.
Apparently, every river, lagoon, and brook along the Florida coast was
searched for the restorative powers of the magical waters that would
reverse the aging process and thus promote immortality (Morrison, 1974).

The appeals of mass migrations throughout human history have
been enhanced by visions of a "promised land" and opportunities for
creating a better life. The myth of the frontier and the myth of Manifest
Destiny were among the many energizing myths in the settlement of the
American West (Slotkin, 1994). The fantastic newspaper accounts following the discovery of gold in 1848 at Sutter's Mill in California precipitated a mass migration of enormous proportions (Starr, 2005). In
response to what was subsequently known as "gold fever," about 400,000
miners migrated to the state of California. Thousands sailed around
Cape Horn in order to get to California; others cut the 12,000-mile trip
from the East Coast in half by crossing the Isthmus of Panama; and yet
others traveled overland by wagon train. By both land and sea, the trip
to the gold fields was fraught with danger. While only a few found the
elusive gold, the real harvest was in rich farmland and in helping to pop-
ulate the Pacific West (Rutter, 2005).

The way in which behavior is driven by ideology is well illustrated
in Henry Nash Smith's analysis in *Virgin Land* of the American westward
movement. Pioneers in search of rich and fertile land that was available
for the taking facilitated the settlement of the West. The frontier
appeared as a salvation for those with troubled lives, as well as for those
who had a preference for the natural environment over the artificiality
of civilization (Smith, 2005). The Oregon Trail was developed as one of
the main migration routes on the North American continent. The wagon
trail from Missouri to Oregon was 2,170 miles long, spanning a vast territory that was later to become the states of Kansas. Nebraska, Wyoming,
and Idaho (Slotkin, 1994).

The phrase "Manifest Destiny" has been used to capture a great
deal of the ideology surrounding the confiscation of Indian lands and
the settlement of the Western United States. The doctrine served as a

justification for extending the American empire from the Atlantic seaboard to the Pacific Ocean. Complex ideas, policies, and actions were incorporated under the label of Manifest Destiny (Tuveson, 1968). Among them were the beliefs that the American people and their institutions were virtuous and favored by God. Further, the nation's primary mission was to spread their democratic institutions and remake the world in the image of the United States.

Those most disenchanted with present circumstances are disproportionately among those who find the myth of new beginnings to be especially appealing. The promise of a better life is to be found in all mass migrations and in all proselytizing social movements. Rather than surrendering to an attitude of despair, religious extremism serves as a buffer against just giving up. Renouncing one's citizenship by going to live permanently in some other country is an attractive alternative to remaining and enduring a sense of estrangement from one's society and the culture it manifests (Neal, 2007). The millions of immigrants who gave up their citizenship in Europe and came to the Americas were energized by the exuberance of the mythology surrounding the opportunity for a new beginning.

We are now on the cusp of yet unforeseen beginnings both on earth and beyond to outer space. Explorations of outer space have produced new and impressive visions of the universe. Here on earth, some of the new frontiers of the modern world are being shaped by the developments in science and technology. Yet others would argue that it is developments in mass communication and mass entertainment that are shaping the newness of modern culture. But in the final analysis, new forms of knowledge and perspectives are expanding all basic social institutions.

2

The Myth-Making
Process

Traumatic events are symbolic in the sense that they represent much more than is directly visible (Duncan, 1968). They grow out of the ambiguous forces and remote dimensions of a social system. A great deal of reflection is required for an extraordinary event to be understood and made coherent (Browne and Neal, 2001). The consequences as well as the causes of traumatic events must be evaluated. Is the event in question an advanced indicator of additional calamities to come? Or is the event simply an ephemeral occurrence that will pass in significance as the general population returns to business as usual? Immediate responses are oriented toward juxtaposing the abnormal event against the normality of everyday life.

Collective memories of traumatic events may be understood as forms of myth-making. Their significance lies less in their accuracy than in the meanings they have for adherents. We construct the world into systems of meaning that can be drawn upon as the need arises (Berger, 1969). The creation of a myth is a pragmatic activity as accounts of tragic events are drawn upon for self-serving purposes. Myths are useful in sustaining personal identities and commitments as well as in supporting a political policy or in documenting the urgency of avoiding a particular line of action. As forms of myth, however, collective memories also become endowed with sacred meanings as they are drawn upon to embellish perceptions of society as a moral community (Durkheim, 1961).

It is through myth-making that societies become endowed with sacred meanings. These sacred meanings have been described by Benedict Anderson (2001) as ingredients for designating the national state as an "imagined community." Modern societies extend over large geographical areas and embrace millions of people. They are bound together by the authority of the state which holds a society together through some combination of coercion and consensus. The emphases on "national unity" and "national identity" are drawn upon to gloss over an enormous range of diversity, pluralism, and cultural conflict.

Prior to the printing press and the widespread use of the written word, mythologies were primarily transmitted by means of oral history. Through the myth-making process, group experiences were passed on from one generation to the next. Stories were told about heroic times and the moral foundations of society. Some degree of social continuity was provided by oral traditions in which narratives were often embellished in order to have a dramatic effect on listeners. New generations were provided with frames of reference for deciding what to do and what not to do in given situations. Then as now, mythical accounts provided the ingredients for shaping a collective identity. The sacred and the secular became inseparable.

Today, we have newspapers, formal documents, photographs, computers, and other sophisticated devices for storing information that may be retrieved when the need arises (McLuhan, 1962). Recorded history provides us with access to information about the collective traumas of the past, how attempts were made to solve what seemed to be overwhelming problems, and the outcomes that resulted. Collective memories serve as a storehouse of knowledge that goes far beyond the information that is stored in the brains of living men and women. The importance of the data from the past, however, is not self-evident; it must be interpreted, given credibility, and constructed along lines that give it applicability to present concerns.

Humans take an active part in determining what their collective memories will be. Events are fashioned through a filtering of experiences. Some experiences are dismissed, while others are elaborated and given high levels of significance. Selective inattention and forgetting is a way of minimizing the risk of cluttering memories with information that is perceived to be trivial or irrelevant. In contrast, we tend to remember what we sense as important for us to remember. Individually and collectively we seek to repeat those activities that were rewarding in the past and to avoid those activities that were associated with pain and suffering. Memories of how a social system was damaged by a traumatic event serve as a reminder of what to avoid in the future.

National traumas provide the raw material for a vast amount of cultural elaboration. The hundreds, even thousands of books, movies, and television productions devoted to national traumas reflect the many ways in which Americans remember their past (Lowenthal, 1985). Like all other societies, our society must pass its heritage from one generation to the next and prepare people for the challenges of changing conditions. The expansive scope of the entertainment industries in serving this function is evident. Collective memories are drawn upon to tap a responsive chord in mass audiences. The self-attitudes, emotions, and predispositions of the viewers and readers shape and refine the content and the entertainment value of the production.

Universally, the ingredients of trauma involve some form of bafflement, some level of suffering, and perceptions of evil in human affairs. The bafflement grows out of an encounter with chaos and an attendant loss of a sense of coherence (Douglas and Wildavsky, 1983). Perceptions of evil reflect the frustration of human effort and an awareness that one's own sense of morality and decency is not shared with others. Because of the suffering engendered by trauma, individuals are unable to remain emotionally detached or indifferent. Experiences suggest that to be human is to be vulnerable and that efforts directed toward mastery and control over events are limited in their effectiveness.

The crises precipitating a collective trauma are of two types. One consists of an acute crisis that impinges upon the normal course of events in an abrupt and dramatic fashion. The acute crisis is an unscheduled event in the sense that it falls outside the range of harmony and order within the social system. Acute crises include such events in the American experience as the firing on Fort Sumter by Confederate forces at the beginning of the Civil War, the assassination of President Abraham Lincoln, the Japanese attack on Pearl Harbor, and the terrorist attacks on the United States. While these events were abrupt disruptions of the social order, they were not isolated events. A great deal of collective stress and tension preceded each of them. However, they were generally perceived as resembling "a bolt out of the blue."

The second type of crisis is chronic, enduring, and long-lasting. A chronic crisis lacks the dramatic beginning of an acute crisis, but builds in intensity with the passing of time. This is the type of crisis that grows out of persisting conditions within the social system. Rather than a volcano-like intrusion into an otherwise orderly system, a chronic crisis grows out of enduring conflicts and the emergence of a crisis of authority. The persistence of Jim Crow policies, the Great Depression, and the duration of the Vietnam War are each prime examples of chronic crises in the social realm. Other examples include the damage to the environment from industrial pollution and an increasing number of endangered species.

An extraordinary event becomes traumatic under conditions in which the social system is disrupted to such a magnitude that it commands the attention of all major subgroups of the population. Even those who are usually apathetic and indifferent to social affairs are drawn into the public arena of discussion and debate. The social fabric is under attack, and people pay attention because the consequences appear to be so great that they cannot be ignored. Holding an attitude of benign neglect or cynical indifference is not a reasonable option.

When a trauma intrudes into our lives, ordinary time seems to stop, and everyday pursuits are temporarily put on hold. The social equilibrium has been upset and engagement in a continuous flow of activities has become problematic. The tragic occurrence is replayed over and over as individuals seek to understand what has happened and why it happened. Through becoming a marker in the lives of individuals, it provides a framework similar to the way in which primitive peoples measured time without clocks or watches. Events that occurred prior to the trauma become mentally separated from the events that occurred after the trauma. This is typically the case when the trauma is of the magnitude of the Japanese attack on Pearl Harbor, the assassination of President Kennedy, or the terrorist attack on the World Trade Center. Turning points occurred in the nation and in the lives of individuals.

Shaping a National Identity

Among Americans, there are three major events that stand out above all others in shaping a national identity: the epic struggles of the American Revolution; the trauma of the Civil War; and the heroic undertakings in winning World War II. Each required extensive personal sacrifices and permanently changed the content of what it means to be an American. Taking an active approach toward mastery and control over events through the pooling of collective resources became embedded in national consciousness. The creation of heroic and legendary figures to symbolize the aspirations of the nation provided sources of inspiration for future generations (Brokaw, 1998).

The trauma of the American Revolution helped to shape the identity of Americans as separate from the British. The Revolution is remembered as a time in which the colonists were oppressed by the British and in which pleas for the redress of grievances fell upon deaf ears. Some of the more militant colonists came to the conclusion that nothing short of a revolution was a viable alternative. Of the many events of the Revolution, few are remembered as vividly as the suffering at Valley Forge and the signing of the Declaration of Independence. Through the Declaration of Independence the moral basis for the Revolution was grounded in the notion that any given group of people have an inalienable rights to alter or abolish a government that is perceived to be unjust. Government, it was argued, exists for the benefit of the governed. The revolutionary ideology held that the right to "life, liberty, and the pursuit of happiness" permitted overthrowing an alien and tyrannical government. The suffering at Valley Forge became emblematic of the long and difficult struggle through which our Founding Fathers emerged victoriously.

While the Declaration of Independence established the revolutionary identity of Americans, it was the development of the Constitution that permitted an opportunity for a fresh start in building a new nation (Lipset, 1963). The Constitution built upon collective sentiments about what a government should be like after the Revolution was over. Guaranteeing certain liberties to all citizens and giving all men the right to vote could downplay elitist values and social class privileges. The new nation emphasized the personal dignity of the individual, drew upon the integrity of the common man, and permitted popular democracy to play a major role in shaping the policies of the nation. The pride of Americans in their new nation provided the foundations for a new national identity built upon revolutionary and democratic principles.

The second major event in shaping American national identity was the Civil War. The nation became deeply divided over the issues of slavery, states' rights, and our revolutionary heritage. The firing on Fort Sumter represented the beginning of an insurrection that would eventually result in the bloodiest war the world had ever known (Faust, 2008). The emotionality surrounding the issues of the Civil War became so intense that the war became a sacred crusade for both the North and the South. The crosses at Arlington, Gettysburg, Antietam, and many other places serve as a grim reminder of what can happen when mass armies meet on the field of battle. It was the Civil War in its many phases and consequences that constituted the dominant historical experience of Americans during the nineteenth century. It was through the coercive power of the state that the unity of the nation was confirmed and reestablished.

Following the Civil War, the assassination of President Lincoln provided the nation with one of its major heroic figures for all times (Naveh, 1993; Schwartz, 1982). The sanctification of Lincoln placed his image on a par with that of the first president. While Washington played a major role in shaping the identity of Americans, Lincoln came to symbolize the leadership of a coherent and organic nation that could not be torn asunder by insurrection. Notions of America as "a confederacy of nations" or as "a league of nations" were firmly rejected. As a result of the heroic and protracted struggles of the Civil War, Lincoln's presidency came to symbolize heroic sacrifices, emancipation, and military victory in affirming the unity of the nation. In the creation of President's Day as a national holiday, Lincoln stands alongside Washington as a major president to be remembered. The traumas and triumphs of the Civil War remain at the forefront of the collective identity of Americans.

A third major trauma for shaping the national identity of Americans grew out of the Japanese attack on Pearl Harbor. The integrity of the United States had been assaulted and the effects were electrifying. The collective sharing of a sense of sadness and a sense of anger produced nationally unprecedented feelings of cohesion, membership, and community. Now that we were at war, we were involved in an historical struggle of epic proportions. The nation was militarily unprepared, and there was uncertainty over what the outcome would be. Previous opposition to involvement in the war vanished, and virtually all Americans reflected on the part they would play in the national objective of winning the war. Group differences that had divided the nation disappeared, or were suspended, as all segments of the population became engrossed in the historical undertaking. National symbols came to be endowed with special sacred meanings. Chills ran up the spines of many Americans as Kate Smith sang "God Bless America." The nation became unified with an unprecedented level of intensity. The war effort became a moral crusade.

The national identity of Americans became permanently altered from the trauma of the war experience (Mosse. 1990). While other countries had suffered far more fatalities and greater damage to their infrastructure, Americans believed that it was their contribution that resulted in the decisive defeat of Nazi Germany and the Empire of Japan. The United States came out of the war strong economically and militarily. The other countries of the world did not. The United States had been thrust into a position of world leadership.

The problems of the world had become our problems. The psychological separation of the United States from the rest of the world went by the wayside. We had supplied the resources that were necessary for winning World War II, and we had the resources for rebuilding the post-war world. The world had become more interdependent and we had found a new place for ourselves among the nations within it. Advances in technology had made all of the areas of the world accessible, and Americans had come to occupy center stage on the world scene. It was no longer a viable option, nor was it seen as desirable, for the United States to maintain a position of aloofness from the rest of the world.

All collective traumas have some bearing on national identity (Edkins, 2003). While in some cases national trauma results in enhancing a sense of unity within a society, there are other cases in which collective traumas have fragmenting effects. Feelings of alienation or social cohesion depend in some measure on the predictions that are made about the outcome of events. For example, during the early years of the American Revolution, the outcome was by no means self-evident. Had the British suppressed the insurgency, the heroic figures that now loom larger than life would have been designated as criminals and punished accordingly. Had the American Civil War resulted in a victory for the Confederacy, we would now have two nations, rather than one. The implications are clear that there is little inevitability in the outcome of historical events. Through the epic struggles of the American Revolution and the Civil War we came to recognize more clearly what it means to be an American.

Generations

As new generations confront the problems of their time and place, the inventory of data from the past is reevaluated. Some experiences from the past become embellished and elaborated in attempts to give them contemporary relevance. Other experiences are relegated to the dustbin of history because they are no longer perceived as useful. It is perhaps because of the human life cycle that societies retain their innovative potential (Mannheim, 1952). New members are added to a social system and older members die off. Through the replacement of members, societies take on dynamic qualities and reflect opportunities for new beginnings.

In popular culture and mass entertainment, myth-making is reflected in the many ways stories are told to new generations about their historical past. In movies, television programs, and fictional writings, storytelling takes an embellished form. Whatever events occurred in the past are now immortalized, and those who tell stories about them are free to shape them as they wish (Grainge, 2003). The constraints surrounding events as they unfolded no longer apply. Plausibility to the reading and viewing audience is of more concern than historical accuracy.

Through mass communications, the historical experiences of specific subgroups of the population are universalized (Landsberg, 2004). For example, the experiences of slavery and the Holocaust are no longer specific to subgroups of the population. The public awareness generated by the drama of movies and novels make them a part of the remembrances of mass audiences. Each reveal the atrocities humans are capable of imposing on each other. Yet the direct traumatic experiences of any one generation can only be transmitted in a highly modified form. Younger generations cannot fully appreciate the emotionality of the direct experiences of their parents and grandparents with news of the assassination of President Kennedy or the Japanese attack on Pearl Harbor.

The members of a generation are influenced disproportionately by what was happening historically during their formative years (Mannheim, 1952). While we cannot say with precision what the boundaries are for the formative years, they would seem to be primarily the years of late adolescence and early adulthood. These are the years in which major life decisions are being made at the individual level about continuing one's education, selecting a career, entering the labor force, getting married, and becoming a parent. The large number of decisions in early adulthood place individuals in positions of hyper-receptivity to the events that are occurring within their communities and the nation. Personal encounters with collective traumas during the formative years tend to have a disproportionate effect on any given generational unit (Neal, 1998).

Sociologists have observed that for an event to have a generational effect it must have an enduring place in the memories of those who experienced it during their formative years (Schuman and Scott, 1989). The emotional impact of the event must be of sufficient magnitude for it to be remembered in a similar way by a large number of people (Brown and Kulik, 1977). Further, the event must generate a sufficient level of public attention that people have a pressing need to develop attitudes and beliefs about it. Subjected to these criteria, the historical events of the twentieth century that have had the more enduring effects on generational memories include the Great Depression of the 1930s, the epic struggles of World War II, the assassination of President Kennedy, the Civil Rights Movement, the collective frustrations over the Vietnam War, and the terrorist attack on 9–11–2001. Other traumas had intense emotional effects on the nation, but were of shorter duration and had less lasting effects on collective memories (Kertzer, 1983).

Those entering early adulthood during the Great Depression of the 1930s had direct experiences with high rates of unemployment and economic hardship. Through knowing what scarcities were like, they became oriented toward saving, investing, and accumulating assets (Elder, 1974). The economic prosperity of the post–World War II era was not taken for granted but seen as an opportunity to increase one's sense of economic security. An increase in income level was seen as an opportunity to prepare for the lean years that might lie ahead. Swings in the business cycle were recurrent concerns, since there was no way of knowing in any given case how far the recessionary swing would go. Perhaps more than previous generations, there was an interest in building wealth in order to achieve financial security and to pass on assets to the next generation to provide for the financial security of children and grandchildren. In contrast, the generation entering into adulthood during the 1950s and 1960s had direct experience with economic abundance and tended to take access to the good life for granted. They tended to see the older generation as overly materialistic and money-oriented (Feuer, 1969). They were more concerned with following impulse tendencies, seeking self-actualization, and making extensive use of consumer credit. "Spend now and pay later" became an accepted practice for this privileged generation. Self-actualization became a more prevalent concern, and hedonistic behavior tended to take priority over long-range financial planning.

Anniversaries and Holidays

The commemoration of heroic events by people dispersed throughout the country is promoted through the news media's giving recognition to anniversaries and the creation of national holidays. Not only does a holiday permit commemoration throughout the nation, it also provides a structure for selectively remembering the traumas and glories of the past. Dwelling routinely on tragic events would reflect a morbid form of anxiety and would be regarded as pathological. Yet those events that had an extraordinary emotional impact on a society cannot be easily dismissed or completely ignored. For this reason, special anniversaries are set aside as times for reflection on the event in question. Reflection is especially necessary for those events that remain unsettled or incomplete.

There are several patriotic holidays in which the unity of the nation is asserted. These include Presidents' Day, Memorial Day, the Fourth of July, and Veterans Day. The holiday is a "holy day" in some respects, but not others. The recreational aspects of holidays suggest their secular character. The running of the Indianapolis 500 on Memorial Day is a prime example of the secular character of holidays. The more intense traumas of the nation are given recognition in setting aside a day of remembrance.

Lloyd Warner's (1962) analysis of Memorial Day is especially relevant to issues related to the sacred character of national holidays. Memorial Day originated in the years following the Civil War as a way to give recognition to the military dead who had served in the Union army. Subsequently, the ceremony was extended to give recognition to those who died for the South as well as for the North. Today, Memorial Day is designed to give recognition to the military dead of all wars. In Drew Galpin Faust's (2008) study of death in the American Civil War, she notes that 620,000 lost their lives in the war at a time the total population of the United States was only thirty-one million. The fatalities of the Civil War exceeded those of all previous wars as well as the future American casualties of World War II and Korea.

Families and friends of the military dead continue to suffer long after a war is over. The sacred symbols drawn upon in the celebrations include the flag, the cross, the red poppy, and the countless objects that stand for more than they really are. The symbols and speeches are designed to invigorate such values as patriotism, duty to one's country, protecting and defending the democratic way of life, and making sacrifices for one's country.

The designation of Martin Luther King's birthday as a national holiday was a way of giving formal recognition to the importance of social justice in the life of the nation. The personal charisma of King came to be associated with his effectiveness as the leader of the Civil Rights Movement. Through his building of a biracial coalition, the entire nation became involved in putting an end to Jim Crow legislation and to the many forms of racial discrimination in the public sector. In recognition of his courageous leadership in the nation's march toward freedom and justice, the memorial to Martin Luther King was located in the National Mall in a vista between the memorials to Lincoln and Jefferson.

For more than 200 years, the speeches delivered on the Fourth of July have served to rejuvenate the values associated with American society as a moral community. The annual commemorations of the Revolution permit a blending of secular with sacred values, linking personal sacrifices with promoting the collective good and expressing devotion to our Founding Fathers. While the specific content of the speeches vary from year to year, all are directed toward promoting the notion that there is a source of unity to American consciousness that cuts across the multiple groups and vested interests within the nation. In view of the heterogeneity of the United States in terms of race, ethnicity, social class, and religion, many foreign observers have been puzzled by the depth of the American belief that there is a common national consensus, almost of a sacred nature, that binds Americans together.

Both the United States and Japan had difficulties with the question of how to properly remember Hiroshima on the fiftieth anniversary of the bombing. The event had such a lasting impact on each of the countries, indeed upon the rest of the world, that some form of remembrance seemed necessary. The trauma of the nuclear holocaust for Japan had become ingrained in collective memories, taking priority over any feelings of humiliation and shame that may otherwise have resulted from losing the war. Americans had their revenge for the surprise attack on Pearl Harbor, while the Japanese were made keenly aware of the negative consequences of permitting the military to gain control of their society.

A storm of protest emerged in Japan in response to plans by the U.S. Post Office to issue a stamp portraying the mushroom cloud over Hiroshima. The stamp had disturbing implications and was regarded as an insult to modern Japan. It commemorated a glorious victory for Americans without considering questions about the appropriateness of using such a weapon on a civilian population. When many Americans agreed with the Japanese, the Post Office canceled plans to issue the stamp.

Monuments and Memorials

Monuments and memorials are designed to give special recognition to great men and women, to selectively elaborate on heroic undertakings, and to acknowledge personal sacrifices for the benefit of the nation. Memorials are created as a form of commemoration for rejuvenating cultural values and promoting images of society as a moral community. For these reasons, the commemoration of public events endow them with sacred meanings and result in the blending of national sentiments with religious ideologies (Bellah, 1975).

In the process of creating memorials, a mixture of selective recall and selective distortion tends to operate. War monuments and memorials typically gloss over the tragedies and horrors of war. The urge to find some higher level of meaning for the suffering leads to justifications for the sacrifices and the losses. The horror of war is replaced by an emphasis on its glory. Encounters with death and destruction are diminished through an emphasis on the sacred task of defending the nation. The speeches at sacred shrines on Memorial Day, the 4th of July, and Veterans Day are all designed to enhance patriotic values through the glorification of war. Emphasis is placed on the men and women who "voluntarily" sacrificed their lives for their country. The underlying meaning seems to be that Americans should be willing to make personal sacrifices for promoting the collective good.

In contrast to previous wars, notions about the proper way to remember the Vietnam War were problematic. The casualties and atrocities of the war and the errors in political judgment were sufficiently painful that most Americans simply wanted to forget about it and move on. Yet the trauma of the war was such that it could not be swept away. Forgetting about it, or denying that it occurred, was not a reasonable option. The mistakes of the war had become a part of the American experience. It was the pressures from the veterans themselves that resulted in the creation of the Vietnam Veterans Memorial. The subtle symbolism of the memorial captures the trauma of the war and permits millions who visit the wall each year to reflect in their own way on the lessons and meanings of the war (Wagner-Pacifici and Schwartz, 1991).

Memories of World War II and the Vietnam War are still vivid in American consciousness, while the Korean War has been described as a "forgotten war." It may be that we remember the wars that provide us with glorious victories or embarrassing defeats, but a war that resulted in a stalemate is hardly worth remembering. When the Korean War ended, the boundaries were drawn at about the same place they had been drawn when the war started. The war was not looked upon as a "real war," but only as a "police action" under the auspices of the United Nations. Despite the fierce battles and the more than 50,000 American fatalities, the Korean War never became a trauma to the nation. Thus, it is not the objective consequences of an event in terms of pain and suffering that makes an event worth remembering, but its impact on the institutional structure of society. During the Korean War, we were neither threatened by an external invasion nor did the war result in deep divisions within the nation. It was a war that provided very little to celebrate or memorialize.

The Vietnam Veterans Memorial, Kennedy's gravesite at Arlington Cemetery, the Tomb of the Unknown Soldier, the Lincoln Memorial, Mount Rushmore, the Martin Luther King Memorial, the Civil War battlegrounds, Pearl Harbor, and the Little Bighorn battlefield are among the frequently visited tourist attractions each year. While by purely objective criteria, these are mundane places and there is nothing particularly special about them, the meanings imputed to them are of a different order. For example, studies of tourists at the Vietnam Veterans Memorial indicate that most visitors have an intensely emotional reaction resembling a sacred or a religious experience. They see themselves in the mirrored reflections on the wall, and whether they opposed or supported the war, they are not able to remain indifferent.

Only a small percentage of Americans make a deliberate pilgrimage to national shrines. More often, a visit to a sacred shrine is a bonus to a vacation. Visiting a monument, memorial, shrine, or museum becomes something to do when convenient.

If one is driving along Interstate 90, a side trip to Mount Rushmore, to the saloon where Wild Bill Hickock was killed, or to the Custer battleground at the Little Bighorn becomes a way to break up the monotony of the trip; however, beneath the superficiality of these visits, there are important latent meanings that are evoked.

The meanings assigned to the Little Bighorn, for example, are richly varied for the many tourists who stop there. For some, the Custer battleground evokes reflections on what is perceived as an American policy of genocide toward an indigenous people; for others it elicits images of Custer as a hero or as a villain; for yet others it is seen as a major military victory by Native Americans who were attempting to protect their tribal lands. In some cases, the reflection may be as specific as imagining the stench of the decaying corpses that were encountered by those assigned to the burial detail. Linking personal lives with historical circumstances is thus a selective process.

We may ask, why undergo the inconvenience of long-distance travel to experience memorials in remote places? We could learn about historical places and events by reading about them, by watching videos, movies, or television programs, or by surfing the Internet. Why travel rather than use some other forms of information-seeking behavior? A partial answer is that being there provides more of an authentic experience than can be derived from reading a book or watching television. Books are abstract and the television experience is vicarious and illusory in a way in which direct encounters are not. While television is much more than moving dots on an electronic screen, it provides only an incomplete experience.

The quest for authentic experiences and knowledge bears an affinity to pilgrimages and the sacred journeys that were prominent at other times and places. The pilgrimages of the past, as well as those of today, offer opportunities for establishing a sense of personal linkage with a set of ultimate values. The sacred journey facilitates separating the genuine from the spurious, the illusion from the reality, and the authentic from the inauthentic. People need to actively participate in a meaningful cosmos in order to satisfy both the needs of the body and the needs of the soul.

3

Religious Extremism

Congress shall make no law respecting an establishment of religion, or prohibiting the free exercise thereof; or abridging the freedom of speech, or the press; or the right of the people peacefully to assemble, and to petition the government for a redress of grievances.
—First Amendment, United States Constitution

The aim of the Founding Fathers was to create a civil society for permitting citizens to become engaged in civic participation on a widespread basis. They did not see establishing a specific state religion for everyone as desirable. Thus, the nonestablishment of a state church became a constitutional guarantee and an assurance that no one particular religion could be imposed on everyone else. The Founders saw a democracy as permitting all segments of the population to become involved in promoting social interests, influencing the course of events, and setting national priorities. The sense of well being was believed to be associated with the feeling among individuals that they could shape their own destinies through their own efforts. The social system was seen as benefiting from grass-roots participation in setting national priorities and mobilizing resources in their attainment. Individuals would be permitted to follow their own religious proclivities or, if they wished, to have no religion at all.

Religion in modern society is not only separated from the state but also from other institutions and the secular affairs of the society. Religious pluralism is reflected in the emergence and development of many groups and organizations. The lack of agreement on such ultimate concerns as the meaning of life and death has resulted in the proliferation of many denominations, sects, and cults, and many more are being established with each passing year. The many claims for the perfectibility of individuals and society, and the validity of one set of claims as compared to others, cannot be resolved at the collective level. Given the relativism of religious beliefs and practices (Berger, 1969), religion becomes primarily a matter of personal choice, and individuals are legally required to tolerate those who make choices that differ from their own.

The separation of church and state is a recurrent issue in our public schools. Controversies over teaching of the theory of organic evolution, over the appropriateness of prayers in the public schools, and over the moral appropriateness of specific library books and textbooks are intermittent ones. In the courts, the issue becomes one of the limits of the separation of church and state and the appropriateness of one religious group attempting to impose their own moral standards on everyone else. From the standpoint of professional educators, the issue is one of who has the right to decide on the educational content of what is being taught. Educators must have the right to draw upon their own expertise if they are to effectively carry out the responsibilities of the educational process.

We are using the term "religious extremism" to refer to beliefs and practices that are fanatical. Beliefs are fanatical if they are held to be infallibly correct and if there is an organized attempt to impose them on the rest of society. This is associated with the intolerance of beliefs and moral convictions that differ sharply from one's own. Such a view represents a rejection of the rights guaranteed by the First Amendment and a dedication to restricting the rights of others to pursue alternative beliefs and opportunities.

Religious extremism is also reflected in a personal willingness to die for a cause. Nearly all religious martyrs fall into this category, as well as others who voluntarily take extraordinary risks in standing up for what they believe in. The willingness to die for a cause is surrounded by overtones of religiosity, sacred values, and perceptions of God's approval (Stern, 2003). Few are able to adequately understand the motives of religious extremists who are willing to die for a cause. With the increasing secularization of modern society, deep commitments to any form of sacred values have become limited.

Instead of engaging the intellect to struggle with the mysteries of existence or the challenges of living in an imperfect world, extremist religious groups insist on blind obedience among their followers. Charles Kimball (2002) observed "veneration of a religious leader becomes dangerous when that leader has unrestricted power and total control." A major example of blind obedience to a charismatic authority figure occurred with the mass suicide among the followers of Reverend Jimmy Jones in the jungle of Guyana in 1978. Other examples of extreme obedience include the Branch Davidian followers of David Koresh at Waco, Texas, and the followers of the Heaven's Gate cult who took their cues from each other in committing suicide in San Diego.

Symbolic Crusades

Extremist religious movements build on and dramatize the strains and contradictions built into modern social living. Being modern implies being up-to-date in one's thinking, making judgments about how the present differs from the past, and recognizing that changes and trends are occurring in the social realm. In some cases modern ideas stand in opposition to tradition and offer challenges to customary practices and existing institutions. While men and women often desire permanence and stability, they necessarily encounter the inevitable realities of instability and change.

The rapid rates of change in modern society are accompanied by selective perceptions of moral decay and the degeneration of social life. It is within this context that cherished beliefs and values are being challenged by new lifestyles and new moralities. For example, Jerry Falwell responded to the terrorist attack of September 11, 2001, by claiming that the destruction of the towers of the World Trade Center represented the voice of God. Falwell claimed that we were being told of God's displeasure with abortion, homosexuality, pornography, and other aspects of moral degeneration (Kimball, 2002). The attempt to stem what is perceived as "the tides of wickedness" frequently develops into a moral "crusade." Members of the crusade insist that their own conceptions of right and wrong must be accepted and applied by the rest of society (Gusfield, 1963). Crusades against the evils of alcoholism, pornography, abortion, and gay marriage are oppositional movements that view the authority structure as being too lenient and permissive. Crusades direct efforts toward upholding moral mandates, restoring traditional values, and restraining the forces of evil.

Joseph Gusfield (1963) described the process of pooling resources and creating a social movement to revive and perpetuate a lifestyle as a symbolic crusade. It becomes a symbolic crusade in that it selectively draws upon some specific symbol that is selected as the master indicator of the degenerative character of modern social life. Earlier in American history, the Temperance Movement focused on the drinking of alcoholic beverages as the master symbol of moral decay. The initial groundswell for the movement stemmed from evangelical preachers who denounced the drinking of alcohol as a sin. As the movement gained momentum, activists asserted that the consumption of alcoholic beverages was responsible for many personal and societal problems, including unemployment, absenteeism in the workplace, violence in the family, and poverty. As a result of the pressure put on state legislators, the Eighteenth Amendment to the U.S. Constitution was enacted in 1920 to prohibit the manufacture, transportation, and sale of alcoholic beverages in the United States.

Herbert Hoover described the Prohibition Amendment as "an experiment noble in purpose." But the consequences of the amendment were far removed from what was intended. Instead of reducing the consumption of alcoholic beverages, the effect of Prohibition was to drive drinking underground. Bootlegging and the illegal sale of alcoholic beverages permitted organized crime to become more powerfully established in the United States. Gangsters used violent methods to acquire and maintain control over a highly profitable bootlegging business. Speakeasies and hidden drinking places became so popular that the nation came to recognize the difficulties and inappropriateness of attempts to legislate personal morality. A sense of relief was associated with enactment of the Twenty-First Amendment in 1933 to repeal the Eighteenth and dismantle "the noble experiment."

Louis A. Zurcher and his associates (1971) found the antipornography campaigns they studied to have several characteristics of a symbolic crusade. Participants in the campaign were concerned about the erosion of several traditional values, such as the growing disrespect for authority, the loss of patriotic sentiment, the perceived decline of religious values, and a weakening of the work ethic. However, the participants selected pornography as the key issue and as the master symbol of moral decay. Their emotionally charged rhetoric included reference to "smut peddlers," "public nudity," "explicit sex," "adult bookstores," and "X-rated movies." The people involved in these campaigns were seeking legislation to ban pornography, not so much to change sexual behavior as to confirm that their own moral values were the official morality of the society.

Some of the more indignant demands of religious extremists grow out of what they see as the erosion of moral imperatives on issues related to sexual identities and practices within the fabric of modern social life. Traditional forms of the family are breaking down and the patterns of intimate relationships are becoming more highly varied (Neal and Collas, 2000). The breakdown of the older cultural blueprints is reflected in greater sexual permissiveness among the unmarried and a weakening of the cultural imperative of heterosexuality. The proliferation of non-traditional family forms includes cohabiting couples, dual-career couples, married noncohabiting couples, lesbian and gay couples, single-parent families (with or without previous marriage) and blended families (Castells, 1997). These variations in intimate family forms provide individuals with a greater range of personal choices than existed previously. The rights of privacy are especially applicable to the control over information about oneself and about behavior behind closed doors. Control over information about oneself and the internal dynamics of intimate relationships is at the center of the struggle over rights of privacy in modern society (Laufer and Wolfe, 1977).

Historical and cultural variations in female/male relationships and forms of sexual expression have raised doubts about what is universal, about God's will, and about what is biologically given. In the modern era of choice (Rosenthal, 2005), it becomes clear that history is not yet finished with exploring the range and forms of intimate relationships. It becomes apparent that if people have the freedom to decide what is in their own best interests, not everyone will make the same decision, nor will siblings and children always make the decisions that their parents would like for them to make. Given the pluralism of modern societies, it is unlikely that modern cultures will ever evolve into uniform patterns of sexual expressiveness.

Extreme emotionality and hostility have surrounded the abortion controversy in recent years. Following the Supreme Court decision (*Roe v. Wade*) that liberalized the opportunities for abortion, many people responded by becoming more tolerant of abortion practices, while the opposition to abortion on the part of others became more firmly established (Jones and Westoff, 1978). The different responses can be understood as stemming from differences in the location of abortion attitudes within the general belief system of individuals. For some, the abortion issue taps sentiments that are central to self-identities, while for others the abortion issue is less closely related to basic beliefs. The beliefs linked to abortion include notions about the creation of human life, the rights of women, the rights of the unborn child, and the will of God. Some look upon abortion as murder and would not approve of it under any conditions, while others are fully tolerant of abortion practices.

Tolerance of abortion is conditional for most Americans. National surveys show that the vast majority of Americans now approve of abortion if the mother's health is endangered, if there is good reason to believe the child might be deformed, or if the woman has been raped. The abortion issue becomes more controversial if the couple wanting the abortion feels they cannot afford another child or if the woman wants an abortion because she is unmarried. The greatest level of opposition to abortion occurs under those conditions in which the couple has had an unwanted pregnancy and simply does not want the child or does not want a child at that particular time (deBoer, 1978).

Religious extremists who oppose the Supreme Court decision of *Roe v. Wade* perceive abortion as the master symbol of moral degeneration. In general, abortion has become more readily available as an alternative to having an unwanted child, and is widely recognized in feminist circles as the right of a woman to have control over her own body. Yet some extremists take a moralistic position and regard abortion as a form of murder. Their perpetrators regard the bombing, burning, and other assaults on abortion clinics as forms of violence "favored by God." Thus, the murder of abortion providers is regarded as justifiable homicide. Thousands of disruptive and violent acts have been directed toward abortion clinics over the past thirty years. Legal and constitutional rights to abortion have been violently opposed by such acts of aggression as harassment, posting pictures of medical records on the Internet, and sending letters through the mail containing substances resembling anthrax spores. Somehow there seems to be a contradiction between endorsing the "right to life" slogan while manifesting a willingness to murder abortion providers.

Antiabortion activists convicted of murder have included members of an underground organization designated as "The Army of God." The terrorist activities of this organization include posting a "Nuremberg File" on the Internet that lists the names of doctors and staff who have worked at abortion clinics. The stated goal of the Web site is "to record the name of every person working in the baby slaughter business across the United States." The aim is to facilitate punishing "these people for slaughtering God's children." Such terrorist procedures are based on beliefs about the infallible correctness of the group member's own position and a commitment to imposing their own morality upon everyone else by means of violence (Kimball, 2002).

Symbolic crusades embrace "true believers" who lay claim to the infallible correctness of their own religious convictions and the inappropriateness of anything else. This may be regarded as holding on to "absolute truth claims" in an age that is generally recognized as one of complexity, change, relativity, and a great deal of uncertainty (Neal, 2007). There are inherent dangers in such rigid and misguided authoritarianism. There is a failure to recognize that we live in a world of multiple realities and that humans are limited as they search for and articulate religious truth (Kimball, 2002). The fanaticism of extremists stands in contrast to the growing belief among Americans that there is no single road to salvation and that no one religious group is justified in claiming that it has a monopoly on truth about the ultimate aspects of the human condition.

Suicide Bombers

In a study of the major forms of freedom, George Hillery and his associates (1979) noted that the willingness to make extreme personal sacrifices for the attainment of a desired goal is a form of *disciplined freedom*. This form of freedom is reflected in an extraordinary dedication to a social cause and to creating a psychological linkage between self-fulfillment and group accomplishments. A well-known historical example is the Kamikaze flyers of World War II. The pilots volunteered for suicide missions fully knowing in advance that their lives would be lost in carrying out the assigned mission.

The linkage of self-fulfillment with self-destruction is perhaps the most extreme form of sacrifice possible in the exercise of disciplined freedom. Jessica Stern's (2003) analysis suggests that suicide terrorists find a clear sense of purpose with their sacrifice in a confusing world of too many choices. Terrorist organizations draw their recruits from the alienated and disenchanted by using religion as both motivation and justification. Once terrorism is embellished with sacred qualities, volunteering for a suicide mission becomes a form of self-actualization and exhilaration. Very few of us would be willing to make the kind of sacrifice required of Kamikaze pilots or suicide terrorists. Such unwillingness may reflect a basic satisfaction with our present life circumstances as well as with the absence of any set of strong personal commitments.

Images of the fanatical commitments of Japanese soldiers were reinforced in the later years of World War II with the surprise and horror associated with the organization of the Kamikaze Corps. The corps was comprised of Japanese pilots who had volunteered for suicide missions that called for diving their planes into American ships and losing their lives in the process. The principle of deliberate self-sacrifice was not new to the Japanese, nor to the ideals of warriors the world over. Extraordinary bravery and self-sacrifice have provided the raw materials for military decorations and awards almost everywhere in the world. Early in the war, a few American pilots had voluntarily dived their planes into Japanese ships, thus sacrificing their lives. But what was new toward the end of the later part of the war was the organization of a suicide corps among Japanese pilots.

In organizing the suicide missions, emphasis was placed upon the legendary beliefs in a sacred shield that had protected the islands of Japan. In August 1281, a Chinese armada of 3500 ships with about 100,000 men aboard had set out for an invasion of Japan. Because of internal wars and conflict, the Japanese were in no position to turn back the assault. The Japanese were expecting defeat, captivity, or death, when a divine intervention occurred. The invasion was halted by the emergence of a sacred wind. A violent typhoon sank most of the ships, destroyed the attacking armada, and preserved the integrity of the islands of Japan. The terrified invaders returned to China, never again to attempt such an invasion. The national mythology of Japan held that their islands continued to be protected by a sacred shield (Millot, 1972).

Drawing upon historical precedent, the term "kamikaze" (sacred wind) was employed to provide inspiration for the Japanese pilots. Implementing their suicide missions resulted in the creation of human gods. Once Japanese pilots volunteered for the suicide missions they were automatically placed into the realm of the sacred, both in terms of self-identities and in the responses of others. An aura of extraordinary and awesome proportions came to surround them. They were elevated above the mundane aspects of everyday life and set apart from ordinary human beings. They came to be admired by the Japanese as "thunder gods" who had no earthly desires (Naito, 1990).

A counterpart to the willingness to die for a cause consists of a sense of dishonor in case of failure. After the Emperor of Japan went on the radio to announce unconditional surrender to the Allied Forces, several high-ranking naval and army officers committed suicide (hara-kiri). Following their failure to protect the islands of Japan from invasion by an alien force, they no longer had any basis for self-respect. Total commitment had been followed by a sense of total failure. The Japanese military code of honor was combined with such a strong sense of obedience that the officers came to devalue their own lives apart from a commitment to victory.

In Emile Durkheim's (1951) classical study of suicide, he noted that suicide takes an "altruistic" form under those conditions in which self-sacrifice becomes a defining trait of those so totally committed to some specific cause that they lose sight of their individuality. While an extreme commitment provides a clearly identified center for a self-identity, it is also a form of risk-taking. Dedication to a single cause often requires giving up the social supports that involvement in multiple group memberships may provide. Disenchantment with a specific cause after investing all of one's psychological resources into it may leave the individual without any sense of purpose or meaning in life.

The motives and commitments of the Japanese Kamikaze are related to the suicide missions of the Islamic terrorists. In each case there was a combination of secular and sacred motives. The modern extremists recognize that the strategies of terrorism provide effective ways of combating the technologically superior equipment of their enemies. The use of suicide bombers requires very few resources for instilling terror and fear in adversaries. We noticed this in the fear engendered throughout the United States following the attack of the suicide terrorists on the World Trade Center and the Pentagon. The date of 9/11 in now firmly etched into American collective memories alongside December 7; each is a "date that will live in infamy."

Acts of violent destruction are driven by the terrorists' claim that God is on their side and that they are privy to scared truths. As a result of their moral certainty, they are obligated to act on the basis of these truths. Those who oppose them are dehumanized and demonized. In acting on their religious fanaticism, they show a disregard for the consequences of their extremist acts. Massive destruction is created for a higher good on the assumption that God will look favorably upon their commitments.

Suicide missions are not carried out from a sense of hopelessness and despair, but by an overwhelming desire to instill terror and fear into the hearts of perceived oppressors. A sense of purpose in life is created to offset a sense of chaos and meaninglessness. Once the individual volunteers for a suicide mission, his or her life takes on an extraordinary degree of coherence and meaning, and the personal experience is one of an intense sense of euphoria.

Charismatic leaders who prepare suicide volunteers for their missions make exaggerated claims that are accepted as valid ones. The indoctrination includes the belief that they will go straight to heaven and that a special place will be guaranteed for their families as well. While there is no support in the Islamic religion for the indiscriminate killing of women, children, and old men in a human bomb explosion, special provisions are provided in the *Qur'an* for those who die "striving in the way of God." The promise for martyrs is that they do not wait for the intermediate stage between death and the Day of Judgment. Instead, martyrs go directly to the seventh heaven, where they will reside with the prophets (Kimball, 2002).

For most people, their political and religious commitments are limited, while for others dedication to a sacred cause becomes a preoccupation and a central life interest. When this occurs, the various parts of a person's life becomes integrated in a positive, coherent, and understandable way. The complexities and confusions of a chaotic world disappear. Developing an extremist commitment involves accepting the persuasive appeals of a charismatic leader as valid and infallibly correct. The individual becomes totally and irrevocably committed to ideology, leadership, and goals as ultimate realities that can be depended on as a basis for understanding and action.

Suicide Cults

Religious extremism is also reflected in the creation of religious cults. These are extraordinary religious groups that become psychologically separated from their host society and the culture it manifests. The separation is based on the belief that the perfection of social life can only be achieved by withdrawing allegiance from the larger society and drawing sharp boundaries to separate members from nonmembers.

The appeal of religious cults derives from beliefs in the certainty and absolute truth of the ideology they have created. Their ideological appeals are based on a doctrine of hope in conjunction with an emphasis on collective mastery and control. Men and women do not embark upon a major religious campaign unless there is a conviction that the prospects are favorable for eventual success. The appeal argues that the attainment of desired outcomes depends on the pooling of collective resources. Alternatives are provided to attitudes of resignation and helplessness by developing a sense of meaning and purpose in life. Through making use of their energies and resources, people themselves can make a difference in their life circumstances. Through building a strong sense of solidarity, religious cults provide a basis for self-pride and concerted lines of action.

Disturbing examples of extreme commitments to religious movements have been revealed in mass suicide and murder among religious cults. For example, on November 18, 1978, a mass suicide of unprecedented proportions occurred in the jungles of Guyana. The fatalities included over 900 people, almost the entire membership of the People's Temple, which was under the leadership of a renegade Protestant minister, Reverend Jim Jones. Initiating plans for mass suicide was precipitated by an investigation of the cult by Congressman Leo Ryan and his staff. The congressman had made the trip to Guyana to investigate the claim that members of the cult were being held against their will. As they approached their plane for a return trip to the United States, the shooting started and Congressman Ryan and all members of his staff were killed (Kilduff and Javers, 1978). It was the first instance in the history of the United States that a member of Congress had been killed in the line of duty.

The People's Temple was a religious cult that required high levels of dedication, loyalty, and sacrifice among its members. Rehearsals for mass suicide and demonstrations of a willingness to die for a cause had been a part of the cult's internal planning. The techniques for producing extreme commitments among the members of the People's Temple were similar to those identified by Rosabeth Moss Kanter (1972) in a study of nineteenth century religious communes in the United States. In Kanter's study, the utopian communities that endured for an extended period of time were those that succeeded in producing strong "we" sentiments among members. The communes achieved solidarity by requiring sacrifices and investments from members. These investments included the time and efforts put into the activities of the movement as well as requirements for financial donations and the assignment of the recruit's property to the community.

There were no refunds for defectors. Furthermore, all activities became centered on the community, which involved renouncing outside friends and family ties. At the same time, internal cohesion was promoted through songs, group singing, confessions, and other ceremonies that tended to separate members from outsiders. Becoming "hooked" on a movement had the effect of reducing the range of options and alternatives subsequently available. Some degree of entrapment resulted from the numerous costs and difficulties associated with dropping out.

Reverend Jones and the People's Temple had expected outside interference and were prepared for mass suicide when Congressman Ryan conducted his investigation. As the People's Temple had grown in size, they had encountered increasing degrees of hostility. It was within this context that they sought to sustain their goals and program through migration. Moving to a more permissive part of the country or to a new country altogether have been frequent historical responses of religious groups to conditions of repression.

Migration under these conditions is associated with an ideology of hope and the perceptions of chances for new beginnings and new opportunities. In the United States, the Mormons migrated from the American Midwest to the Territory of Utah. In Canada, the Dukhobors followed the movement of the frontier westward to their present location in British Columbia. The movement of the People's Temple from Indianapolis to San Francisco to Guyana reflected efforts to find a friendlier environment for conducting an experiment in group living.

The fear of cults generated by the episode at Jonestown was expressed in several ways. The greatest fear for many middle-class parents was that a son or daughter would join a religious cult. Such religious organizations provide a strong sense of community, a clear sense of purpose in life, and a buffer against the many forms of alienation experienced by young adults (Neal, 1970). Many parents had a conspiratorial view of "brainwashing" as a device used by charismatic leaders in producing an extremist commitment among their members. The widespread fear of cults may have influenced the responses of federal marshals in their assault on the arsenal of the Branch Davidians at Waco, Texas in 1993. The criminal justice system and particularly law enforcement officials are faced with the problem of how to deal with religious extremists who are heavily armed and willing to die for what they perceive as a just cause.

The Branch Davidians had emerged from a schism of the Seven Day Adventists and had established a religious commune with David Koresh as their charismatic leader. Koresh had taken control of the commune and his claim to be a reincarnation of Christ was accepted by his followers. He taught that the prophecies of the Bible were being fulfilled and that the Apocalypse would begin with the American army attacking Mount Carmel, the name given to the Branch Davidian compound. In preparation for the final days, the Davidians buried a school bus to be used as a bunker, stored a huge quantity of food, and developed an arsenal of impressive military weapons. The arsenal included assault weapons, both automatic and semiautomatic rifles, .50 caliber machine guns, and a large supply of hand grenades.

Concern on the part of the Bureau of Alcohol, Tobacco, and Firearms (ATF) stemmed from reports about the noise associated with training both men and women to fire the weapons in the Branch Dividian arsenal. There were rumors that the weapons were being enhanced for military purposes and that chemical weapons were being developed. A series of articles appeared in a local newspaper on "The Sinful Messiah." The newspaper articles were based on information from defectors who were willing to talk about what was going on in the compound. Defectors claimed that Koresh severely abused children, had sex with minors, and practiced polygamy, all in the name of God.

A showdown occurred when ATF agents attempted to arrest Koresh on charges of possessing illegal firearms and explosives. While there is uncertainty over who fired the first shot, a heavy exchange of gunfire took place over the next forty-five minutes. Twenty ATF agents were either killed or wounded, while there were an undisclosed number of casualties among the Branch Davidians. Although the ATF assault team had been trained at the military base at Fort Hood, Texas, the firepower of their weapons could not match that of the Branch Davidians.

Over the fifty-one-day siege that followed, attempts were made by the FBI to negotiate a solution to the crisis. Although the FBI employed several harassment techniques, such as playing loud and offensive music and turning off the electricity, it became evident that Koresh and his followers could not be persuaded to come out. A planned final assault on the compound was launched on April 19, 1993. After becoming aware that a tear gas attack was imminent, the Branch Davidians started shooting. The gas attack was continued for several hours before tanks were used to smash into the buildings. Several fires were started and quickly engulfed the entire compound with intense heat. About eighty members of the Branch Davidians perished along with their leader David Koresh (Linedecker, 1993).

The incident at Waco was one of the most disturbing episodes in the history of federal law enforcement. Many saw the episode as clear evidence of state tyranny and egregious violation of the constitutional guarantees of freedom of religion and the right to bear arms. In subsequent court proceedings, the FBI was exonerated and responsibility was placed exclusively on David Koresh and his followers (Reaves, 1995). Following his conviction for the 1995 bombing of the federal building in Oklahoma City, Timothy McVeigh noted that the terrorist attack was planned and carried out as retaliation for what happened at Waco. The bombing of the Alfred P. Murrah Federal Building was deliberately timed for April 19, the second anniversary of the Waco incident. According to McVeigh, the bombing was in retribution for the war the government had declared on its own people.

Since religious cults stand outside the framework of institutional religions, their ideology and practices may take extraordinary forms. This was evident with the Heaven's Gate Cult in San Diego, California. Selecting passages from the four gospels and the Book of Revelation, their charismatic leader, Marshall Applewhite, taught that the earth had had UFO visitations, that evil forces were controlling the planet, and that the apocalypse was near. When the comet Hale-Bopp approached the earth, this was taken as a sign that the time had come to die.

On March 26, 1997, the police encountered a shocking sight behind the closed doors of an ornate mansion located in the community of Rancho Santa Fe, a suburb of San Diego. Twenty women and nineteen men were found dead with purple shrouds covering their faces and bodies (Hoffman and Burke, 1997). Cult members had believed that there was a spacecraft behind the comet waiting for them. By committing suicide their souls could be liberated from their bodies and beamed up to the spacecraft for transport to a higher plane of existence.

All of the 39 suicide victims were proficient in the use of computers and actively involved in elaborating Web pages on the Internet. The lack of response to their Web pages by the rest of the world provided a basis for promoting solidarity within the cult. The cult was deeply involved in cyber culture, science fiction, and millennial influences (Robinson, 1997), as a result of which it was easy for them to believe in UFOs, and to have difficulty in distinguishing real life from "virtual reality."

Several of the cult members, including their leader Marshall Applewhite, had undergone voluntary castration in the weeks and months leading up to the mass suicide. Physical bodies were seen simply as "containers." There was a rigid authoritarian rule that Applewhite imposed upon everyone. They were required to give up their worldly possessions, their diets were strictly regulated, and sex was strictly forbidden. In response to the tragedy, many commentators have pondered the depth of their beliefs that space aliens had for generations been sending envoys to earth to abduct humans.

Extremist cults, particularly suicide cults, are not typical of religious cults in general. Many of the established religions of today had their origins in zealous cults. Yet there are several characteristics that all religious cults share in common in addition to their charismatic leaders. Their appeals derive from a sense of certainty in a world characterized by chaos. The charismatic group serves as a buffer against alienation and isolation by providing a strong sense of cohesion, membership, and belonging. The pooling of resources provides a collective sense of mastery and control to offset previous beliefs in personal helplessness and powerlessness (Neal, 1970; Galanter, 1989).

Religion as Evil

A primary source of evil in a pluralistic society stems from a failure to recognize the First Amendment rights of individuals. The First Amendment of the U.S. Constitution recognizes the rights of individuals to develop their own particular religious beliefs and to organize in order to pursue their implementation. From the diversity of religions it is clear that there is no single religion upon which there is consensus or that is equally applicable to all. What seemed to be direct and apparent realities of religion in the past have now been replaced by cultural relativism and a diversity of beliefs about what constitutes a set of solid facts.

The multiple realities of religion are reflected in the variety of lifestyles among segments of the population. Each lifestyle includes a worldview, notions about appropriate ways of doing things, and a set of beliefs about the ultimate conditions of human existence. Most men and women in the modern world now reject notions about the infallible correctness of any particular truth claims. For example, one study found that only two percent of young people in a modern society agree with the statement "All religions are respectable, but only mine is true" (Hervieu-Leger, 2006).

Charles Kimball (2002) observed that all of the major religious traditions tend over time to move in an evil direction. This occurs when there is a claim for a monopoly of truth in matters pertaining to God's will. These are the extremists deeply involved in proselytizing and seeking to impose their own beliefs on everyone else.

Such efforts reflect a refusal to recognize the rights of individuals to make personal choices and decisions about consequential life events. Conditions of complexity, uncertainty, and diversity become intolerable.

In the introduction to Charles Kimball's book *When Religion Becomes Evil,* he observed that "more wars have been waged, more people killed, and these days more evil perpetrated in the name of religion than by any other institutional force." The historical record shows that the sense of community (Durkheim, 1961), acts of self-love, and being of service to others are deeply embedded in religion. But at the same time, the historical record also shows human sacrifices to a bloodthirsty god, contrived witchcraft trials, tragic wars, crusades, and predatory priests are among the many evil manifestations of religion.

The cruelty of charismatic leadership in religious groups is another manifestation of evil. The insistence on blind obedience among followers fails to recognize the importance to individuals of struggling with the mysteries of existence and of developing coping mechanisms for living in an imperfect world. Although claims of being of divine origin are fraudulent, they are frequently imposed upon and accepted by willing followers. Blind obedience to a charismatic leader, however, is not always voluntary, but grows out of extreme isolation and the lack of suitable alternatives.

4

The Problem of Evil

The concept of evil does not have a direct empirical referent. It is not an inherent characteristic of any person, any group of individuals, or any particular set of events.

It is a mythological concept that is imputed to persons, places, or events that are presumed to be extraordinarily immoral, dangerous, sinful, or harmful (Hart, 2004). Accounts of evil arise from the fear of unknown threats to worldviews and personal lifestyles. Extreme forms of evil in the modern world are attributed to war crimes, serial murders, sex offenders, and murders committed by children.

In a study of media representations of evil, Kathy Ann Farr (2001) concentrated on newspapers and magazine articles about 35 women on death row. The women designated as evil were depicted as unrepentant, remorseless, and lacking in empathy for their victims. The harmfulness and destructiveness of these women were described as intentional, "inhuman," and "beastly." Almost half of the women were convicted of the murder of a husband or lover. Variations in depictions of these women as evil included describing them as "black widows," "cold calculators," "depraved partners," "explosive avengers," and "robber predators." After receiving the harshest of state sanctions, the women on death row were treated as extreme cases of gender-deviant women and as the worst of evil.

In their analysis *Frames of Evil*, Caroline Joan Picart and David A. Frank (2006) emphasized that fear and fright, stalking and injury in horror movies are implicated in the harm caused to individuals by the abnormal conduct of perpetrators. The authors make a comparison between the evil depicted in horror films and the evil reflected in movies on the Holocaust. Sharp separations are made between good and evil, perpetrators and victims in both the horror movies and those on the Nazi Holocaust. The dual themes of sex and violence in cinematic productions are drawn upon both for audience appeal and to symbolize the processes of birth, life, and death. In contrast to the eroticized female bodies, the evil perpetrators are depicted as masculine monsters. The movie *The Silence of the Lambs* hints at male brutality as an outgrowth of a monstrous childhood involving years of violent abuse. Viewing the many movies depicting horror may very well intensify perceptions of evil in the modern world as well as reflect the importance of the sense of society as moral community.

At many times and places evil has been explained as the work of the devil, Satan, Lucifer, or some such linguistic equivalent (Pickett, 2005). While Satan or the Devil may not exist as a literal entity, he is a metaphor for describing the worst of the worst in human conduct. Demonic evil is invoked to symbolize the smoke and flames pouring out of the Twin Towers on September 11, the piles of emaciated bodies observed by Allied soldiers upon the liberation of the Nazi death camps, the little naked girl in Vietnam running screaming toward the camera with her body seared by napalm, and the school shootings of classmates and a teacher at Columbine High School.

In primitive societies evil was attributed to socially disapproved uses of the supernatural. While shamans drew upon the supernatural for beneficial effects, sorcerers developed their proficiency in the supernatural to use for antisocial purposes. The sorcerer could use his magical powers to produce a voodoo death and to wreak havoc on the personal life of an adversary. This magical power could be drawn upon for either good or evil purposes.

Several of the Western fundamentalist religions emphasize the epic struggle between the forces of "good" and "evil." Such dichotomous thinking has been drawn upon to designate certain individuals as malevolent or dangerous. Humans may be successful in acquiring supernatural powers of a demonic nature. The supernatural powers may be used to destroy or to seriously damage the lives of adversaries or enemies as well as the lives of ordinary citizens. In the mythology of religion and folklore, a demon is a supernatural entity that is endowed with a malevolent spirit. Demons are oriented toward inflicting damage or harm to the innocent (Frankfurter, 2006).

In his State of the Union address in January 2002, President Bush designated as "evil" those enemy nations that were devoting their resources to the development of weapons of mass destruction. He applied the term "axis of evil" to Iraq, Iran, and North Korea. Such a designation was based in part on those nations' presumed support for the terrorist attacks and in part on their research programs to enhance their capacities for waging chemical, biological, and radiological warfare. Shock at the president's remarks derived from his use of the term "axis of evil" and from the expectation that he was presenting a justification for launching air strikes at targets within the countries designated as "rogue nations." Placing the emphasis on rogue states may have served as a substitute for the inherent difficulties in locating and destroying terrorist networks.

Demonizing an enemy is drawn upon as a justification for the random destruction and killing of civilian populations during times of war. Notions about evil are used to reduce the complexity of events and to provide a public framework for the illusions of clarity and understanding. The concept of evil with its demonic overtones has almost completely disappeared from academic discourse in modern society. The current emphasis on cultural relativism and pluralism has resulted in discomfort with such terms as "bad," "immoral," and "evil." While the concept of evil lacks precision, the closest modern equivalent appears to be the psychiatric term "abnormality," which is drawn upon to describe unusually deplorable and harmful behavior (Peck, 1998). Rather than an attack on society as a moral community, abnormality is regarded as a form of mental illness.

The Witchcraft Craze of Western Europe

An example of a religion turning evil occurred with the witch craze of Western Europe between the fourteenth and seventeenth centuries. During this time, an estimate of more than 200,000 people were executed as witches (Ben-Yehuda, 1980). As witchcraft beliefs spread throughout Europe, a demonic supernatural order was created, women were disproportionately selected for execution, and the moral boundaries of social conduct were redrawn. In several books about witchcraft, church officials elaborated theories about a demonic order. The Church maintained that humans can and do enter into the worship of Satan, engage in sex orgies with demonic beings, and gain magical powers through a pact with the Devil. The creation of a demonic order established an epic battleground between the forces of good and evil. Public officials vigorously pursued the witch-hunts in an effort to stamp out hidden enemies and to purify society.

The invention of the printing press permitted the book *Malleus Maleficarum* (*The Hammer of the Witches*) to be widely circulated. The two authors, Heinrich Kramer and Jacob Sprenger, were Dominican friars and had been Inquisitors. The main purpose of their book was to establish that Satan directly intervenes in human affairs, to prove that witches were more often women than men, and to educate magistrates on the procedures for finding and convicting witches (Williams, 1959).

The treatise held that the Devil had power to do extraordinary things and that his greatest power is where human sexuality was concerned. It was believed that women have insatiable carnal lust, and loose women were especially susceptible to the persuasive appeals of the Devil. It was the relationships of women to the Devil that paved the way for the development and elaboration of witchcraft. Evil women had the power to cast spells and had astonishing abilities to tempt young maidens to be susceptible to the prowess of young devils. The document argued that witches engaged in the practices of infanticide and cannibalism in addition to having the power to cast spells for stealing the penises of males and producing male impotence.

The witch craze grew out of the efforts of church officials to create new moral boundaries for regulating conduct. The authority of the church was eroding, new moralities were developing, and fear of impending doom was growing. The execution of women as witches developed from the increased involvement of women in roles other than those of wife and mother. For example, a growing percentage of adult women were without family attachments; the practice of birth control had become widespread; and prostitution increased with the growth of cities. The witch hunts, cruel tortures, and execution may be understood as a form of scapegoating directed toward reasserting the authority of the church.

While the conviction and execution of witches had a long history in the West, it was the specific conditions of the 14th century that generated an unusual degree of suspicion and distrust in human relations. The Black Death had decimated the population of Europe, and no explanation was forthcoming. The germ theory of disease had not yet been elaborated, and supernatural explanations were sought. There was a demand for credible explanations, but the church was unable to offer one. The promised cures and treatments failed to work and led to disillusionment. It was within this context that the church promoted the fear of witchcraft in an attempt to reassert its moral authority.

The charge of witchcraft was not made randomly against those within the community (Erikson, 1966). Instead, the accusations were directed toward those individuals the accusers thought deserved to die or without whom the community would be better off. Those charged with witchcraft were said to be responsible for natural disasters, unsolved murders, or any misfortune reported by an ill-willed neighbor (Mair, 1969). Associates who attempted to defend those accused were also thought to be guilty of witchcraft.

Levels of suspicion and distrust increased in tempo and ferocity during the 15th century as thousands were handed over to authorities for trial and execution (Hughes, 1965). The persons charged with witchcraft were generally assumed to be guilty and to have actually made a pact with the Devil. Torture and trial by ordeal were employed to obtain confessions. In one form of the trial by ordeal, the accused was held by ropes and dunked into a tank of water. The failure to sink was taken as clear evidence of guilt, since water was considered pure and would reject the impure (Mair, 1969). Because of the importance of obtaining a confession, the accused was often tortured if a confession was not obtained voluntarily.

The most frequent penalty on the Continent for those found guilty of witchcraft was that of burning at the stake. In England and North America witches were hanged, while elsewhere the most common form of execution was burning. The penalties were sometimes less severe for those who admitted their guilt and expressed regrets. These were killed before their bodies were consigned to the flames. Eventually being burned alive was considered to be an extreme and unusual form of punishment, except in Spain and Italy where the practice was continued for a longer period of time. The executions often became spectacles attended by several hundred who came to see the popular event.

All of the American colonies prior to the Revolution had enacted laws prohibiting the practice of witchcraft. However, it was in Massachusetts that witchcraft trials became notorious. Between February 1692 and May 1693, over 150 people were arrested and imprisoned. The courts convicted twenty-nine people of the capital offense of witchcraft. Nineteen of the accused, fourteen women and five men, were taken to Gallows Hill near Salem and hanged. By the early eighteenth century the witch craze in Western Europe and their colonies had run its course. Yet beliefs in witchcraft and the violence surrounding claims of witchcraft still persist in many parts of the developing world.

We now know in retrospect that the evil embedded in the witch trials of Western Europe and Salem, Massachusetts, resided with the church officials and magistrates who persisted with their extremist views and who were determined to carry out their convictions and executions. The thousands of victims could not have been guilty of the crimes with which they were charged. The Devil is a mythical creation without an empirical base and thus could not have engaged in alliances with human beings. The confessions were sought as justifications for the burnings and hangings, not as a means for revealing the truth about a conspiracy.

The suspected witches were subjected to inhuman forms of torture until they confessed, and these confessions were then taken as clear evidence of guilt. Then, as now, any information obtained by means of extreme coercion or torture lacks validity. People will usually say anything to avoid or minimize additional pain or torture. For example, under forceful interrogation, American POWs in Korea falsely confessed to our use of biological warfare. While the torture of prisoners of war is prohibited by international agreements, it is still widely employed in attempts to obtain useful and strategic information.

The 200 years following the burning of witches in Europe witnessed remarkable developments in human affairs. The past was no longer regarded as an adequate guide to the future. The philosophical developments of the Enlightenment were either directly or indirectly aimed at the evils of the church as a dominant institution. The scientific method and an empirical approach to the world was elaborated as an alternative to prior claims of divine wisdom and *a priori* knowledge. Truth claims were to be validated through a combination of human rationality and the empirical methods of science. The emergence of the Protestant Reformation paved the way for eventual freedom of religion and religious pluralism. With the creation of civil society, an emphasis came to be placed on the rule of law, human rights, and the creation of democracy (Neal, 2007).

With the emergence of modernity, there was a loss of the supernatural component of evil. Today, evil is likely to be defined as a deplorable and egregious violation of social norms (Erikson, 1966). Evil as abnormality is associated with mental illness, with an abusive and lamentable childhood, or with being a victim of unresolved traumatic stress. Increasingly, evil is looked upon as a problem in collective morality, rather than as a problem of individual misdeeds and conduct.

"Crimes against humanity," the "genocide" of indigenous people, the Nazi Holocaust, and the brutality of modern warfare have taken on a prominent place in collective memories and in the guilt of nations (Barkan, 2000).

The Nazi Holocaust

Allied soldiers who took part in the liberation of the Nazi death camps at the end of World War II in Europe were shocked by what they saw. Human corpses were stacked on top of each other and the emaciated bodies of those scheduled for the gas chambers conveyed a story of gruesome horrors. Coping with the trauma of the war experience had not prepared combat veterans psychologically for what they now confronted. The notion that the authorities of the state could do whatever they pleased within their borders seemed to no longer be applicable.

The secrecy surrounding the creation of the German death camps had been remarkably successful. There had been a great deal of information available to the rest of the world about the intentions of Hitler and the Nazi Party to exterminate the Jewish population of Europe, but the available information was generally dismissed as wartime propaganda. Even the German people living in towns adjacent to the death camps claimed that they had no knowledge of what was taking place there. General Eisenhower issued orders to line up the members of the communities and march them through the death camps for them to see directly the evidence of barbarity. He also suggested that photographers take an extensive array of pictures to document the atrocities. Eisenhower anticipated that there would be an eventual attempt to deny the scope and realities of the German death camps. Subsequent denials of the Holocaust by right wing groups in Europe and America verified Eisenhower's concern (Lipstadt, 1993).

Samantha Power (2002) has described the Nazi policy of Jewish genocide as *A Problem from Hell*. There was no term in modern vocabularies to adequately describe the German death camps. The inhumane treatment of civilians in occupied countries and the brutal treatment of prisoners of war by the Japanese army had been described as "atrocities." But the term "atrocities" seemed inadequate for the policy of systematic apprehension and annihilation of the Jewish populations of Europe. Subsequently, the term "genocide" was drawn upon to describe any national policy that attempted to justify the systematic persecution, coercion, and murder of a subgroup of the population based on nothing more than their ethnicity (Fein, 1993).

The Nazi plan to exterminate the Jewish population of Europe was clearly reflected in Adolf Hitler's autobiography, *Mein Kampf*, and in the development of his political career. He drew upon the anti–Semitism in German society and used the Jews as scapegoats for advancing his career. They were blamed for Germany's losing the First World War, for the unfavorable terms of the peace treaty, and for the uncontrollable deterioration of the German economy. After all of these years and the many attempts of social scientists to explain the rise of German fascism, it remains unclear why the unsubstantiated claims and speeches of Adolf Hitler tapped into such a responsive chord (Payne, 1980; Gregor, 1974).

Soon after Hitler came to power in 1933, the Nazi Party developed a policy of "racial hygiene." This policy was based on beliefs about the desirability of a purification of the German people by removing "racially unsound" elements, which included the mentally defective, those with physical disabilities, Gypsies, communists, and all who expressed opposition to the Nazi regime. Many of the assumptions underlying this policy were widespread in the eugenics movement of the 20th century in Europe and the United States. In effect, Hitler favored killing those he believed to be "unworthy of life," "unworthy of reproduction," and as a source of contamination in the general population. The research of Robert Jay Lifton (1986) documented the widespread cooperation of German physicians in the medical killings and mass murder.

The Jews of Europe constituted the central focus and the most specific victims of the Nazi mass-murder dynamic. Under the cover of World War II, the Nazis elaborated a policy labeled the "Final Solution." Previously, the Nazis had worked vigorously to encourage the Jews to emigrate. In the early years of the war, the psychology of hate was promoted with the objective of carrying out the mass murder of all the Jews in Europe. Extermination camps were established to carry out the killings efficiently and at the lowest cost possible. The policy called for transporting all Jews in Germany and in the occupied countries to the extermination camps. In addition, killing squads were sent to the occupied countries to round up all of the Jews and slaughter them. The death toll was staggering.

Hitler maintained that history would look favorably upon their accomplishments. Instead, the brutality and inhumanity were of such a magnitude that it could not be ignored. In August of 1945, representatives from the United States, England, France, and Russia met in London to establish the first International Military Tribune and to announce that war crimes trials were to take place (Gallagher, 1961). Those holding key positions of authority in the Nazi regime were charged with "crimes against humanity" (Taylor, 1992).

The war crimes trials at Nuremburg were grounded in the assumption that there are universal principles of morality that transcend the cultural diversity and sovereignty of the national state (Donnelly, 1989). The United Nations subsequently adopted the Declaration of Human Rights to codify a new set of principles as universal and thus binding on the nations of the world. The major significance of the human rights declaration was the moral authority it provided for the condemnation of such practices as slavery, torture, rape, and genocide (Perry, 1998). The sovereignty of the national state is no longer an adequate justification for institutional practices that are offensive to the rest of the world.

Over time, the mass killings of the citizens of a state in the Nazi Holocaust came to be regarded as a unique form of evil in the human experience. The Holocaust also came to be designated as a world historical event and as a universal event that belongs to all of humanity. The systematic murder of six million Jews dramatically illustrates what human beings are capable of doing to each other. It was through universalizing the event that it came to be designated as the "Holocaust." The trauma of the Jewish people became a trauma for all of humankind.

Raising the Holocaust to the status of a dominant myth challenges both the ethical and the instrumental basis for modernity (Alexander, 2004). Collective guilt, obedience to authority, the use of technology in the killing process, and modern forms of transportation have all been implicated in observations on the Holocaust. Both the promises and the pitfalls of the human condition generate a collective need for remembrance. Museums are created to challenge all of us to experience the tragedy and to seek redemption.

The United States Holocaust Memorial Museum was created to link the collective memory of the American people with the Holocaust. Its location adjacent to the Mall in Washington, D.C., provides a connection to other components of the American repertoire of memory. The long lines that followed the opening of the museum in April 1993 exceeded everyone's expectation. The intense emotional experience of visitors to the museum serves as a reminder that evil is inside all of us and in every society. We thus all become victims as well as perpetrators as we relive the questions of "How did it happen?" and "Why did it happen?" The horrors and atrocities inflicted upon human beings by other human beings in Nazi Germany became ingrained in historical memories as one of the major traumas of all times. In reflections on the Holocaust, it becomes clear that the range of worlds that humans are capable of creating is very vast indeed.

The place of the atrocities of the Holocaust in the national consciousness of Germany continues to be surrounded by controversy and uncertainty. What happened at places like Auschwitz, Dachau, Buchenwald, and Treblinka still defies adequate explanation. How was it possible for a nation that produced some of the world's finest contributions to philosophy, music, and literature to also produce an Adolf Hitler? Why did the German people comply with the mandates of the Nazi Party when it was not in their own best interests to do so? Most Germans would prefer to forget about their ugly past and just move on and leave the explanations of what happened to professional historians. The lessons of the Holocaust are of such a magnitude, however, that selectively forgetting is not a reasonable option. The issue continues to surface and resurface in intellectual discourse, both in Germany and in the rest of the world.

The debates over the Holocaust frequently center on whether this event was unique among the atrocities in human history or whether it was simply a reflection of the type of event that has occurred at many other times and places. Those who relativize the Holocaust by seeing it simply as another case of atrocities in human affairs tend to downplay its lasting significance for German national identity. In contrast, those who perceive the Holocaust as unique in human affairs maintain that Germany must confront in some major way the significance of the event for the German national identity. In the absence of an adequate historical resolution, some degree of collective guilt is likely to remain, along with the question of what form of atonement would be appropriate for remembering such a difficult past.

Banality of Evil

In reviewing the trial of Adolf Eichmann in Jerusalem, Hannah Arendt (1963) coined the term *banality of evil*. Her central thesis was that the great evils of modern history, and particularly the Holocaust of Nazi Germany, are not carried out by fanatics and sociopaths, but by ordinary people who accept the premises of their state and regard their personal actions as normal and appropriate. Arendt noted that Eichmann was not ideologically driven, was not particularly anti–Semitic, and was only zealous through his obedience to a totalitarian regime that had inverted human morality. Yet he knowingly and willingly participated in genocide and thus became a criminal whose actions offended all of humanity (Cesarani, 2004).

In a desire to improve his career, Adolf Eichman accepted the mandate from Adolf Hitler to carry out the Final Solution. In his trial Arendt noted that Eichmann showed no trace of anti–Semitism or guilt and remorse. The psychiatrists who examined Eichmann during his imprisonment found no evidence of an abnormal personality. It thus appears that the most ordinary of people are capable of committing horrendous crimes with the proper incentives (Milgram, 1969).

From 1941 to 1945, Adolf Eichmann organized the deportation and execution of Jews in Europe. He was the center of the Nazi genocide and orders originated in his office for the transport of millions of Jews from their homes to death camps (Cesarani, 2004). He has come to be associated with Hitler, Himmler, Heydrich, and Hoess as central figures in the persecutions and mass murders in the Nazi genocide. Arendt's analysis indicates that he was essentially an amoral bureaucrat who was not ideologically driven. His motivation consisted of little more than advancing his personal career through conformity to the directives issued by a malevolent authority.

Arendt's thesis clearly demonstrates why we cannot view advances in science, technology, and rationality as unqualified evidence of human progress. The science and technology that are sources of pride in the modern world are ethically neutral and may be applied to any set of problems. In contrast to the optimism of an earlier generation about social change as progress, modern technology permits totalitarian control of large populations over large geographical areas. The evil of Nazi Germany and the evil of the former Soviet Union grew out of state control of the technology that permitted the mass murder of its own citizens. The brutality, torture, and murder under the purges of the Stalinist regime resulted in a number of deaths that may have exceeded that of the Nazi Holocaust.

In recent years, heated debates among German scholars have centered on issues related to the part played by ordinary people in the atrocities of the Holocaust. Drawing upon the movie *Schindler's List* (1993), some focus on the Germans who resisted the Nazis and did what they could to shield and protect the victims. But it is also clear that many Germans enthusiastically cooperated. Daniel Jonah Goldhagen's (1996) research suggested that ordinary Germans willingly and zealously served as the executioners for the Nazi Party. To the extent that this is the case, issues of collective responsibility and collective morality become implicated in the Holocaust. Without widespread support from the German people, neither the policy of military expansionism nor the policy of genocide would have been possible.

There are few places in the contemporary world in which evil is manifested more clearly than at both the macro and micro levels of modern warfare. For example, during the Vietnam War, Americans were shocked at the news that an army platoon under the leadership of Lt. William Calley had rounded up all the unarmed men, women, and children of the village of My Lai and shot them. This episode raised disturbing questions about what a soldier should do if he were in Lt. Calley's platoon and given an order to carry out such a mission. A national survey indicated that the majority of Americans agreed that the soldier should "follow orders and shoot" (Kelman and Lawrence, 1972).

In a subsequent trial, Lt. Calley did not deny that the order was given and that compliance with the order was responsible for the killings that took place. Instead, it was argued that Calley was doing what any good soldier would do—namely, follow the commands received from higher officers, even if this included killing defenseless civilians who may or may not have aided the enemy. In this respect, the trial of Lt. Calley was seen as unfair because it held an individual accountable for the performance of military duty in a combat situation.

While most Americans agreed with Calley's defense, a substantial number of people believed that the individual soldier must be accountable for personal actions in the conduct of war. If an improper order is given, there is a moral obligation to disobey. The individual soldier obviously is not responsible for the overall conduct of a war, but is accountable for his or her own personal actions. In recognizing that war crimes had been committed, the jury head Colonel Clifford Ford pronounced Calley's sentence: "To be confined at hard labor for the length of your natural life; to be dismissed from the service; to forfeit all pay and allowances." President Nixon ordered that Lt. Cally be removed from the stockade, after spending only a weekend there, and placed under house arrest. Subsequently, the Secretary of the Army announced that Lt. Cally would be paroled. Calley was released, later married and found employment in a jewelry store in Columbus, Georgia.

During the American occupation of Iraq, both Americans and the rest of the world were shocked by the publication of pictures revealing cruelty and unusual punishment of prisoners by American soldiers at the Abu Ghraib prison outside of Baghdad. The humiliation and abuse included stripping prisoners of their clothes, stacking them on top of each other in the nude, and forcing them to engage in sexual acts. An exceptionally offensive picture showed a naked prisoner being led by a female guard with a leash around his neck. The photographs revealed what human rights activists had long suspected. Some of the forms of humiliation, fear, and physical deprivation that had been used by American interrogators in Afghanistan and Guantanamo Bay were now being applied in Iraq. Indignant Americans clamored for an investigation to establish responsibility for these atrocities.

The rules of the Geneva Convention in 1949, which was endorsed by the United States, banned the torture of prisoners of war for the purpose of extracting information. Publication of the pictures generated collective memories of Nazi Germany and the former Soviet Union. In such totalitarian societies, individuals designated as enemies of the state were tortured without mercy before they were killed. But as a self-proclaimed civil society, the United States was bound by the rule of law and by the United Nations Universal Declaration of Human Rights. Initially, the Department of Defense attempted to dismiss the abuse as "criminal misconduct" by a small number of individual soldiers. However, subsequent investigation revealed that the several hundred cases of known abuse were deeply embedded in the U.S. policies for waging war on terrorism.

The ugliness of the past may be found in the social heritage of all countries of the world (Nytagodien and Neal, 2004), but it is during times of war that the more extreme forms of evil become apparent. While rape, slaughter, and plunder may be nearly universal aspects of warfare, they were manifested to an extreme degree among Japanese soldiers during World War II. Perhaps their exalted samurai tradition also promoted the view of captives as defective people who deserved to be abused and maltreated. About fifty years passed before the world became aware that tens of thousands of young Korean women had been raped and subsequently coerced into serving as sex slaves for the Japanese army (Hicks, 1994). In the conquest and occupation of Nanking in 1937, thousands of women were raped, and perhaps as many as 350,000 civilians were slaughtered by Japanese soldiers (Chang, 1997). While many Japanese today claim to have no knowledge of such practices, historical evidence for the brutality of the Japanese army in occupied countries is well established.

Institutional Violence

The major forms of evil in the modern world have little to do with the supernatural demonism prominently drawn upon as an explanation during so much of our past. Nor are the major forms of evil expressed through the motives, intentions, and behavior of specific individuals. Instead, overwhelmingly the major forms of evil in the modern world grow out of the institutional violence endorsed, promoted, and elaborated in the name of the state.

Acts of state terrorism, mass murder, covert assassinations, bombing raids in the deliberate killing of civilians, and other forms of brutality are facets of life in virtually every country and continent on this planet. Such forms of destructive behavior are among the more urgent of the unresolved problems faced by the modern world. Institutional violence is a form of violence growing out of the functioning of social systems at all levels of organization (Neal, 1976). The forces promoting the centralization of power in the modern state do not provide a ready-made justification for the present allocation of priorities and the directions in which social life is moving.

In all societies, a crisis of authority develops when those in positions of power become malevolent and the moral fiber of society crumbles. For example, in the maintenance of a system of racial and ethnic segregation, both law enforcement officials and members of organizations such as the Ku Klux Klan and the White Citizens Council frequently employed terrorist measures. In the American South, lynching was an extreme form of terror directed toward the social control of black males. In his discussion *The Lineaments of Wrath*, James W. Clarke (1998) observed that the burning of crosses, beatings, stabbings, and other forms of physical abuse, torture, and property destruction were widely employed for maintaining a caste system in race relations.

The practices tolerated and approved by law enforcement officials violated both universal human rights and the specific constitutional guarantees of a civil society. This became evident in the voter registration campaign of Selma, Alabama, during the Civil Rights Movement. Plans were made for a fifty-mile march from Selma to Montgomery to call national attention to the discriminatory voting laws of Alabama. The nation watched with shock and disbelief as the peaceful demonstrators were met with violent resistance from the sheriff's department and the state police (Neal, 1998). The police waded into demonstrators with billy clubs, fixed bayonets, and tear gas. The police brutality observed on television was incompatible with American conceptions of justice and legitimacy. The brutal exercise of power stood outside the boundaries of legitimate authority.

While many of the forms of brutality in American race relations originated with either organized or semiorganized hate groups, endorsement and participation by the police themselves accompanied the insidious practices. No black male could rest assured of freedom from victimization. The effectiveness of terror was based on the uncertainty growing out of its arbitrary and unpredictable character. As a result of the culture of fear, blacks were required to endure in silence many forms of abuse and injustice (Grier and Cobb, 1969). The collective trauma could not have occurred without the support of those in positions of power and authority.

Under malevolent political rule, torture, plunder, rape, and murder have taken on enormous proportions. Dramatic cases of genocide and mass murder of their own people by agencies of the state have included hundreds of thousands of deaths in Rwanda, Uganda, Sudan, East Pakistan (now Bangladesh), Bosnia, and Cambodia. The murder of people by their own government is often based on little more than their ethnicity, race, national origin, religion, or tribal membership. In many cases state-generated murders were based on a presumed criticism of the government or on some expression of opposition to the prevailing political regime.

The "killing fields" of Cambodia have become a major tourist attraction. International tourists are stunned to silence as they observe the 8,000 human skulls enshrined under glass about eight miles from the Cambodian capital. The horrifying and fascinating attraction was arranged to document and highlight the mass murder of approximately two million people during the reign of Pol Pot and his Khmer Rouge soldiers. The slaughters of innocent people was arbitrary, designed to instill fear in the general population, and intended to elicit the total allegiance of everyone to a malevolent government.

The unnecessary killing of civilians has become a regular feature of modern warfare. The total number of American soldiers killed in Iraq was reported on the nightly news, but there was a ban against reporting civilian fatalities. The U.S. Defense Department regards the civilian fatalities in Iraq as necessary "collateral damage." But while the Americans have lost a little over 4,000 soldiers, the civilian fatalities may have reached 100,000. As the killing machines of modern warfare have become more efficient, they have also become more indiscriminate.

The dehumanization and impersonality in the killing of civilians was evident in the bombing raids on the North during the Vietnam War. The bomber crews could fly their missions over North Vietnam, drop their bombs, and return to base for cocktails prior to the evening meal. In this process they were "just doing their job" and had no direct experience with the slaughter and suffering on the ground as a result of their mission. Frequently there was no military target because no identifiable military targets were known. Instead, the objective was to get the enemy to recognize our military superiority and to coerce them into submission. Such brutality in warfare did not achieve the desired objective in Vietnam, nor did it achieve its objective at other times and places. The Nazi V-2 rockets launched indiscriminately against London during World War II did not lead the British to negotiate a settlement with Germany, but only increased their determination to resist.

During the course of the 20th century, the number of people who died violently is greater than for any previous century in the history of mankind (Elliot, 1972). In the first half of the 20th century, social life was shattered by two major world wars. If both civilian and military casualties are included, the fatalities from World War I exceeded 18 million. The loss of life stemming from World War II was approximately 62 million. An additional estimated six million people were annihilated as a result of the purges in the Soviet Union. Single bombing raids during World War II produced 100,000 fatalities or more.

The rules of engagement changed dramatically during World War II. Modern warfare became "total war," and as a result the civilian casualties exceeded those of military personnel (Aaron, 1955). The civilian toll of the war was around 37 million, while the military fatalities numbered about 25 million. Modern warfare had become much more than armies meeting on the field of battle. The total population of the countries at war was defined as they enemy to be exterminated.

The brutality of the armies of Germany and Japan were directed toward the killing of civilians in the countries occupied. Under the onslaught of the German army, the civilian fatalities of the Soviet Union were about 16 million, or about double the Soviet military casualties. The brutality of the Japanese army in China resulted in civilian fatalities that were about five times greater than the military fatalities. The intent of these policies was to demonstrate the moral superiority of the Japanese and to terrorize the occupied countries into compliance with the conquering army (Chang, 1997).

The killing of unarmed civilians has become a part of modern warfare. The massive fire-bombing of Dresden, Hamburg, and other German cities toward the end of World War II was not necessary, since Germany was already a defeated nation (Knell, 2003). Under the command of General Curtis LeMay, massive fire-bombing attacks were launched against Japanese cities. The civilian fatalities of a single incendiary attack on Tokyo may have exceeded that of the atomic bombing of Hiroshima. While the full scope of the motives for conducting such attacks remains somewhat obscure, the justifications were for weakening the capacity of the Japanese to resist and to hasten the date of surrender. General LeMay once made the statement that if the Americans had lost the war, the chances are pretty good that he would have been tried as a war criminal.

As repugnant as the unnecessary killing of civilians in warfare may be, it is only one of the many deplorable forms of evil in the modern world. According to R.J. Rummel (1994, 1999), the purposeful state killings of its own members, which he calls *democide*, exceeded 160 million people in the 20th century. A large percentage were victims of genocide, while others were victims of mass killings of political groups as well as state massacres. The total number of victims exceeds the population of all but five of the largest counties in the world. The fatalities from genocide and political killings have taken the lives of more people than the number killed in all of the wars of the past century. This is evil in an historically unprecedented form.

5

Terrorism

A special exhibit at the International Spy Museum in Washington, D.C., in 2004 focused on the history of terrorism in the United States from the American Revolution to the present. At the start of the exhibit, terrorism was defined as the "unlawful use of force or violence against persons or property to intimidate or coerce a government, the civilian population, or any segment therof in furtherance of political or social objectives." The exhibit drew upon visual representations to depict the many expressions of terrorism in American history. Images from a turbulent past provided potential insights into contemporary forms of terrorism.

Extraordinary turbulence was evident in the United States before, during, and after the Civil War. For example, historians have noted that that before the Civil War there were more than 200 slave uprisings involving ten or more people (Rasmussen, 2012). While slave revolts could not topple the institution of slavery, the violence did succeed in instilling high levels of fear in slave owners and their families. The immediate proximity of slaves permitted food poisoning and other acts of retribution for abuse and brutality.

Terrorism was also expressed in deep social and political divisions between the abolitionists and the defenders of the institution of slavery. On October 16, 1859, a raid led by John Brown captured the federal arsenal at Harpers Ferry, Virginia. The raid was intended to provoke a general uprising among slaves and to provide the insurgents with weapons in support of a war against slavery (Horowitz, 2011).

A military unit under the command of Colonel Robert E. Lee surrounded the arsenal and nearly all of the insurgents were killed or captured. A severely wounded John Brown was hastily tried and convicted as a traitor. Before he was hanged, Brown declared that his actions were in accordance with God's commandments,

The distinguishing feature of terrorism is the illegitimate use of violence to promote a social or political cause. The cause is often endowed with sacred qualities, and there is a strong sense of dedication and commitment. The explosive character of violence is expressed in killing others to dramatize a societal need for remedial action (Stern, 2003). Since terrorism is designed to instill fear in the general population, the specific victims are intended to be randomly and indiscriminately selected (Vetter and Perlstein, 1991). The victims of random acts of violence are often innocent spectators. Such events as the bombing of abortion clinics, the burning of black churches, and the indiscriminate bombing of the Boston Marathon are dramatic and unusual happenings that reflect troubles in the social realm.

The primary terrorist organizations in the United States in recent years include racial hate groups, neo–Nazis, militia groups, right-wing radicals, and extremist religious groups. Their commonality stems from advocating and preparing for the use of violent methods to express their anger and sense of discontentment. There is no single ideological cause or set of special concerns that unify these hostile and threatening groups. Their objectives are as diversified as the pluralism of society in which they express their disenchantment. While the specific motives of perpetrators and the forms of violence are highly variable, each episode of violence intensifies the sense of vulnerability and fear of living in modern society. The effectiveness of terrorism depends to a very large degree on it arbitrary character and it lack of predictability.

Traumatic events impinge directly into the life-worlds of individuals without the cushioning effects of intermediate layers of social organization. There are no filtering or cushioning effects for such dramatic events as the school shootings at Columbine, the mass suicides of a religious cult, the anthrax scare, or the bombing of the Federal Building in Oklahoma City. The effects of such events on the nation are direct and immediate. They remind us that it is possible for our darkest fears to be validated here and now at any public place and at the least expected time.

While conditions of isolation and privacy are among the rights of individuals in a democratic society, they also permit secrecy and planning for clandestine operations. Privacy permits a cover-up of activities that would be regarded as immoral and reprehensible if they were known. For example, from a cabin in an isolated region of Montana, Theodore Kaczynski engaged in acts of terrorism over an eighteen-year interval before he was apprehended as the "Unabomber" (Lacqueur, 1987).

Kaczynski used the U.S. Postal Service to deliver bombs to intended victims. His sophistication was reflected in developing an explosive that would be detonated when the package delivered by a mail carrier was opened. His actions were those of an alienated individual who had no affiliation with a terrorist organization. The target of his bombs were scientists who were among the nation's elites and located in different parts of the country. The Federal Bureau of Investigation (FBI) spent eighteen years working on the case without a clue to his identity. It was only after his brother turned him in as a suspect that the FBI was able to locate and apprehend Ted Kaczynski.

Kaczynski was exceptionally intelligent, had been educated at Harvard, and was totally disillusioned with modern society. In his trial, he expressed a desire that his lawyers not pursue a mental illness defense. Instead, he wanted his acts of terrorism to focus attention on a manuscript he had written that developed theses on the deleterious effects of modern technology. After pleading guilty to thirteen counts of bombing and murder, he received several consecutive life sentences. Few people paid attention to his manifesto, but throughout the country the presence of an unidentified package became a sufficient reason to evacuate a building.

Racial Vigilante Hate Groups

In contrast to the above sporadic acts of violence, racial terrorism has beenpervasive and persistent in generating fear among African-Americans as This is a form of terrorism that operates outside the legal framework of courts, legislative assemblies, and law enforcement agencies. Hatred-based terrorist groups have taken the basic functions of government into their own hands. Their activities become clandestine through using such tactics as secret membership, secret meetings, and the wearing of hoods in public places. Since the Civil War, the dominant form of terrorism in the United States has consisted of the terrorism of the racial hate s directed toward African-Americans.

Instead of being able to enjoy the freedom promised by the Emancipation Proclamation, and the privileges of citizenship guaranteed by the Thirteenth Amendment, the maltreatment of blacks took on an extreme form with the emergence of the Ku Klux Klan (KKK) and other vigilante organizations. Hooded night riders burned crosses and destroyed the homes and property of African-Americans. The encounter with terror on the part of former slaves was accompanied by fear among whites that the emancipated slaves would retaliate against their masters who had previously abused them. The turbulence of the times promoted an atmosphere of reciprocal fear and distrust.

The ideological justification for slavery persisted and provided support for the continued maltreatment of African-Americans. The freed slaves were vulnerable and became objects of scapegoating for venting the pent-up anger and hostility over the South's defeat in the Civil War. Former Confederate officers and enlisted men created and joined vigilante organizations in order to support the notion that they were not among those who had surrendered at the end of the war (Poole, 2004). As members of the KKK, they were able to wear hoods to conceal their identities as they engaged in acts of violence and aggression for instilling fear in African-Americans.

The forms of violence employed by the KKK and White Citizens Councils were tolerated and approved by local community leaders and law enforcement agencies. No black could rest assured of freedom from victimization for any minor infraction of the unwritten rules concerning their subordinate status. The effectiveness of terror as a form of social control depended to a very large degree on its arbitrary character and its lack of predictability. Acceptance of minority status by black Americans required recognizing that color lines were not to be crossed and that many forms of humiliation, brutality, and injustice were to be endured in silence (Blackman, 2008).

The racial forms of terrorism not only inflicted immediate physical damage but also sent symbolic messages to the black community. News reports of racial crimes had serious consequences for minority perceptions of vulnerability, risk and danger as well as for imposing serious restrictions on freedom of movement. The damage involved feelings of anger, depression, physical ailments, and other symptoms of stress disorder (Grier and Cobb, 1969).

The message being sent was that racial and ethnic minorities were unwanted and regarded as inferior and undesirable. On balance, racial crimes did more damage to perceptions of society as a moral community than all other crimes combined. The effects of such violations had unmistakable effects in aggravating community conflicts and tensions (Beck, 1999).

In 2000 the nation was shocked by an unusual exhibit at the Rose Horowitz Gallery in New York City. The exhibit consisted of a collection of picture postcards depicting lynching in the United States (Allen, 2000). Between 1882 and 1968 an estimated 4,742 blacks met brutal and violent deaths at the hands of lynch mobs. The lynchings were the culmination of the extreme measures vigilantes were willing to take to instill terror in black populations. Many of the postcards in the exhibit were worn from their circulation through flea markets and antique shops.

Images on these postcards indicated that racial terrorism had the full support of leading citizens in the towns and villages where the lynchings occurred. Rather than reflecting indignation, the activities of spectators in the picture postcards displayed a festive, carnival-type atmosphere. Most viewers of the depictions in this gallery exhibited experiences of pain, anger, and collective guilt. Some pictures displayed the burned bodies of black men who had been brutally mutilated, and in some cases, castrated before being lynched. The message on the backside on one postcard read "This is the barbeque we had last night." Others contained reference to the "Protection of White Womanhood of the South."

Historically, lynching had been one of the major forms of terror directed toward black males. Self-appointed defenders of racial purity and the status quo had directed incredible forms of violence toward black citizens. The burning of crosses, beatings, stabbings, and other forms of terror had long been drawn upon as forms of terror for maintaining the caste system in race relations. Extreme measures were used by both law enforcement officials and the white majority who were committed to "keeping blacks in their place." Racial terrorism continues to be expressed in the thousands of race-based hate crimes that still occur each year in the United States.

The openness of terrorism depicting a lynching and a viewing audience stand in contrast to the clandestine character of burning crosses in front of residences and the bombing of black churches. The burning and bombing of black churches escalated with the emergence of the Civil Rights Movement. The black church was the primary institution for offering a sense of catharsis for the agony and despair in a hostile and unfriendly environment. In this way, churches provided stable anchoring points as the soul of the black community. Many of the churches worked collectively to address such issues as racial discrimination, segregated schools, and the special concerns of their members. It was perhaps because of the symbolic meaning of churches in black communities that they became primary objects of racially motivated violence.

The firebombing of the 18th Street Baptist Church in Birmingham, Alabama, became symbolic of racial terrorism in America (Hewitt, 2003). The destruction of this church had a profound effect on the black community as well as the entire nation. This attack evoked sympathy for the four children killed as well as for the several people injured. The sense of security provided by the church could never again be taken for granted. Unfortunately, this act of terror was not an isolated event. Episodes of burning African-American churches persisted into the 1990s. For example, between January 1995 and July 1996 more than seventy black and multiracial churches were burned. Recurrent episodes of racial terrorism are still an ugly reality of our society.

Further expressions of racial terrorism include the large number of armed militia that have been organized in recent years. These groups combine racial hatred with selected religious ideologies and hostility toward the federal government. The basic beliefs of many of these groups are designated as "Christian Identity," which holds that only those of the white race are God's chosen people. All others are regarded as impure and defective. The armed militia have assembled arsenals of weapons to draw upon for implementing their objectives when the appropriate time arises (Dyer, 1998; Koppelman, 2001).

The Oklahoma City Bombing

Before his execution, Timothy McVeigh indicated that he had planted the bomb in the federal building at Oklahoma City to avenge the deaths at Ruby Ridge and Waco. Each episode had previously become linked in public discourse over the rights of individuals and the imperatives of law enforcement. A great deal of anger was directed toward agencies of the government that were perceived as using excessive force against the Weaver family at Ruby Ridge and the Branch Davidians at Waco (Bock, 1996).

On April 19, 1995, a rented Ryder truck heavily loaded with explosives was detonated outside the Alfred Murrah Federal Building in downtown Oklahoma City. The car bomb virtually destroyed the building and severely damaged six other buildings in the vicinity. The explosion left 168 people dead and 500 injured. The fatalities included 19 children who had been in a day-care center on the second floor. Subsequently a nurse was killed during the rescue efforts. At that time, it was the most serious single episode of terrorism in the history of the United States.

The news coverage was extensive, and the nation responded as it had to other national traumas of the 20th century (Neal, 1998). Fear and anger were combined with intense feelings of empathy for victims and their families. The concern was primarily with the ways in which individuals could be blown to smithereens while involved in the most ordinary of daily pursuits. It was particularly disturbing that the damage was intentional and that it occurred in our own country. Oklahoma City did not seem to be a likely target for a terrorist act of this magnitude.

Prior to the Oklahoma City bombing, most of the terrorist attacks within the United States had been on a relatively small scale and were generally perceived to be ineffective in calling attention to a social cause or a political objective. The sense of safety and security Americans had about living in their society was diminished by the bombing. Previous acts of terrorism by alienated indivuals were insignificant by comparison. Public concerns were expressed in clamor for decisive action in the quest for apprehending suspected perpetrators.

About ninety minutes after the blast, Timothy McVeigh was pulled over by a highway patrolman for driving a car without a license plate. Timothy McVeigh, a highly decorated soldier in the Gulf War, was arrested on traffic charges and for carrying a loaded semi-automatic pistol. When FBI agents inventoried his car they found pages from right-wing books and magazines and a futuristic novel glorifying an anticipated racist revolution. It became clear that he was steeped in militant anti-government ideology. Two days later he was charged with the Oklahoma City bombing.

After his military service, McVeigh had symbolically withdrawn his allegiance from the United States. He no longer paid income tax and drove his car without a driver's license. He had carefully considered right-wing books on how to disappear from the government's view, go underground, and make bombs. He and an army buddy, Terry Nichols, provided psychological support for each other. Apparently McVeigh suffered from an exaggerated sense of justice and felt that the federal government should be punished for what he saw as the slaughter of innocents at Waco.

Following his conviction, McVeigh was given an opportunity to make a statement before his sentencing. He used this occasion to claim that he had acted in retaliation for what happened at Waco and that he had timed the second anniversary, April 19, as the date for his retribution. McVeigh claimed that he had declared war on a government that had declared war on its own people. He asserted that he and he alone was responsible for planning and carrying out the attack.

Serious doubts were raised by many people about the possibility that McVeigh alone could have developed such a complex bomb, loaded with several thousand pounds of explosives in a rented truck, and detonated it without blowing himself up. He did not receive any special training on explosives during his military service. Demolition and military experts expressed doubts about the possibility of a single bomb, of the type that was used, bringing down the federal building without supplemental demolition charges.

Terry Nichols was subsequently found guilty of conspiring with McVeigh, although he did not participate in the slaughter itself. They had become close friends during their military service because of their fondness for guns and their hatred of the government. Both McVeigh and Nichols became avid readers of extreme right literature, with special emphasis on conspiracy theories of power and antigovernment literature. Although Nichols was in another state at the time of the bombing, he received a life sentence for his role as a conspirator in planning the attack.

Following the Oklahoma City bombing, strict security measures were initiated for federal buildings. Barriers were constructed to prevent unauthorized trucks or cars from entering the vicinity of the buildings. The easy entry of citizens into federal buildings was terminated. Security systems, including armed police and metal detection systems, were installed. Even federal employees were required to go through security systems on their way to work.

Separately and in combination, the episodes at Waco and Oklahoma City became important symbolic referents for a variety of constituencies. Antigovernment activists imputed special meaning to these events, along with religious extremists, law enforcement personnel, authority figures, and people in general. As with other forms of terrorism, these events confirmed that we livin a dangerous world and that the safety and security of everyday life are not self-maintaining.

The terrorist attack on the federal building in Oklahoma City became an advanced indicator of calamities to come. With the subsequent destruction of the twin towers of the World Trade Center and the bombing of the Pentagon, the age of terrorism was fully launched (Lacqueur, 1987). The vulnerability of our complex civilization was illustrated and the world could never again be the same. The continuity of everyday life, as it was known and understood, could no longer be taken for granted.

The Terrorist Attack of September 11, 2001

The initial responses to the events of September 11, 2001, were those of shock, disbelief, and incredulity. The tragic news from New York and Washington hit the nation hard. The world had lost its predictability, and from the encounter with chaos, it seemed like anything could happen next. Americans were jolted out of the sense of complacency that followed the ending of the Cold War.

Airplanes commandeered by terrorists crashed into the twin towers of the World Trade Center. Each of the planes contained approximately 10,000 gallons of highly flammable fuel. The heat generated by the explosion approximated the eneregy output of a nuclear power plant and reached temperatures as high as 2,000 degrees. The intense heat softened the steel columns and reduced their capacity to support the buildings (9/11 Commission Report, 2004).

Many of the 35,000 people who were usually at work by 9:15 had not yet arrived. Among those there, it became evident that they needed to get out of the building as quickly as possible. Those above the impact area were not able to escape and some jumped from the top floors rather than suffer death from the heat and flames. More than 2800 people from 115 countries of the world were identified as having died from the attack. Bravery and heroism were reflected among the more than 200 firemen and poilicemen who lost their lives in helping people evacuate the buildings.

The routine journey to work had become a journey to death and destruction. The deaths were seen as senseless events that should never have occurred by the standards of what is normal, natural, and just within the social realm. Anxiety levels were high among those who had an intimate friend or relative who failed to return from work and was presumed dead under the rubble at the World Trade Center. Photos of the missing were prominently displayed at Ground Zero and subsequently published in New York newspapers along with brief bio-sketches. Initially, the losses were estimated at almost double the fatalities at Pearl Harbor.

Shortly after the collapse of the towers of the World Trade Center, the White House was evacuated. All incoming international flights to the United States were diverted to Canada. The primary elections in New York City were canceled. The headquarters of the United Nations in New York was fully evacuated. And the international airports in San Francisco and Los Angeles were evacuated and closed. Four businessmen stranded in Los Angeles found it necessary to rent a van and share the driving in order to get back to Florida.

About half an hour after the attack on the World Trade Center, a third hijacked plane crashed into the west wall of the Pentagon in Washington, D.C. The Pentagon and the World Trade Center were primary symbols of world dominance by the American economy and military. While the Pentagon had been designed to withstand a terrorist attack, a section of it collapsed and burned upon impact of the plane. There were more than 20,000 civilian and military workers in the Pentagon at the time. The casualties included the 184 people at the Pentagon who died along with the 59 aboard the hijacked plane.

A national tragedy of intense proportion was developing. All commercial planes were grounded throughout the country, and thousands of passengers were stranded in airports. Anxiety levels were high about how it would be possible to get home. In the absense of any immediate course of action, the nation became engrossed in reports from the news media. Few people had ever thought of the possibility of using a commercial airplane as a rocket or as a military weapon.

The tragedy of the attack continued to unfold in a fourth hijacked plane over Western Pennsylvania. It was suspected that the next target would be the White House or the nation's Capitol Building. In a series of phone calls, the passengers aboard the plane learned about the destruction of the World Trade Center. The heroic efforts of the passengers twarted the plans of the terrorists, even though they were not able to save themselves. They personally gave their lives in order to save the lives of other people. Following their assault on the terrorists, the plane crashed in a field about 80 miles southeast of Pittsburgh.

If the objectives of the terrorists were to instill fear in the general population, they could not have been more successful. The fear response centered not only on the dangers inherent in commercial flights, but also in the possibility that subsequent acts of terror would be directed toward contaminating urban water supplies, blowing up buildings, dynamiting bridges, or exploding bombs in subways. The prior sense of confidence in our infrastructure and its interdependency was called into question.

Throughout the country, Americans raised the question, "Why do they hate us?" While most Americans thought they were admired and respected by the rest of the world, this turned out not to be the case in all sectors. Americans thought of themselves as the ones who had liberated Europe from the tyrannical domination of Nazi Germany. They saw their benevolence as reflected in the Marshall Plan, which helped to rebuild countriies devastated by the destruction of World War II. They also saw themslves as providing leadership for the world throughut the Cold War. Americans were puzzled as they noted the strong sentiment of anti–Americanism in some parts of the world.

The secular and sensate lifestyles reflected in modern movies and television programs turned out to be particularly offensive to religious fundamentalists in many parts of the world. The traditional norms and values of many Islamic societies conflicted with the individual freedom and hedonistic values depicted in American popular culture (Huntington, 1997). Yet the satellites that circled the globe several thousand miles above the equator made American television available to the rest of the world (Anderson, 2004).

Political boundaries are permeable, and there is nothing Islamic or other countries can do to prevent the sexual themes from soap operas and other forms of popular culture from being available to their viewers. Through Hollywood, television, and other forms of popular culture, the United States is seen as reflecting the degeneracy and decay of Western civilization.

Religious Underpinnings of the War on Terrorism

The terrorist attack provided a dramatic illustration of the vulnerability of the nation that had the world's largest defense budget and unsurpassed military capability. It led to an awareness that the major threats to the security of the United States did not stem so much from the threat of adversarial nations as from alienated and disenchanted individuals. A relatively small number of indivduals armed only with box cutters and a willingness to die had disrupted the world's most powerful nation.

Initial casual explanations of the terrorist attack drew heavily on the theme of evil in attempts to make sense of what happened. Osama bin Laden was assumed the mastermind in back of the attack. The training of terrorists and the mobilization of resources for an assault on American institutions had accompanied his declaration of *jihad* (holy war) against the United States. As an added emphasis on the evil explanation, a comparison was made in public discourse betwen bin Laden and Adolf Hitler. It was a comparison that served to reduce the complexity of events and to provide a public framework for clarity and understanding.

The concept of evil has demonic overtones and, to a very large degree, has disappeared from academic discourse in modern society. The current emphasis on cultural relativism and pluralism has resulted in discomfort with such terms as "bad," "immoral," and "evil." While the concept of evil lacks precision, it usually refers to intentional acts of destructive and harmful behavior, perpetrated by a person or a group. The individual evildoer is seen as unrepentant, remorseless, and lacking in any redeeming social value (Morrow, 2003). Invoking the notion of evil has a labeling or a name-calling quality. It is interesting to note that Islamic extremists promoting a *jihad* against the United States draw heavily on a similar vocabulary.

Others qualified the designation of evil by maintaining that the terrorists were not so much evil as misguided religious extremists. As religious extremists they were regarded as idealists who believed in the rightness of what they were doing. For example, in an address to his followers in 1998, bin Laden observed that his brand of terrorism was commendable for it was a religious war directed against tyrants and the enemies of Allah. The brand of religion espoused by bin Laden provided a sense of meaning and direction for acting in accordance with mandates received from God.

Acts of violent destruction are driven by the claim that God is on their side and that they are privy to sacred truths. As a result of their moral certainty, they are obligated to act on the basis of these truths. Those who oppose them are dehumanized and demonized. In acting on their religious fanaticism, there is a disregard for the consequences of their extremist acts. Massive destruction is created for a higher good on the assumption that God will look favorably upon their commitments.

As true believers, terrorists achieve a high purpose in life and are honored for their dedication and willingness to die for a holy cause. Suicide as an extreme form of self-sacrifice becomes a form of self-realization. Few Americans are able to adequately understand the motives of of religious extremists who are willing to die for a cause. With the increasing secularization of modern society, deep commitments to any form of sacred values have become limited. Yet it is important to note that there are more people in the world who die from suicide each year than from all the wars that are fought. The World Health Organization reported that suicide is the third largest cause of death among people aged fifteen to thirty-four worldwide (Willims, 2004). From an individual standpoint, it would seem prefeable to voluntarily sacrifice one's life for a holy cause than to take one's life out of a sense of despair. The suicide terrorists of 9/11 may very well have believed that following their violent deaths they would go directly to heaven.

The War on Terrorism

The intensity of the fear and anger among Americans resulted in a call for a militant course of action. Americans were outraged and determined to go after the terrorists. Nothing could be done directly about the suicide bombers, but a great deal could be done about the extremist leaders and organizations that had planned and orchestrated the attack on the United States.

Under the known leadership of bin Laden, the objectives of the terrorisats were to maximize the number of people killed, to maximize the societal disruption, and to destroy major economic military and political symbols of the world's uncontested superpower. The new forms of terrorism stemmed from religiously inspired groups that lacked firm commitments to any specific national state. Since their organization was global in scope, their activities were not subjected to the usual state sanctions for criminal conduct. Within a religious framework, the leadership of global terrorism had the capacity to draw upon relatively large numbers of young adults who were willing to volunteer for suicide missions.

In order to locate and destroy terrorists, it became necessary to take military action against those nations that harbored and provided financial support for them. It was within this context that Americans launched an assault on terrorist organizations located in Afghanistan. The organization of al Qaeda under the leadership of bin Laden had found a sanctuary in Afghanistan. The Taliban leaders who had gained control of the country gave al Qaeda a high degree of freedom for training and indoctrinating terrorists with other *jihad* groups and leaders. The general headquarters of international terrorism had been established for planning and carrying out attacks on the United States and other nations.

Initially, Congress had supported President George W. Bush in his declaration of war on terrorism. Such a designation served to indicate that those in positions of power were taking decisive action. We were becoming engaged in a permanent war without a clearly identifiable enemy. There were no battle lines, as there had been in World War II and Korea, and there were no identifiable gauges that would indicate when the war was over. We were engaged in a new kind of war, and the war designation was drawn upon to mobilize society through promoting national security and a sense of patriotism.

While terrorists lack the resources for developing sophisticated nuclear weapons, they do have the capacity for developing "dirty bombs" (King, 2004; Dershowitz, 2002). A dirty bomb is a conventional explosive device of the type used in the Oklahoma City, but it is packed with radioactive substances. With an explosion, the radiation could become airborne and spread contamination, death, and injury over a large area. While such a weapon is limited in its effectiveness, it has an enormous capacity for instilling fear in a large population.

American intelligence reports suggested that Iraq was actively engaged in the production of weapons of mass destruction, and that these weapons could be made available to terrorists. The appeal to the United Nations for endorsement of our plans for air strikes and a ground invasion failed to meet with approval. The United Nations inspectors had not found any evidence of weapons of mass destruction in Iraq and requested more time before the United States and its allies launched a military attack. Most of the western democracies, including those that had been close allies with the United States since World War II, were opposed to the planned invasion.

A preemptive strike was based on what was presumed to be the motives, intentions and plans of an enemy nation. Why wait, it was argued, for another Pearl Harbor in which an enemy might use weapons of mass destruction against the United States? Since we are the world's only military superpower, why not go ahead and crush an enemy before they strike first? To do so would set an example for the futility of any other nation following the course of action presumed to be have been taken in Iraq.

The military invasion of Iraq was swift and decisive. The president of the United States appeared aboard an aircraft carrier in front of a banner that read "Mission Accomplished." However, dismantling the world's largest army did not mean that the war was over. There was widespread looting following the collapse of authority in Iraq. guerrilla warfare sporadically erupted and led to intense fighting with the army of occupation.

Americans were becoming more highly divided than at any time since the Viet Nam War. Although several thousand weapons of mass destruction were ultimately found, the Pentagon blundered by keeping their discovery classified information for years. It became apparent that no adequate plans had been made for either nation-building or for the occupation of Iraq after the war was over. Many of the soldiers in the National Guard units sent to Iraq felt that they were not adequately trained for the nuances of an army of occupation in a hostile land.

Culture of Fear

Before the terrorist attack of September 11, numerous books suggested that a culture of fear had developed in the United States (Furedi, 1997; Glassner, 1999). The collective perception of risk and danger stood in contrast to the primary emphasis of Americans upon mastery and control of their destinies. Popular culture and mass entertainment, as well as the news media, pointed toward the mishaps, tragedies, and dangers of living in the modern world.

A casual inventory of everyday fears before 9/11 would have been a very long list. The health field includes fears about the safety of the water we drink, the food we eat, and the air we breathe. The fear of AIDs, Ebola, and mad cow disease suggests the importance of taking extraordinary measures in everyday life. Perceptions that human beings were not in control of the consequences of their own actions surfaced in the fear of nuclear power plants and in fear of exposure to radiation in the use of computers. Because of the fear of criminal victimization, enormous resources went into the construction of prisons. The list could go on and on.

The collective fear generated by the terrorist attack of 9/11 built upon and extended the culture of fear in our society. Many of the measures intended to increase the level of national safety and security had the reverse effect at the individual level. For example, color-coded alerts from the FBI and Homeland Security can contribute to increased levels of fear. At airports, travelers are required to produce a photo ID to establish their identities, to remove their shoes and belts, and to empty their pockets. They are also required to prove that their laptop does not contain a bomb and to send their briefcase or pocket book through a machine to prove that it does not contain a weapon. Any comment regarded as offensive by the security officers may provide a basis for detention, special treatment, or a missed flight. The message of these procedures serves as a reminder that we are living in a dangerous world and that travel on any specific flight without extraordinary precautions may turn out to be a lethal undertaking.

The consequences of high levels of fear, sustained over long period of time, are likely to be maladaptive. The sense of vulnerability leads to a preoccupation with defensive measures, avoidance behavior, and restrictions of freedom of movement. It is out of our collective fear that paranoia is directed toward neighbors and hate crimes are directed toward strangers and immigrants. It may be that terror can be induced not by the terrorists so much as the fear we create for ourselves. Intensifying the level of fear within the general population cannot, in and of itself, be an effective strategy for defeating the terrorists.

The global character of modern terrorism requires us to recognize that the incubation of terrorist plans and strategies may originate at any place in the world. We saw on September 11 the kind of damage to our society that could be inflicted by the clandestine activities of only a small number of individuals with very few resources. Preventing a terrorist attack from ever occurring is beyond the capacity of either our intelligence-gathering agencies or our military institutions. In a world that has become interdependent, we may not be able to increase our sense of safety and security by enhancing our military sophistication.

Most people are aware that there is no place to hide from the risks and dangers of the modern world. The rhetoric of mastery and control over events is necessarily a part of the political process of instilling confidence in a nation's leadership, but its fraudulent character is apparent to many people. Increased surveillance of the personal lives of individuals will not eliminate the threat of terrorism. A suspension of the civil liberties guaranteed by the U.S. Constitution will neither increase our sense of national security nor prevent unidentified individuals from smuggling weapons of mass destruction into the United States.

We know from anthropology that human beings have a remarkable capacity for creating and adjusting to a wide range of cultural conditions. However, there are limits. We do not know, for example, the long-range effects of intense and prolonged levels of fear in the general population. We have no way of knowing what the full range of those effects will be, but there is a high probability that they will be deleterious. Neither the creativeness of modern civilization nor the well-being of individuals can long endure under extreme conditions of collective fear.

6

Born Again

The term "born again" is a metaphor for the process by which adults are converted to a particular religious group. The origin of the concept lies in the early phase of Christianity: the Gospel of John describes how Jesus told a Pharisee named Nicodemus, "You must be born again"—a reference to a spiritual experience. In the Book of Acts, Saul has a very dramatic supernatural experience on the road to Damascus. To symbolize the transition from his hostility toward Christianity to becoming a strong supporter of the new religion, his name is changed from Saul to Paul.

The modern intensity of the "born-again experience" is highly variable. For some it is a fairly mild form of simply confessing one's sins and taking whatever vow is required for becoming a member of a particular group. For others, it is very dramatic and interpreted as an extraordinary supernatural visitation. In these cases, personally following the instructions received becomes mandatory. There is no decision to be made. The imperative is reinforced by a divine mandate.

The social significance of the born-again phenomenon derives from eliminating the need for church officials to serve as intermediaries on the road to salvation. It confers a direct relationship between the individual and God. The born-again experience is found among those religious groups that confer formal membership only on adults. Other religious groups in a pluralistic society have formal ceremonies for conferring membership status during infancy, childhood, or the transition from childhood to adulthood. Whatever the case, the church is seen as binding individuals together into a moral community and providing reinforcements for each other in pursuing the will of God on the road to salvation.

The born-again experience is interpreted by church officials and the individual as a sudden and dramatic transition of self-identities.

Such a possibility does not fit consistently with any of the learning theories in social psychology. The self is shaped over an extended period of time from interactions within the family, within the peer group, and from the many significant others that enter into the individual's field of vision.

Religious adherents interpret the sudden conversion experience in terms of "charisma," "possession of the Holy Ghost," "the gift of grace," or some other supernatural explanation. Both the convert and those in contact with the convert view him or her as a changed person and regard the change as stemming from a sudden and dramatic change in self-identity. To investigate the difference in religious and social psychological perspective on the sudden transformation of self-identity, James V. Downton (1980) made a study of converts to the Divine Light Mission.

The conclusion of Downton's study indicated that identity transformations were an outgrowth of an evolutionary development rather than the result of sudden changes in personality. The developments included growing feelings of personal inadequacy; disillusionment with the prevailing lifestyles of modern society; increased faith in spiritual solutions to personal and social problems; more frequent interactions with "spiritual people"; futile attempts to attain spiritual fulfillment through personal efforts; and increased involvements in the activities of a religious community. The eventual conversion involved surrendering to spiritual authorities and accepting the problem-solving perspectives of the religious movement.

However, the conversion experience may be understood as a sudden change in levels of awareness and reality perception. The willingness to make personal sacrifices for a cause intensifies and the individual makes a sharper separation between "insiders" and "outsiders." Rather than a radical transformation of self-identity, the conversion symbolizes individual integration into a religious movement as the culmination of a gradual development.

Several historical observers have noted that joining social movements, religious or otherwise, provides "an escape from an unwanted self" (Hoffer, 1951). "The permanent misfits," wrote Hoffer, "find salvation only in a complete separation from the self, and they usually find it by losing themselves in the compact collectivity of a mass movement." In a similar vein, Erich Fromm (1941) argued that with the increased individualism of modern men and women, they have become isolated, powerless, and instruments of purposes outside of themselves, alienated from themselves and from others; and furthermore this process makes them ready for submission to new kinds of authority.

Relatedly, Theodore Adorno et al. (1950) maintained that those characterized by feelings of personal inadequacy tend to depend excessively on authority, to impute an exceptional degree of mastery and control to charismatic leaders, and to locate the controlling mechanisms of their own destiny in external forces. Thus, the sense of significance derives from the born-again experience and joining a religious group is presumed to compensate for feelings of self-inadequacy.

In some cases the born-again experience is preceded by an intense sense of estrangement from modern society and the culture it manifests. Cultural estrangement refers to a sense of disdain or a rejection of what is seen as the lifestyles that prevail in one's own society. This includes, for example, assigning a low reward value to mass entertainment, competitive sports, vacation travel, or other activities regarded as meaningful and rewarding by most people. Estrangement is reflected in a rejection of materialistic values and consumer-oriented lifestyles. A rejection of psychological modernity occurs with attitudes of nostalgia and a personal preference for living at some idealized time and place in the past. Estrangement is further expressed in thoughts about suicide or leaving the United States and going to live permanently in some other country.

Other attempts to discover self-fulfillment and meaning in life turn out to be futile. These frequently consist of seeking the pleasures of the moment, such as indulgence in alcohol or other drugs or becoming involved in impersonal and indiscriminate sexual relations. Following such impulse tendencies and the sequential quest for ephemeral pleasures frequently results in an overall lifestyle of aimlessness and drift (Neal and Groat, 1980).

Out of a sense of despair, attempts are sometimes made to find spiritual fulfillment through one's own efforts. These attempts are typically of limited effectiveness without frequent interactions with people who have succeeded in developing a spiritual life. Under these conditions, a dramatic and extraordinary supernatural experience may have an exhilarating effect and provide the decisive moment for changing the direction of one's life.

The conversion process reflects an attempt to make the tenets of a religious group the central values around which one's personal life is organized. The new forms of ego-involvement have a much greater degree of social acceptability than the previously destructive attempts to find meaning in life. A buffer is provided against the sense of aimlessness and drift stemming from following impulse tendencies. Taking drugs or engaging in indiscriminate sex frequently grows out of a futile quest for happiness. The redemption offered by conversion is well reflected in the comment by Mario Meadows (1990) that "God may hate sin, but he loves the sinner." At the time of making the comment, Marlo Meadows was the madam at the Mustang Ranch, a brothel in Reno, Nevada.

Crisis of Meaning

A crisis of meaning is expressed in feelings of confusion, an experience with chaos, an inability to see the interrelatedness of events and in the lack of a sense of coherence. Under these circumstances, men and women become uncertain about what to believe and how they ought to act. The core component of a crisis of meaning is the many ways in which uncertainty may be encountered. These conflicts find expression in the feeling that one's personal life lacks direction, in the perception that social life as it is known and understood is unlikely to continue in the future, and that major life decisions cannot be made with confidence.

The world has not become more coherent and orderly as a result of the vast changes that occurred during the 20th century. Perceptions of uncertainty are reflected in a process by which all societies operate with a combination of confidence and fear (Douglas and Waldavsky, 1983). In any given case, some dangers are selected for emphasis while others are relegated to the background. In general, humans are not very good at selecting the right things to worry about. This is not a matter of the grasp between reality and perception, but an inability to know the lurking dangers in any given case until after a calamity has occurred. The combination of uncertainty and incompleteness of information are foremost among the experiences of individuals in the modern world.

For those who find social life to be uncertain, there are two major forms a crisis of meaning may take. One kind emerges on a situational basis in which the individual is clobbered by an unwanted and unexpected event, such as an unplanned pregnancy, the breakup of a love affair, or the accidental death of a friend. The second kind is more pervasive and occurs in conjunction with feelings about the enduring forms of chaos in social life. Under conditions of crisis, individuals become unclear about what to believe, about how they ought to act, and about the goals worth pursuing.

Sensitivity to the variations in the world's cultures grew out of several developments of the 20th century. These included a dramatic increase in the interdependency of the world's economies, the growth of international travel and tourism, and other forms of global connectivity, such as the World Wide Web and the published reports of anthropologists. Ethnocentric beliefs about the superiority of one's own culture and the inferiority of all others still persists but is diminished within the general population. Our educational system requires at least a partial awareness of the diversity of human beliefs, values, and practices around the world.

Recognizing the diversity of cultures around the world was important for an appreciation of cultural pluralism within large and heterogeneous societies such as our own. Modernist views reject the notion that there is a single, objective reality that is shared by everyone. Ideas about relativity are elaborated to give recognition to the diversity of beliefs, practices, and experiences among groups that differ in terms of such variables as age, sex, race, ethnicity, socioeconomic status and religion.

Vulgarization of the principle of cultural relativism takes several forms. Foremost among them are the views that "anything goes," "everything is relative," and "there just aren't any definite rules to live by." Recognizing that morality is relative does not provide a justification for disregarding the normative standards of one's own society. As a result of the increased personal freedom in the modern world, individuals have more choices about how to live their lives (Rosenthal, 2005). In view of the increased pluralism of the modern world, most religious fundamentalists now reject notions about the infallible correctness of their own truth claims.

The ideology of evangelical religions serves to reduce the complexity of modern social life and thus provide a sense of purpose and meaning. Focusing selectively on the religious domain provides a way of simplifying the complexity stemming from concern with all other social institutions. Charismatic leaders provide a convincing doctrine for pointing the way to personal salvation, which serves as an alternative to personally being pulled in many different directions at the same time.

Rick Warren's book *The Purpose Driven Life* (2002) has sold over

30 million copies by laying out a religious formula for personal fulfillment, satisfaction, and a sense of meaning in life. In a modification of President Kennedy's Inaugural Address, Warren exhorts: "So, my fellow Christians, ask not what God can do for your personal life plan, ask what your life can do for God's plan." The book is not intended to be a "how-to book," nor about the range of consequential life decisions. Instead, it is only about "personal devotion to a Christian God."

Evangelical churches not only provide a sense of meaning in a chaotic world, but membership, belonging and community. Rick Warren, founder of the Saddleback Church in Southern California, is the pastor of what is often described as the largest congregational church in America (Sheler, 2007). His sermons provide an inspirational manifesto for a "wonderful, church-driven life." In his view, the tenets for the purpose-driven life include the importance of worship, fellowship, discipline, ministry, and mission. These elements are elaborated to produce meaningful outcomes that are compatible with God's plan for the individual and for the church. The appeal of Warren's book and the Saddleback Church derives from its degree of success in reducing personal stress, giving a focus to personal energy, and offering hope for a rewarding eternal life.

Those converted to an evangelical religious group are disproportionately among those seeking a sense of meaning and coherence in a mundane world. According to Max Weber (1958) and most other intellectuals, the realm of the sacred has become diminished with the growing emphasis on science, technology, and rational approaches to problem solving. Weber expressed concern about "the disenchantment of the world" with a potentially exclusive emphasis on the empirical realm. In his view, science advances at the expense of religion, rationality at the expense of the mysterious, and the secular at the expense of the sacred.

Moral Community

Robert D. Putnam (2000) reported in his book *Bowling Alone* that far more Americans are socially isolated today than they were just a few decades ago. Several research studies reveal that increasingly Americans report that they have no one to turn to or confide in when faced with a problem. In the absence of social supports, an increasing number of people are required to rely exclusively on their own resources in times of trouble. Social ties are seen as less dependable and, as a result, people have to look out pretty much for themselves.

Social isolation is manifested in a rejection of institutional behavior (e.g., family values, religiosity, the political process) under the expectation of few rewards from them. When this happens, men and women cannot assume that their own values, assumptions, and interests are likewise held and applied by other people. This occurs when feeling lonely in the midst of a crowd; feeling intensely sad during the Christmas holidays; sensing a generation gap with one's parents; or thinking about leaving the United States and going to live permanently in some other country. Confusion, bewilderment, and disbelief are frequent responses when personal assumptions fail to be confirmed by the unfolding of events or in relationships with other people.

Zygmunt Bauman (2010) has described modern intimate relations as a form of "liquid love." They are liquid in the sense that they are constantly changing and seldom endure. Even marriages are becoming increasingly fragmented as couples break up and go their separate ways, and many marriages that endured have turned sour and become bereft of meaning. Social relationships have become increasingly problematic. In the more modernized parts of the world, it does not matter where individual men and women live, since the qualities of their lives are shaped by an urban way of life.

With urbanism, communal values are replaced by individualism, tradition is replaced by personal choice, and a shared identity is transformed into collective anonymity. In recent years the private sphere has been elaborated at the expense of the public domain (Fischer, 1981). In the urban way of life, public interactions typically take place around focused activities and among strangers who share no ongoing relationships. Experiences with the city involve a vast jumble of shifting fragments and glimpses (Alter, 2005). Individualism in urban life permits a high degree of freedom of movement, yet it is a type of freedom that is based on the lack of social bonds and enduring social relationships.

Within the fabric of modernity, the family as an institution has grown increasingly fragile, and its traditional patterns are breaking down. Family members go their separate ways: they seldom eat meals together, or listen to the same music, or watch the same television programs. The increased involvement of individual members in media-produced entertainment serves as a way of reducing conflict by avoiding conversations and hence social interactions with each other. The lack of shared values and interests is likely to be among the many reasons that fewer Americans are married today than ever before in American history.

Humans are indeed social animals, but the quality of their social attachments is highly variable. Most people at some time or another are likely to feel a sense of apartness from others, just as under other circumstances they are likely to experience a strong sense of membership and belonging. The degree of comfort with one's society relates closely to the overall qualities of social relationships. These are shaped through engagement in events and activities with others (Bernikow, 1986). The lack of rewards in social relationships, the sense of apartness from others, and the loss of social attachments frequently are serious problems.

The classical work of Emile Durkheim suggested that the common denominator of all religions was that they bind men and women together into a sense of moral community. Whether a church, synagogue, or mosque, members develop a sense of solidarity that is embellished with sacred qualities. Participation has a special meaning since it provides the social cement for bringing people together and thus offering a buffer against the profane character of everyday life.

Basic to Durkheim's theory is the notion that religious phenomena are communal, rather than individualistic. According to his formal definition, "A religion is defined as a unified system of beliefs and practices relative to sacred things, that is to say, things separate and forbidden— beliefs and practices which unite in one single moral community called a Church, all those who adhere to them" (Durkheim, 1954, p. 49). Sacred activities are valued by the community of believers because of the transcendental and extraordinary meanings that are bestowed upon them.

In viewing religion as a social creation, Durkheim maintained that religious worship is implicitly a worship of society itself. Accordingly, the collective consciousness is the highest form of psychic life, since it is placed outside and above the individual and local constituencies. Religious rituals provide men and women with the necessary discipline and motivations to make personal sacrifices for the common good. The many religions of the modern world encompass representations of the multiple realities of social life. Religious observances have a euphoric function in that they counteract feelings of frustration and provide the believer with a sense of well-being (Alpert, 1939).

A type of religious fervor frequently characterizes extremist political movements (Neal, 1956). The ideologies and persuasive appeals become accepted as realities that are binding on the conduct of members. For example, in Ralph Chaplin's autobiography, *Wobbly: The Rough-and-Tumble Story of an American Radical*, he makes the following observation on his conversion to the I.W.W. (International Workers of the World):

> Here it was all wrapped up in one neat package stamped with the I.W.W. emblem. Here, I thought, was the revolutionary creed, which supplied all the answers to our questions, plus a crusading fervor, which would fill to overflowing the ideological vacuum created by previous disillusionment. We few against the world, regardless of creed, color, or nationality, united in proletarian fellowship to overthrow capitalism and usher in the "industrial commonwealth" ... to bring peace, happiness, and security to the disinherited of the earth ... to end war, injustice, and exploitation [Chaplin, 1948: 148].

The I.W.W. was a revolutionary movement with religious overtones seeking to unify the members of the working class in order to overthrow the capitalist system. The "wobblies," as they were called, refused to register for the draft during World War I. This refusal stemmed from the assumption that military service may require members of the working class to kill members of the working class in other countries. As a result. Ralph Chaplin and other members of the IWW were arrested and spent the First World War locked up in prison for acting on their convictions. Chaplin observed, "Never since the early days of the Christian martyrs were men more willing to sacrifice for a cause they believed in (p. 150)." The euphoria generated by charismatic leaders, the solidarity provided by group membership, and the receptivity to social change are among the many conditions contributing to commitment and dedication. When plunging headlong into an undertaking of vast change, men and women must have a strong conviction that both human beings and social institutions are amenable to improvement and perfectibility.

Through persuasive appeals, evangelical groups attract an assortment of constituents. Some are sympathetic to the religious message but are unwilling to participate actively. Among those who do participate, there are variations in the kinds and degrees of social and psychological involvements. The level of commitment is limited for some, while for others dedication to a cause becomes a preoccupation and a central life interest.

Commitment to a cause may provide an overall sense of purpose in life. If this occurs, in any given case, the individual may become highly dedicated and willing to make extensive personal sacrifices. The various parts of a person's life become integrated into what the individual perceives as a positive and coherent way. Becoming committed involves accepting the persuasive appeals as valid ones. The individual accepts the group's ideology, leadership, and goals as realities to be depended upon and as a basis for understanding and action. Commitments bind individuals to others in ongoing social relationships, and interaction patterns are built up that have consequences for the well-being of the individual. The formation of commitments derives from an initial process of attraction and the subsequent development of bonds that restrict the range of options available.

The concept of commitment has two distinct meanings (Becker, 1960). One is the sense of a positive commitment, which refers to embracing or dedicating oneself to the pursuit of some particular course of action. The positive aspects of a commitment relate to the rewards anticipated from the promotion of a cause or the pursuit of a goal or a set of social relationships. On the other hand, there are the negative aspects of commitment, and these consist of the penalties associated with "backing out," "reneging on a promise," "being undependable." People are likely to associate the positive aspects of a commitment with the selection of a goal, while the negative aspects of a commitment include the constraints that prevent "being a quitter," "giving up," or "changing one's mind."

People do not necessarily make commitments at the conscious level but more often experience them as an occurrence or as something that "just happened." The difficulty in terminating a commitment is analogous to the difficulty in walking up a down escalator. Continued interactions with the same people over an extended period of time tend to produce consistent lines of behavior. It frequently becomes more expedient to continue than to terminate a relationship. Howard Becker (1960) observed that the development of a commitment is analogous to "making a side bet." The side bet consists of all those considerations that emerge to promote consistency in a line of action at the same time providing obstacles to the pursuit of other alternatives. The unwillingness to change affiliations is apparently tied in with the development of routine patterns of behavior that individuals do not wish to give up because it is inconvenient to do so.

Commitment to continuance of any course of action is promoted through the development of identities that the individual's significant others know and understand. Through church affiliations, the individual acquires stable anchoring points in broad networks of social relationships. By knowing where an individual stands, others are able to relate to him or her in a predictable manner. Or in contrast, if aspects of an individual's identity become unclear, social supports may grow weak and become undependable.

The constraints accompaning commitments account for a great deal of consistency in social behavior. Becoming committed involves accepting the persuasive appeals of a religious movement as valid ones. This involves accepting the group's religious ideology, leadership, and goals as realities that can be depended on as a basis for understanding and action. While some religious groups do not require high levels of dedication and commitment, there are many that do. The utopian religious communities that endure for long periods of time are those that succeed in producing strong "we feelings and sentiments" (Kanter, 1972).

These communities achieved solidarity by requiring sacrifices and investments from members. The investments included the time and efforts put into the activities of the movement as well as requirements for financial donations and assignment of the recruits' property to the religious community. There were no refunds for defectors. Furthermore sacrifices were required in terms of individual lifestyles. These included giving up such things as tobacco, alcohol, sex, personal adornment, and personal property. All activities became centered on the community, which involved renouncing outside friends and family ties. At the same time, internal cohesion was promoted through songs, group singing, confessions, and other ceremonies that tended to separate members from outsiders.

The techniques for producing commitments in utopian religious communities are found to some degree in all social movements. Producing the commitments of members is achieved through a combination of procedures relating to social control and social cohesion. Some degree of entrapment frequently occurs because of the costs associated with dropping out. Becoming "hooked" sometimes has the effect of reducing the range of options and alternatives subsequently available.

In his autobiography, *Witness*, Whittaker Chambers (1952) makes the following observation on his dedication and commitment in joining the Communist Party:

> I was willing to accept Communism in whatever terms it presented itself, to follow the logic of its course wherever it might lead me, and to suffer the

penalties without which nothing in life can be achieved. For it offered me what nothing else in the dying world had power to offer at the same intensity—faith and a vision, something for which to live and something for which to die. It demanded of me those things which have always stirred what is best in men—courage, poverty, self-sacrifice, discipline, intelligence, my life, and at need, my death [Chambers, 1952: p. 196].

The commitment of Whittaker Chambers is another examples of what George Hillary (1977) described as "disciplined freedom." The willingness of individuals to make sacrifices for a religious or a political cause is perceived as the highest form of self-fulfillment (Hoffer, 1951). Without strong commitments life is seen as falling into fragments and becoming meaningless. Discipline, personal sacrifice, and group sharing are seen as necessary for self-actualization as well as for promoting religious or political values.

Defection

The excitement surrounding the conversion experience stands in contrast to the intense sense of disillusionment when participation in a religious or political group fails to work out as expected. The sense of purpose, community, dedication, and commitment falls by the wayside with emergence of the despair that often accompanies defection or dropping out. Richard Crossman's book *The God That Failed* (2001) provides excellent discussions of these contrasting emotions in his collection of essays by writers who had once been affiliated with the Communist Party and subsequently defected.

After six years in the American Communist Party, Whittaker Chambers repudiated Communism and was faced with the loss of group identity, fear of retaliation by former comrades, and feelings of social isolation: "No man lightly reverses the faith of an adult lifetime, held implacably to the point of criminality. He reverses it only with violence greater than the force of the faith he is repudiating" (Chambers, 1952: p. 444). In evangelical religions, the term "backsliding" is used to describe the lapse of morality on the part of a member who no longer adheres to the moral mandates of the faith. The backslider is no longer assured salvation and is viewed by officials of the church as reverting to a worsened condition. Advice to converts and members on how to avoid backsliding include staying daily in communion with God, regular reading of the Bible, and maintaining friendship and fellowship with other believers. The defectors are perceived as disloyal, untrustworthy, undependable, and dangerous.

Deep divisions within congregations may develop from controversies over religious doctrine, from conflicts over leadership struggles, or over a strong dislike for a specific member of the congregation. The reasons for leaving are many and varied. But, whatever the case, it is much easier to get into a religious group than it is to disaffiliate. Leaving the collectivity threatens the integrity of the group itself, and severe sanctions are often imposed on defectors.

Disenchantment may result from the cumulative effects of a crisis of faith. Dropping out of a particular religious group may stem from intense doubts and internal conflicts triggered by a single episode or by a gradual buildup of a general sense of discontent. Strongly opposed views on such moral issues as abortion, homosexuality, or sexual expression may lead to doubts about an unbending, official position of a church or congregation. A fanatical insistence on the correctness of a universalistic ideology may conflict with the relativism of the modern age. The interplay between certainty and doubt is being acted out in many religious denominations during our time and place (Berger and Zijderveld, 2009).

Serious doubts about the ideological correctness of one's church may lead to retaining nominal membership while holding personal views of a different order. For example, the part of the "baby boom" generation from Catholic families was keenly aware of the victimization of their parents by the mandate from the Church on birth control issues. The consequences of having to live with an exceedingly large number of siblings, and observations on the stress of their parents in raising a large number of "unplanned" or "unwanted" children, were central to their consciousness.

A crisis of authority surfaced when the Church refused to bend its position on birth control, even after the introduction of the birth control pill. Many of the younger Catholics resolved to disobey the authority of the Church on the issues of sexuality, birth control, and family planning (Groat, Knisely, and Neal, 1975). They had decided to make major life decisions on the basis of what they saw as being in their own best interests. As a result, there was a sharp decline in Catholic fertility and a convergence in levels of Catholic and Protestant fertility in all of the modernized countries of the world.

7

Illness and Wellness

The devastations visited upon individuals by unexpected and unanticipated disease, disability, or deaths are foremost among the crises of the human experience (Knowles, 1977). The crises stem in part from their unexpected appearance and from their debilitating consequences. Uncertainty about what is going to happen next precludes an inability to remain indifferent in confronting tragic circumstances. The tragedy and crisis surrounding illness and death are among the main reasons that myth-making is necessary. These two crises have been accompanied by a variety of magical and myth-making activities throughout human history. While cultures have unique ideologies and mythologies about sickness and healing, they also have conceptions about personal efficacy and the conditions promoting well-being.

The scientific treatment of illness is primarily a development of the past 200 years. Throughout most of the human past, illness was regarded primarily as a supernatural occurrence and the treatment of illness was primarily magical. While biomedicine has become the dominant element in the modern diagnosis and treatment of illness, magical and supernatural myths and rituals still abound with even the most modern forms of medical practice. Since sickness and illness are universal attributes of the human condition, all societies are required to establish and maintain the sick role in some way or another. This is because illness involves much more than physiological malfunction; family members, the work group, and sometimes the entire community are required to participate in defining and managing any given health problem.

In contrast to the scientific underpinnings of modern medicine, up until modern times, the sacred realm was elaborated to account for the uncertainty and mystery implicit in the human condition. Elaborations of the sacred included the mythical creation of supernatural entities, supernatural forces, and supernatural places. Emile Durkheim

(1961) observed that mountains and rivers may be endowed with sacred qualities as they have at various times and places. Or they may be regarded as the more mundane of the objects in the physical world. Not only gods and spirits are to be found among the sacred, but also things like rocks, trees, pieces of wood, or the special performances of artisans, athletes, or shamans. Sacred things are surrounded with a sense of awe and the extraordinary as well as with taboos and rules about what must or must not be done. The adherents of any cultural group are subjected to the moral authority of sacred beliefs and practices; social imperatives are projected onto sacred things.

Stonehenge, Mt. Fuji, Machu Picchu, and the pyramids are among the many geographical locations that were designated, at some time or another, as sacred places. Spiritual and pilgrimage travels to sacred places were for the purpose of having access to invisible energy and the mysteries of the supernatural. From ancient to modern times, people have visited sacred sites for healing, spiritual inspiration, and guidance. Ancient legends held that extraordinary things happened to people while visiting these places. Among the ancient Greeks, the shrine at Delphi was regarded as a sacred place located at the center of the earth. It became a hallowed location for consulting an oracle for guidance in making critical decisions that had life-shaping consequences.

A peasant girl of the small village of Lourdes in Southwestern France in 1858 allegedly encountered an apparition of the Virgin Mary. The location subsequently became a sacred place where large numbers of people came to drink the miraculous water from a spring and to pray for miracles of their own. While the many reported cures had no natural basis, the desired outcomes may have stemmed from the power of suggestion and from the power of the mind over the body. The medical profession of the day rejected the notion of miraculous cures and speculated that a reasonable explanation was to be found in crowd psychology. Those presumably cured had joined other believers who were "immersed in the multiple sacred symbols of healing" (Harrington, 2008).

In primitive societies, conceptions of the sacred played an important part in how people defined and reacted to illness. The mysterious powers of the sacred entered into the *mana* of the shaman and his or her special qualities that were drawn upon in the treatment of illness. The notion of *mana* in the Oceanic cultures of Melanesia, Polynesia, and Micronesia referred to the extraordinary impersonal forces that resided in people, animals, and inanimate objects. Impersonal supernatural forces provide the "stuff by which magic operates," as well as the substance inherent in the human soul. The presence of a high degree of *mana* in humans was presumed to account for superior power, influence, and ability. The *mana* possessed by an unusual stone, when placed in a garden, could lead to an unusually successful crop. The *mana* of the warrior's spear increased with each death that it inflicted. The prestige and reputation of the shaman was enhanced with each success in the treatment of illness.

Extraordinary events, such as accidental death or serious illness, evoke responses of shock, disbelief, and incredulity (Neal, 1998). Such were the responses in primitive societies to the occurrence of injury, illness, or death. In the absence of rational, empirical knowledge about the causes, primitive societies drew upon the supernatural for explanations. Consistently with explanation of illness and the rest of life, extraordinary and sacred qualities were imputed to such prescribed methods of healing as sweat baths, bloodletting, cathartics, massages, trepanning, and bone setting. People draw upon whatever knowledge they have at their disposal for solving the problems they confront, but when their rational empirical knowledge is exhausted, they draw upon the supernatural or the extraordinary to fill in the missing gaps (Malinowski, 1954).

In addition to the gods and deities that were created, the sacred also resided in the souls of individuals. A duality was seen as occurring among humans through the distinction between the body that is visible and occupies space and the soul that is invisible. It is the soul that animates the body, gives it vitality, and is liberated after life has been terminated. According to the classical writings of Sir Edward R. Tyler (1873), the soul concept was central to the development and evolution of religion. In his view, the soul concept stemmed from human experiences with sleeping, dreaming, illness, and death.

A widespread belief in primitive societies held that it was the presence of the soul that animated the body and gave it decisive and fundamental qualities. In going to sleep at night, it is the departure of the soul that places the body in a quiescent state. While sleeping, the soul goes on a journey, interacting with other souls, and even with the souls of people who are no longer living. The soul must re-enter the body in order to animate it before the person wakes up. It was for this reason that American soldiers stationed in the Pacific during World War II were surprised at the fear of alarm clocks that was held by the natives. The fear stemmed from the belief that a sudden awakening of a sleeping person may cause his soul to become disoriented and thus unable to re-enter the body prior to awakening. Dreaming was often interpreted as actual experiences from the journey of the soul while the person was sleeping. Accordingly, death stems from a permanent departure of the soul; it leaves the body never to return. Such a belief was a variant on the modern notion that death occurs with a permanent loss of consciousness.

Supernatural Explanations of Illness

In shamanistic practices, soul loss was one of the major interpretations of illness. The symptoms of soul loss include eating and sleeping disorders, a lack of energy, difficulty in performing everyday tasks, a sense of detachment or estrangement from others, and feelings of vulnerability. In modern psychiatric terminology, these are the symptoms of exposure to a traumatic event. In such cases, the soul may not return to the body on its own, and the tasks of the shaman were to intervene, to determine the reasons for the trauma responses, and to return the essence of the soul to the person's body. An attempt was made to restore wholeness and completeness following fracture from the struggle with a traumatic shock or "magical fright" (Gillin, 1958). While we would not use the term "soul loss" today, we do know from studies in medical sociology that there is an empirical connection between severe levels of depression and the onset of physical illness (Asneshensel, Frerichs, and Huba, 1984).

The shaman was a forerunner of both the modern physician and the modern priest, and his skill in treating illness was based on his proficiency in the use of the supernatural. The underlying assumption of shamanism held that certain individuals could serve as an intermediary between members of a community and the supernatural. But if humans are capable of attaining extraordinary powers through their proficiency with the supernatural, their powers could be used for evil as well as for benevolent purposes.

The belief that witchcraft or sorcery could be used to produce illness in an adversary was widespread in ancient societies as well as in many parts of the world today. Illness in primitive societies was not generally viewed as a natural event. In the absence of any other suitable explanation, notions about witchcraft and sorcery were often invoked. The use of charms, the wearing of amulets, and avoidance of the evil eye were among the many protective practices for offsetting the effects of evil influences.

Numerous anthropologists and travelers in various parts of the world have noted accounts of death following a voodoo curse. Walter V. Cannon (1972) made an important study of the mechanism by which a magic curse can result in the death of an otherwise healthy person. While voodoo was presumed to be the cause of death, we now know that the death resulted from extreme levels of fear that extend over a relatively long period of time. An intense fear response is accompanied by several physiological reactions. These include an acceleration of heartbeat, contraction of blood vessels, an increase in the production of adrenaline, and an increased release of sugar into the bloodstream. These reactions are adaptive if the fear is of short duration, but if fear is intense and extends for a protracted period of time, physiological deterioration can occur very rapidly. In modern terminology, an extreme degree of psychological stress can result in serious illness (Aneshensel, 1992; Turner and Lloyd, 1995).

Another prominent interpretation of illness was the intrusion of an evil spirit into the body of an individual. Prior to modern times, mental illness was defined primarily as an affliction stemming from demonic spirit possession. In some cases, malevolent ghosts haunted the localities where they lived and died and subsequently sought revenge on the individuals or families they had issues with while they were living.

It was often assumed that anyone meeting with a sudden and violent death would become a vengeful ghost. The disembodied spirits of the restless dead were presumed to latch onto specific persons in order to complete unfinished tasks or to live vicariously through them (Opler, 1958). The symptoms of demonic spirit possession included low energy levels, sharp character shifts or mood swings, poor concentration, sudden onset of severe depression, inner voices, unexpected physical or verbal aggression, and physical problems with no obvious cause. Such symptoms were frequently viewed as clear evidence of spirit possession.

Sometimes the malevolent spirit speaks through the victim and thus provides information about the source of discontent and what must be done before the spirit will leave. In other cases, the shaman is required to enter into a trance state in order to contact the malevolent ghost or demonic deity to diagnose the nature of the possession and to determine the means for influencing or otherwise persuading the invader to leave the body of the victim. The practices of the shaman in ancient times resemble the modern practice in some religious revivals or providing a "laying on of hands" for the purpose of driving out demonic spirits.

There was a series of movies in the 1970s that depicted "devil babies" and monster children who were possessed by demonic spirits. Such movies as *Rosemary's Baby, The Exorcist, The Omen, Damien, The Devil Within Her,* and *Audrey Rose* were designed to have a shock effect on their audience (Jackson, 1984). For example, in *The Exorcist,* the demonic child vomited green bile at the priest, masturbated with a crucifix, screamed obscenities about the young priest's mother, and rotated her head 360 degrees. In the monster movies, children lost the inherent innocence projected on them during the baby boom generation and reflected changing attitudes toward the family size and the increased perceptions of the disadvantages of children (Neal, Groat, and Wicks, 1989).

The box-office success of the movies about demonic spirit possession apparently stemmed from tapping into a responsive chord. Despite the success of science and technology in solving basic human problems, religious ideologies and beliefs in the supernatural still persist. If a benevolent God does intervene in human affairs, it seems plausible that demonic or satanic forces can also do likewise. If human beings offer prayers to a High God, either on a ceremonial occasion or in privacy, it meets with social approval. But eyebrows are raised today when either men or women report that God talked to them. Political leaders are suspect if they claim to carry on direct conversations with God on a daily basis.

Taboo violation is another of the frequently perceived causes of illness in primitive societies. The permitted and the prohibited of any given culture shape perceptions of both self-preservation and what is necessary to protect the integrity of society as moral community (Farberow, 1963). Taboos are created to protect the past. They are social norms that automatically convey supernatural punishment if they are violated. Sacred authority lies in back of taboos and avoidance of the prohibited behavior is mandatory.

The term taboo is of Polynesian origin and was first noted by Captain Cook in 1777. After its introduction into the English language it achieved widespread currency. Taboos are found in all cultures and some form of punishment automatically follows violations of them. A major way in which the punishment is manifested is through the onset of illness, either on the part of the person who violated the taboo or a member of his or her family. Taboo violations are also expressed in some type of calamity to the community. In our society, the taboo against cannibalism is sufficiently intense that most of us would associate it with mental illness, unless in an extreme situation the choice was between cannibalism and death through starvation.

The taboos of any given culture are presumed related to the ultimate conditions of the human existence. The sacred qualities of taboo are to be found in attitudes the group holds toward the rules of conduct. They are treated with respect, regarded as having supernatural support, and embedded in notions about what is necessary for sustaining order and stability. Through being held to be sacred, taboo violation has a belittling effect, and punishment is likely to occur even if others do not detect the violation or bring it forward for any kind of official action. The authority behind taboos rests on supernatural power, and punishment comes from some undefined, vague, extraordinary source.

Among the Inuit, illness or a calamity stemming from taboo violation required an assembly of the entire community. The assembly was under the supervision of a shaman who had contacted the supernatural to determine that a taboo violation had occurred (Rasmussen, 1979). The solution to the crisis resided with a public confession of the guilty about the violations that had occurred. The ceremony usually started with individual confessions of violations of rather minor offenses. These were then rejected by the shaman as not serious enough to cause the calamity of concern. The confessions would continue until more serious violations were admitted and brought out into the open. This ceremony had the effect of both tuning up basic values and promoting a sense of moral community. Social control and the treatment of illness were closely interconnected.

There were several reasons for the success of the supernatural treatments of illness. Foremost among them is the observation that most people would recover from illness most of the time if nothing at all were done. The human body has within itself remarkable curative powers. Further, the power of suggestion is important for mobilizing physiological responses. In seeking the services of a shaman, the patient temporarily becomes the center of attention. The extensive rituals surrounding the curing ceremony all point toward recovery for the patient. Social and psychological forces are mobilized to provide support in bringing about the desired result. The definitions of the situation are all organized to work in favor of the patient's recovery.

Further, the uncertainty and mystery associated with illness are diminished through the shamanistic diagnosis and treatments. Stress levels are reduced when an explanation is given and appropriately corresponding treatments are initiated. The patient develops a sense that something is being done to correct a serious, personal problem. In contrast to modern times, the diagnosis and treatment of illness was closely integrated with the dominant values and beliefs of a particular culture. Since the biomedical model as an explanation of illness had not yet been developed, the success of primitive medicine was mainly due to the placebo effect.

The Placebo Effect

A placebo is an inert substance which, when taken as medication, results in an improvement for the patient. The success of a placebo primarily depends on the belief of the patient that taking medication will help. The desire for relief from the symptoms of illness is usually a strong one among patients, and this contributes to a basic faith in the ability of physicians to provide help. Prescribing a placebo is not so much an act of dishonesty on the part of a doctor as it is doing what he or she can under the circumstances. Up until the beginning of the 20th century, the history of medicine was primarily the history of the placebo effect (Shapiro, 1959).

The improvement following the taking of a placebo may lead the patient to conclude that taking the "medicine" helped. Today we would regard the medicine shows that our great-grandparents saw at county fairs as a form of quackery, but in their time, such performances were defined as a form of consumer education. Previous generations relied on Lydia Pinkham's compound, hadacol, and other patent medicines that claimed to have impressive healing powers. The seller packaged such medicines for immediate use; instructions were included for proper dosage; and exaggerated claims were made for the curative properties. From the modern standpoint, we know that the patent medicines did not have the curative properties claimed for them, but the compounds did have enough alcohol to make our grandparents feel better, whether they were cured or not.

Historical evidence that many of the medicines of the past were placebos has not reduced the level of confidence in the medical profession. To the contrary, medicine serves as a tonic of reassurance, and people seek out medical experts when they are faced with health problems that they cannot handle themselves. They expect to improve after seeing a doctor, and the use of socially defined symbols of healing has important implications for recovery from many types of illness. The optimal condition for the self-fulfilling prophecy is when neither the patient nor the doctor is aware that the substance prescribed is a placebo.

In recognition of the placebo effect, the empirical testing of new pharmaceuticals often consists of using a double-blind research technique. In this method the researchers minimize the physician's power of suggestion by keeping knowledge of which substance is active and which is a placebo from the physician as well as from the patient. A careful analysis of the physiological responses may then indicate the degree to which the outcomes are due to the patient's pharmacological reactions to a particular drug rather than to social psychological factors. There are sufficient variations in the management of illness at all stages of its development that we cannot adequately understand illness by considering its physiological attributes alone. How people define and react to problems of illness are matters of attitudes, constructed meanings, and social supports (Segall, 1976).

For example, definitions of pain and pleasure depend to some significant degree on an interaction framework. This may be illustrated in the fact that in normal childbirth, some women describe it as a pleasurable experience, while others describe it as extremely painful. The research of Doering, Entwisle, and Quinlan (1980) suggested that the social supports expectant mothers receive influence the definitions of childbirth. The quality of the birth experience may be enhanced through adequate training and preparation for the delivery. Individuals may take classes in a hospital setting to assist them in defining child delivery in positive terms. The presence of the husband in the delivery room also seems to help, since there is a sharing of experiences and the mother receives social support. If the expecting mother has not been prepared, or if social supports are lacking, childbirth is likely to be a very painful experience; but if the positive definitions of childbirth are worked out in advance and supported in social relationships, the delivery of a baby can be a pleasurable and fulfilling experience.

During World War II and the Korean War, members of the medical staff observed that some soldiers died from relatively minor battle wounds; these deaths could not be fully explained on physiological grounds. In other cases, soldiers who received serious battle wounds demonstrated remarkable recovery although the medical odds were clearly against them. The underlying variables seemed to be attitudes toward one's physical condition and assessments of the prospects for recovery (Frank, 1964). Thinking that one will die may very well act as a self-fulfilling prophecy. Extreme attitudes of fear may produce a condition of shock and set physiological processes in motion that result in rapid deterioration and death.

Some surgeons recognize the important part the patient's attitudes play in the success of an operation. In some cases, they will not perform surgery if the patient holds a dim view toward the likely outcome. The technical skills of the surgeon may not be enough; they must be reinforced by the patient's favorable attitude toward the prospects for recovery. Doctors recognize that physical well-being is intimately connected with self-attitudes as well as with actual physiological conditions. Some paraplegics think of themselves as being physically and vocationally disabled, while Franklin D. Roosevelt as a paraplegic went on to become president of the United States. Thus, attitudes and behavior are closely linked in an individual's sense of well-being.

Doing Better But Feeling Worse

Perceptions of the quality of life vary widely among human beings, often bearing little relationship to objective circumstances or past accomplishments. People in good physical health are sometimes bored with the monotonous routines of everyday life, and people who work in high-paying jobs are often dissatisfied with other aspects of their lives. The gap between the objective circumstances of life and subjective responses to them represents an important starting point for understanding the myth-making process underlying human perceptions and behavior.

The notion of quality implies evaluations and judgments about what is desirable. Quality is an attribute of one's personal thinking rather than an inherent characteristic of persons, objects, or events. For example, by purely objective standards those living at the poverty level in modern industrialized societies of the West have standards of living that exceed those of the nobility in fourteenth-century Europe. The qualities of food, housing, and health care, for example, have improved for nearly everyone. But there is no evidence that these advances have been accompanied by corresponding increases in human happiness.

Reports from the surgeon general recurrently indicate that Americans are doing better healthwise than at any previous time in their history. For example, during the 20th century alone, more than twenty-five years were added to the life expectancy.

Several diseases, such as smallpox, polio, and tuberculosis, were brought under control through the results of medical research, and improvements in nutrition and sanitation have contributed to the better health of the nation. However, improvements in health at the community and national levels have not been accompanied by perceptions of physical well-being at the individual level. Collectively, we may be "doing better but feeling worse," as researchers in the field of health have frequently noted. A significant gap exists between the objective facts about health and the subjective responses of individuals.

If we concentrate only on objective health indicators, we would likely conclude that impressive gains have been made in recent years. But such a conclusion would not be fully warranted. Improvements in health have occurred along with increased demands for medical services and new forms of anxiety about health-related problems. The lack of exercise, the consequences of cigarette smoking, the presence of air and water pollution, and the use of chemical food preservatives are among the recent health-related concerns of Americans. Exercising, jogging, taking vitamin supplements, and participating in weight-watching programs are among the activities that reflect efforts to improve health and correct the deficiencies in lifestyles (Glassner, 1989; Hayes and Ross, 1986).

In response to modern health anxieties, Americans are inclined toward overmedication. The assumption is frequently held that there is a pharmaceutical or chemical solution to all health problems. As a result, when patients go to a doctor, they often feel that nothing has been done unless a prescription has been given. In many cases, however, medical practitioners clearly recognize that the best medicine for patients is reassurance rather than a prescription. The pharmaceutical companies have a vested interest in having doctors promote their products, and doctors frequently prefer to give patients what they want.

Patients also bear a responsibility for overmedication. They sometimes take more of a medication than is prescribed on the label; they face interaction effects by taking prescriptions along with over-the-counter medications. Both doctors and patients often fail to take into account the interaction effects of multiple medications. Overmedication is frequently an acute problem among the elderly and among children. The overuse of drugs is counterproductive through increasing dependency and the probability of allergic reactions. The overuse of antibiotics has not only led to allergic reactions for the patient but also to the evolution of bacterial strains that are resistant to antibiotics.

Uncertainty is inherent in medical knowledge and medical practice (Fox, 1980). The uncertainty stems from the limits of what is known to the medical profession as a whole as well as from limits to the grasp of the available medical knowledge by any given practitioner. In a large percentage of the cases in which the services of a physician are sought, there is no readily identifiable organic disorder. Apparently, many people become ill as a result of their inability to cope with the stresses of everyday life. Under these circumstances, establishing a definition of the patient's illness becomes a bargaining process between the doctor and the patient.

The transaction is one in which the patient proposes various illnesses that the physician may reject, and the diagnosis continues until an illness has been identified that is mutually agreeable to both the doctor and the patient. In some cases the physician may influence the outcome of the medical diagnosis independently of the patient's actual condition. This may stem from the doctor's notions about the kind of illness that is proper for any specific patient to have. Once a label has been established for characterizing an illness, the patient often feels relief in being freed from the uncertainty of not knowing how to describe his or her condition (Neal, 1983).

How people define and react to problems of illness are matters of social definitions derived from social supports in an interaction framework (Segall, 1976). However, in the diagnosis and treatment of illness, the realities constructed by the physician and the patient may differ in fundamental ways. The patient tends to have a global orientation toward health problems; something has occurred that interferes with normal functioning and remedial action is sought. The physician, by way of contrast, is trained to think in terms of specific maladies for which there are specific remedies. If there is a physiological basis for the illness, there is a physiological remedy.

The physician is able to perform effectively the expected role if he or she is able to identify specific problems. In many cases, however, an identifiable, organic malfunction cannot be found and consequently a clear-cut remedy cannot be established. Or the physician may not be able to locate any specific problem, or may identify a specific problem for which there is no known cure. In either of these cases, several outcomes can occur: the physician may prescribe a "best guess" medication; the physician may refer the patient to a diagnostic center for further testing; or the physician may suggest to the patient the lack of any apparent medical problem. The realities defined by the doctor may be unacceptable to the patient; the patient may become angry with the doctor; the patient may seek the services of another physician for "a second opinion"; or the patient may seek remedies that lack endorsement by the medical profession.

If there is a physiological basis for an illness, there is a physiological solution. But many, perhaps most, of modern illnesses do not stem from germs or viruses. Instead, they grow out of the many forms of stress inherent in modern social living (Harrington, 2008). These include communal levels of stressors, such as being stuck in congested traffic, standing in long lines at the supermarket, being fearful of criminal victimization, and living in the midst of environmental pollution (Stockwell and Neal, 1991). Serious personal troubles include the stress associated with the death of a spouse or a close friend, getting a divorce, being in an automobile accident, becoming a rape victim, or losing one's job. A great deal of research reported in the *Journal of Health and Social Behavior* indicates that the health-related problems growing out of conditions of communal and personal stress are not readily amenable to solution through applications of the bio-medical model.

Antidepressants are the most widely prescribed drugs in the United States today. This is in part because a large number of people think that there is a chemical solution to all of their problems. Rather than using the medical criteria for clinical depression, doctors frequently write unnecessary and inappropriate prescriptions in order to give patients what they want. As a result, the extension of medicalization has had the effects of suppressing the range of human emotions and thus limiting what it means to be human. According to Eric G. Wilson (2008), Amer-

ican obsession with happiness accounts for the spiraling use of antidepressants to suppress such emotions as melancholia and sadness.

The dominance of the bio-medical model has not worked very well
in treating the traumatic stress of combat veterans, rape victims, or bro-
kenhearted lovers. These are among the illnesses for which there are no
quick fixes. With the ending of the Vietnam War, the nation became
more clearly aware of what came to be called *the post-traumatic stress
syndrome*. Thousands of veterans returned from the war victimized by
their tragic experiences. The trauma of the war continued in recurrent
nightmares, in the resurgence of intense feelings of sadness, and in the
enduring sense of numbness. Psychologically, the war had not ended
for the returning veterans. Through being required to suspend the normal guidelines for morality, decency, and humanity, combat veterans of
all wars necessarily become changed persons (Shay, 1994).

In order to compensate for the deficiencies in modern medicine,
an increasing number of people are turning to the spiritual mythology
of Eastern religions (Worsley, 1997). Echoes from ancient religions are
being combined with modern medical practices. The traditional systems
of Eastern medicine that developed over many centuries include herbal
medicines, meditation and relaxation techniques, acupuncture, spinal
manipulations, spiritual therapies, and massage. Eastern medicine
emphasizes a holistic approach, and attention is directed toward obtaining an optimal balance between the physical, mental, emotional, and
spiritual aspects of health.

Several decades of research on social indicators suggest that Americans derive greater satisfaction from family life than from any other
social domain. Among married couples the overwhelming majority
(about 75 percent) report being "completely satisfied" or "very satisfied"
with their marriages. No other domain of social life evokes such a positive response, suggesting that married couples find greater sources of
reward and meaning within marriage than in any other area (Campbell,
1981). The high levels of satisfaction within family life are perhaps due
to the importance of emotional supports that intimate relationships provide. Along these lines Angus Campbell (1981: 75) made the following
observation: "Marriage, of all human experiences, appears to have unri-
valed potential for joy and torment, fulfillment and frustration. For most
people the positives outweigh the negatives, and their feeling of the quality of their marriage contributes crucially to their perception of the quality of their lives."

But a large percentage of the marriages in the United States today do not work out. The divorce rate has increased dramatically, and the consequences for the most part have been disastrous for the quality of life. Negative typifications of relationships between men and women abound in popular music, in mass entertainment, and in everyday patterns of speech. Men frequently complain of women: "We can't live with them, and we can't live without them, so what the hell are we going to do?" The comments of women mirror a similar sense of despair: "There are a lot of rotten men out there," and "You have to kiss a lot of frogs before you find a prince." The pathos and tragedy surrounding love affairs reflect a pantheon of troubles: marital discord, disloyalty of a spouse or partner, having wants and desires that remain unfulfilled, wanting someone you cannot have, receiving promises that are not kept, dealing with the abuse of alcohol, confronting marital infidelity, and suffering the tragedy of breaking up are among the staples in the mood states evoked by popular culture (Neal and Collas, 2000).

While the themes of country music are individualized in that they portray personal troubles of individuals in specific situations, the generalized context is one of a sense of malaise in male-female relationships. Rather than a neutral set of observations about the borders and boundaries of sexual conduct, the messages more nearly reflect generalized themes of despair and resignation. A study by Steven Stack and Jim Gundlach (1992) of forty-nine metropolitan areas found that those areas devoting a greater amount of airtime to country music had higher suicide rates. Apparently, the mood states of country music can build upon and accentuate the sense of despair in heterosexual relations that prevail on an everyday basis. The mythology of "romantic love" and "living happily ever after" leads to expectations in intimate relationships that cannot be fulfilled.

Yet the quality of life is compromised with the severance of social ties. Marriage, friendships, and employment are forms of social attachment that provide psychological stability in the sense that predictions can be made with confidence about the normality and continuance of social life. But if this stability is shattered through divorce, the loss of a job, the breakup of a friendship, or the death of a spouse, the individual is thrown back on his or her own resources and is likely to experience feelings of isolation and a sense of meaninglessness. The disruption of marriage through divorce or the death of a spouse produces high levels of emotional stress irrespective of the quality of the marriage or the desire for its dissolution.

In the later years of life, the most critical adjustments women have to make is coping with the severance of marital bonds through the death of a spouse. This adjustment is more likely to be required of women than men because of two basic facts: life expectancy is greater for women than for men, and most women marry men who are older than they are. Thus overall patterns of mate selection and longevity converge to make coping with the death of a spouse a special problem for older women. Data from the United States Bureau of the Census indicate that the odds were nearly five to one that the surviving spouse will be the wife rather than the husband.

We may understand the social isolation produced by widowhood as deriving from numerous sources of meaning and commitment that have been built up over a long period of time. The meanings include both recurrent interactions in the more intimate spheres of married life and the linkage of the couple as a unit to broader networks of social relationships. The interior of family life includes the development of such joint enterprises as coordinating daily schedules, sharing work tasks, planning vacations, making love, and pursuing hobbies. Externally the marital unit tends to become an influential social link, and others come to view the couple in terms of a common front, which the two present to the outside world.

Without her husband, the wife cannot reproduce certain interaction patterns, and other people do not treat her as they did before. For example, friends of the widow's husband often avoid her because they are uncomfortable in her presence and do not know how to relate to her. She does not receive invitations to certain events because the events are organized for couples. The difficulties in coping with these disruptions are reflected in higher suicide rates for the widowed compared to the continuously married; among the widowed the suicide rates are higher for men than for women. Apparently for men the isolating effects that accompany the loss of work attachments intensify with a loss of the marital bond. The greater difficulties of men in coping with the death of a spouse suggest that under normal circumstances men are more emotionally and socially dependent on their wives than most would care to admit.

In contrast to the importance of intimate relationships for the quality of life, a sense of well-being is less correlated with the impersonal domains of social life. Satisfaction with family life, marriage, friends, and work account for a great deal that is known about the sense of well-being. These are the areas of life that generate intrinsic rewards for many people. The domains relating to the external environment exert less influence on overall evaluations of the quality of life. The community, the neighborhood, housing, the amount of wealth, and conditions in the nation at large are certainly important in the thoughts and actions of individuals, but these domains contribute less to general life satisfaction than do the more intimate spheres of social relationships.

With the loss of a sense of community in our increasingly urbanized society, there are encounters with impersonality, detachment, atomization, and anonymity. Georg Simmel (1950) demonstrated the experiences of individuals in the modern metropolis by drawing upon the concept of "the stranger" as one who is physically close to many other people while psychologically feeling far away. The combination of "nearness" and "remoteness" is not conducive to having a sense of well-being. We are precluded from assuming that there is a correspondence between our own understanding of norms and values and those held by other people.

Extending the life expectancy to 100 years would be a remarkable accomplishment if certain conditions were met in the life circumstances of individuals. These include sufficient physical well being that major life objectives can be pursued; sufficiently rewarding social attachments to provide a sense of membership and belonging; and adequate financial resources for being able to pay the bills without being stressed out. Finally, it is important for the elderly to have a sense of purpose in life and to be engaged in activities that are intrinsically rewarding. But if the above conditions are met, the quality of life is pretty good, regardless of age level or stage of life.

8

Death and Immortality

Death is one of the major tragedies of the human experience, stemming from the recognition among humans that all living things are born, grow old, and die. It is our consciousness that sets us apart from all other animals and produces the tragedy of death. Awareness of death and dying is not problematic for the deceased, but only for the living. If death is the permanent loss of consciousness, then when we are dead we will never know it. The tragedy of death is for the survivors and those who are required to go on living without a valued spouse, friend, or other group member.

The fundamental absurdity of the human condition is that each of us has an awareness of our own mortality. We go through the journey of life without knowing how or when death will occur. As a result of our incomplete information, we go about business as usual as though we were immortal. At the same time, lurking in back of our minds is the recognition that sooner or later each of us will die. It is against this background of not knowing the death date on our tombstones, if we have one, that serves as a reference point for assessing the meaning of life.

Only the individual deliberately terminating his or her own life can eliminate the uncertainty of not knowing when death will occur. At the time of this writing, suicide with the assistance of a medical doctor is illegal in most states. The state of Oregon enacted the Death with Dignity Act on October 27, 1997, to permit terminally ill patients to end their lives voluntarily with lethal medications that were prescribed by physicians for that purpose. Deciding on the timing of death by lethal medication permits individuals to set their affairs in order, to obtain relief from pain and suffering, and to have a sense of personal mastery and control over one of the more consequential events of the life course.

The tragedy of death grows out of our experiences with time as one-dimensional and irreversible. We are born, pass through the stages of infancy, childhood, adolescence, and then become young adults. With human biological reproduction in early adulthood, the biological life cycle has been completed and the species continues. This now occurs before half of the modern life span has been completed. We experience the stages of the life span as intervals along a one-way street as we grow old and die. As noted on tombstones, the journey of life has a clear beginning and end. The reality of death as final is a part of our empirical experience.

As human beings, we have difficulty with notions of life as one-directional and irreversible. We make mistakes, do stupid things, and have regrets, but as Omar Khayyam (1048–1131), a Persian mathematician, astronomer, philosopher, and poet, wrote:

> The Moving Finger writes; and, having writ,
> Moves on; nor all thy Piety nor Wit
> Shall lure it back to cancel half a line,
> Nor all thy Tears wash out a Word of it.

The recognition of events as irreversible places a heavy burden of responsibility on the individual. While we have increased the freedom for making choices (Rosenthal, 2005), we do not have the opportunity to undo or to reverse some of the more crucial life decisions we make. We are often left helpless and dissatisfied from the promiscuous amount of choice we are now permitted to have (Schwartz, 2004). Because of the irreversibility of such decisions as those leading up to an unplanned pregnancy or an unfortunate marriage, individuals suffer from the tragic decisions that are made. Yet, as a result of trying too hard to make the best decisions possible, there are others who suffer from regrets, missed opportunities, and feelings of inadequacy.

But if we experience the journey of life as a one-way street with a dead end, we also have experiences with time as repetition. This is characteristic of the oscillation between night and day and the circular movement of the seasons from fall to winter, to spring to summer to fall, and thus in a continuous circular motion. Such repetitions provide opportunities for new beginnings and hence offer more hopeful possibilities than time only as unidirectional. The renaissance of spring clearly indicates that in the natural world certain phenomena repeat themselves.

Religious repudiation of the finality of death frequently implies that life is a series of repetitions: life follows death and death follows life. The ticking of a clock, the rise of the morning sun, and New Year's Day are all a part of the human experience with repetitions (Leach, 1975). The notion of time as repetition is built into the regular celebration of such societal events as Christmas, the 4th of July, and Martin Luther King's birthday. It is also built into the repetition of such family events as birthdays and wedding anniversaries. We know in advance when these events will occur, plan for them, and alter everyday activities to give special recognition to them.

The above time perspectives serve as underlying frameworks for assessing and evaluating the meaning of death. Biological and genetic conceptions of the life cycle do not recognize the abrupt beginning of an individual life or the finality of the end. Both birth and death are simply episodic occurrences within a broader evolutionary scheme. An extremely long evolutionary process lies in back of the creation of a human being and this process will be continued long after a specific death has occurred. From a biological standpoint, animal life forms are interconnected; humans share a large part of their genetic structure with chimpanzees and even lower life forms such as worms.

From a sociological standpoint, specific individuals come and go, but specific societies remain. In this sense a society is a super organic entity in that its origin and continuance are not fully dependent upon specific individuals or even upon a specific generation. The social heritage of any given group of people has deep roots extending into a remote and unknown past. While the future is always surrounded by an inherent uncertainty, we go about our everyday activities by assuming that social life as we know it will continue into the future.

Yet within the biological and sociological contexts, the death of specific individuals is frequently surrounded with intense emotionality, especially among close friends and relatives. We are not able to remain indifferent when we encounter the meaninglessness of death. The crisis is more intense when it falls outside the predictive framework within which we orient our commitments and aspirations. For example, the premature deaths of college students in automobile accidents or in drug overdoses are events that should never occur by the standards of what is normal, natural, and just within families and within the social system. Such untimely deaths preclude the fulfillment of the hopes and aspirations of both parents and the students. To have lives ended abruptly and without warning is an encounter with absurdity that has no place in a just world.

When Death Is Out of Place

The sting of death has a more intense impact when it is unpredictable and out of place. We have a collective awareness of the proper time to die. For example, death is more acceptable after a long and productive life than when the promise of youthful idealism is terminated. Death is more readily accepted for those in old age who are suffering from chronic pain and an incurable illness than for those who are young and healthy. The tragedy of the political assassinations of the 1960s was heightened by their shocking effects and their assaults on the leadership of the nation.

The collective sadness shared by Americans following the assassination of President John F. Kennedy was unprecedented in the history of the nation. The collective sadness was in part an outgrowth of the continuous coverage of the events surrounding the assassination by the relatively new medium of television (Zelizer, 1992). Everyday activities around the country were drawn to a halt upon the involvement of the entire nation in the four-day mourning process. The nation watched as the heads of state arrived in Washington to pay their respects. The funeral possession from the National Cathedral to Arlington Cemetery was three miles long and included such world figures as General Charles de Gaulle, Emperor Haile Selassie, and the presidents of the Philippines and South Korea. The emissaries represented nearly all the major noncommunist countries of the world. In some respects, the tragedy of Kennedy's death resulted in one of the most impressive summit meetings in history.

The youthfulness of Kennedy added to the intensity of the trauma. He was only forty-three years old when he was elected president, the youngest man ever elected to that office. The aura he brought to the presidency was one of youthfulness, vigor, energy, and idealism. He was the first president born in the twentieth century and was admired by the youth of the nation and regarded as the central spokesman for a new generation. Politics had been elevated to a new level, and Kennedy's style was oriented toward enhancing optimism, idealism, and commitment.

The sanctification of Kennedy as an ideal man and as an ideal president was frequently associated with collective memories of President Lincoln. Each had been assassinated under conditions of crisis and tension. In Lincoln's case, the Civil War had recently ended and his assassination was linked with the deaths of thousands of soldiers who had lost their lives on the field of battle. His assassination had provided a climax to the end of a bitter war in which mass armies met on the field of battle and the casualties ran into the hundreds of thousands (Faust, 2008). The tragedy of Lincoln's assassination added to the trauma of the war itself. The enormous task of rebuilding a divided nation remained unfinished. By elevating Lincoln to the status of a martyr, his assassination provided the world with a sanctified model of what a great leader ought to do in the quest for social justice and human rights.

A little more than four years after Kennedy's death, the nation was again shocked by the assassination of one of America's major political leaders. A sniper shot Martin Luther King, Jr., as he stood talking on the balcony of a motel in Memphis, Tennessee. He died shortly afterward in St. Joseph's Hospital from wound in the neck. He was only thirty-nine years of age at the time of his death. King had been in Memphis to lend his support to a strike by sanitation workers. As the symbolic leader of the Civil Rights Movement, he had delivered hundreds of speeches and sermons in the quest for social justice. He had succeeded in transforming the politics of social change into a moral and religious responsibility. The trauma of his assassination brought into sharp focus the epic struggle for racial equality. He had mobilized a large constituency to address the question of how to bring about an end to the blatant forms of racial discrimination in our society (Neal, 2005).

The nation was shocked and saddened by the death of an American who had received the Nobel Peace Prize for his contribution to human rights and social justice. The moral conscience of the nation was brought under examination as Americans reflected on the violence that seemed endemic to American life. Comparisons were made between Kennedy and King. Both were seen as martyrs with strong convictions, with idealistic visions for the future of the country, and with personal commitments to the cause of social justice. It became noteworthy and symbolic that King's assassination took place on Good Friday, a day recognized as the day of death of another great religious leader.

The largest category of the premature dead consists of the civilian and military fatalities of modern warfare. The trauma of the military dead has its more intense impact on family members. This is because the motives for having and rearing children are geared toward having durable and meaningful relationships over the life course. To have these social ties terminated by the death of a son or daughter in the Korean

War, the Vietnam War, or the Iraq War is not what parents had in mind in their family planning.

The significance of the slaughters in modern warfare perhaps derives less from the military objectives than from the discontinuities stemming from notions about the proper end of life. Drew Gilpin Faust (2008) describes military fatalities as an issue of who should die, when and where, and under what circumstances. In addition to the uncounted civilians, modern warfare abruptly takes the lives of healthy men and women who have only reached the promising years of early adulthood. To parents and siblings the absurdity of losing a child or a sibling to modern warfare is intensified by the increasing life span within the general population. The tragedy is further intensified for those who believe that the specific war was immoral and unnecessary. The process of mourning is one of efforts to come to grips with the reality of an irreplaceable loss (Gorer, 1967).

Through a collective attempt to come to terms with the trauma of premature death, rituals and ceremonies are elaborated. Each year when the flowers are blooming, Americans celebrate Memorial Day. It is both a holy day for commemorating the military dead and a holiday. For some it is a long weekend for such pleasurable engagements as an extended outing, attending athletic events, watching the Indianapolis 500, or involvement in other rewarding activates. It is also a time for solemn rituals and ceremonies and for visiting cemeteries.

Memorial Day originated in the North shortly after the end of the Civil War. It was designed as a sacred day to show respect for the extremely large number of Union soldiers killed in the war. It subsequently became a holy day for giving recognition to all Americans who lost their lives in all of the nation's wars (Warner, 1962). The speeches and ceremonies in small-town America, as well as at Arlington Cemetery and the Tomb of the Unknown Soldier, elevate the military dead to heroic status and emphasize the theme that they voluntarily gave their lives for their country. Patriotic rituals and ceremonies are thus designated to tune up national values and to give solemn recognition to the tragic loss of some of the nation's best and brightest.

The public glorification of dying for one's country stands in contrast to the meaninglessness of young people dying as a result of random killings on college and high school campuses. We usually think of college campuses as among the more idyllic, safe and secure places in our society. Yet one of the more shocking episodes during the Vietnam War surfaced when the Ohio National Guard fired indiscriminately into students on campus at Kent State University without regard for whether they were protesting against the war or not. Four students were killed and several others severely wounded. The anger of students and faculty over the senseless killings resulted in the largest strike in the history of the country. Most colleges and universities in the United States were required to suspend normal operations for several days.

Another traumatic example of death out of place occurred on April 20, 1999, at Columbine High School near Littleton, Colorado. Two teenage students, Eric Harris and Dylan Klebold, carried out a planned shooting spree that killed 12 other students and a teacher before they committed suicide. They had planned to detonate bombs they had placed in the cafeteria when about 500 students would be on their lunch break. The detonators on their bombs failed to work, or the calamity would have been even more severe. Their journals also included plans for a massacre in the neighborhood before hijacking an airplane that they intended to crash into a building in New York City.

The school shootings at Columbine became an important symbolic event in the life of the nation. In elaborating on the symbolism of the tragedy, Michael Moore's documentary filmed *Bowling for Columbine* concentrated on the gun culture that has been elaborated in our society. The ready availability of guns becomes manifested in the aggregate data on homicide, suicide, and accidental death. Studies funded by the U.S. Department of Education revealed the many ways that the gun culture has an impact on children and adolescents. Almost a hundred children are expelled in the United States each week for bringing a gun to school. While the motives remain unclear, it is somewhat evident that they frequently bring guns to school with the intention of using them.

Whatever the basis for the indiscriminate killing in school shootings, it is clear that the death of victims has traumatic and long-enduring consequences for family and friends. The motives for bearing and rearing children often consist of an interest in promoting family continuity. The pleasures of watching children grow and develop and the emotional interactions with them were circumvented by their premature deaths. Schools are expected to provide valuable learning experiences under protective and secure conditions, rather than the context for the senseless loss of life.

Funeral Practices

All societies are characterized by a ritualistic or ceremonial disposal of the dead. The emotional impact of the death crisis is sufficiently intense that simply tossing the corpse on a garbage dump is not a reasonable option. The ritualistic disposal of the dead follows cultural patterns that are deeply embedded in the social heritage of any given group of people. Funeral ceremonies help to confirm the reality and finality of death. As such, they provide for a declaration that a life has been lived and that a death has occurred. The funeral often serves as a gathering place for family and friends to share the loss and to give emotional support to each other. While the death of a family member is a very personal loss, the death also has consequences for distant family members, friends, and the community at large. The funeral rituals provide a way of tuning up group values, giving recognition to a transition in the life course, and providing a standardized way of dealing with a tragic event.

In all cultures, responses to a corpse are ambivalent ones. Universally, the person is remembered as a valued group member at the same time it is noticed that a gruesome transformation has occurred. In some cultures, the corpse is held and passed from one person to another, along with wailing and the expression of grief. In other cultures, the corpse is immediately placed into the sacred realm of taboo and is avoided as much as possible. The ambivalence toward the corpse is manifested in a wide range of cultural beliefs and funeral practices.

Morris E. Opler's (1958) study of the traditional Mescalero and Chiricahua Apache cultures noted an extraordinary fear of the dead and funeral practices that involved disposing of the corpse on the same day as death, if that was possible. Only a few people participated in the disposal of the dead, and those who did were required to undergo a decontamination ritual afterwards. The contact between the living and the dead was reduced to a minimum. The possessions of the dead were disposed of with dispatch. It was incumbent upon relatives to dispose of those things the deceased used during his lifetime. The place where the diseased lived was burned to the ground. The location of the grave was not discussed afterward, and visiting the grave was unthinkable. These procedures grew out of a deep underlying fear of "ghost" or "darkness sickness." Serious attempts were made to suppress or to obliterate the memory of a diseased relative. Yet there was a prolonged expression of grief by a spouse, by a sibling, or by a friend. This often involved tearing the clothing from one's body upon hearing of the death of a close friend or relative.

Among the Apache the fear of ancestral ghosts was very intense. In this culture one of the most serious insults was to mention the name of a deceased relative in one's presence. It was believed that just through mentioning the name of the deceased it would cause their evil spirit to arrive at that spot. The Apache were also frightened by the appearance of an owl in camp. Ghosts come back in the shape of an owl, and the owl is the ghost of a departed relative. Ghosts trouble people mostly at night, and when the owl leaves camp it is only a short time until the death of a close family member. The owl was interpreted as a physical representation of the dead. It was a serious omen of an impending death in the family, and when the owl departed it would soon take the soul of a living relative.

Rebecca Green's (2000) study of funeral practices in Madagascar provides a striking contrast to those of the Apache. Instead of obliterating memories of the dead, funerary practices revere them and consider them essential to the stability and well-being of the living. Caring for ancestors is believed to be reciprocated by the deceased with benevolence and gratitude. Accordingly, the main point of interaction between the living and the dead occurs with the rewrapping ceremony. The four-day ceremony involves going to the caves and bringing the deceased into the community for feasting, flowery speeches, and celebration. The dead are reshrouded, given gifts, spoken to softly, touched, carried, and danced with. Before the ancestral dead are returned to their caves, the reburial involves enveloping them in new shrouds. New silk cloths are wrapped around the old ones. As long as the deceased are remembered and honored, social life as it is known and understood will be perpetuated.

The traditional Irish wake, which was commonplace in Ireland up until about 1970, involved giving a great deal of immediate attention to the deceased. Neighbors assisted in washing and laying out the body in the house where he or she lived. The body was placed in a coffin and carried into the living room. Relatives, friends, and neighbors would gather in the home, and large quantities of food and drink were consumed to assure that the deceased would have a good sendoff. The wake was as much of a party as it was a funeral ritual. Those who came would both socialize and remember the life of the departed. There was a norm against saying anything negative about the person who had died. The corpse must not be left unattended for the duration of the wake. On the next day the corpse was taken to the graveyard for a second funeral and burial.

Jessica Mitford (1963) observed that the traditional American funeral resembled the Irish wake in many respects. It was not until the 20th century that the American funeral industry became professionalized and replaced the role of family members and friends in preparing the corpse for burial. Up until the end of the 19th century, simplicity was the guiding rule in funeral preparations, almost to the point of starkness. After a death occurred, friends would gather with family members to lay out the corpse in a pine box, usually made by a neighbor. After an optional wake, friends and relatives bore the coffin to the graveyard for a funeral and for placing the coffin in a grave that had been dug by neighbors. Once the mortuary industry became professionalized, funerals became much more impersonal, complicated, and expensive (Harmer, 1963).

In a study of modern American funeral practices, Ronney E. Turner and Charles Edgley (1976) drew upon Irving Goffman's distinction between "front stage and backstage regions" of theatrical performances. The front stage region is the setting in which some prearranged performance is enacted for a viewing audience; the backstage region is an "off limits" area where the background work is performed. The backstage areas are designated as private spheres not only for getting the necessary work done without interference but also to keep the activities taking place there from discrediting the impressions made in the front stage area.

In an analysis of funeral directing, Turner and Edgley demonstrate the importance of the backstage setting for the theatrics surrounding the death crisis. From their description of the backstage setting in which the corpse is prepared for viewing, it becomes evident that most of us would prefer to be excluded from such areas or activities:

> Here the corpse is washed, shaved, sprayed with disinfectant, sliced, pierced, creamed, powdered, waxed, stitched, painted, manicured, dressed, and positioned in a casket. Embalming involves the draining of blood via the major arteries while simultaneously refilling them through an injection point in the neck or armpit with fluid. Through the use of other chemicals the flesh is softened, stretched, shrunk, restored, colored, and even replaced [Turner and Edgley, 1976: 381].

Observing such procedures would likely have a shocking effect on the friends and relatives of the deceased. The front stage area, by way of contrast, is characterized by a widely different set of performances and definitions. People speak softly to one another; they attempt to control their expression of grief; and they make reference to "the loved one" as looking "natural" or as appearing to be in "a deep and tranquil sleep." Such images are supported only by shielding observers from the activities connected with preparing the corpse for viewing. As a result of modern funeral practices, very few contemporary Americans have ever seen an untreated corpse. Preparing the corpse to look lifelike is a form of a denial of the reality of death.

In contrast to most funeral practices, the ancient Egyptians believed that the corpse must be prepared for eternity and that the body of the deceased should bear as close a resemblance to the living person as possible. Many elements of embalming and preservation of the body were associated with the mummification process (Pinch, 2004). Techniques were elaborated for minimizing the putrefaction process. Features of the face and other parts of the body were modeled with linen bandages. Amulets were placed in the bandages to provide magical protection for the hazardous journey through the afterlife. The Egyptian mummy was more than a preserved corpse: it manifested an image of what the person had been. Placing a golden mask over the face of the deceased was believed to facilitate turning a mummy into a supernatural being. The preservation process was so remarkable that mummified bodies have been found in good condition thousands of years after their death.

Mummification and cremation represent extreme opposite forms of response to a corpse. Mummification is oriented toward preserving the body as a representation of the person. In contrast, cremation focuses on the gruesome transformation and the corpse is no longer regarded as a person. Being human requires consciousness, and without consciousness the corpse has become an undesirable and gross entity. The untreated human corpse starts the process of decomposition very quickly. For example, complex chemical reactions, bacteria, and enzymes begin breaking down cells and the destruction of body organs. Soon after death, brain cells die within three to seven minutes, while skin cells can take over 24 hours. Cremation accelerates the decomposition and putrefaction that would occur under natural conditions of exposure to the air, being submerged in water, or being buried in the ground.

The custom of cremation is an ancient one among the Hindu of India. Prior to modern refrigeration, the cremation was held without delay, usually within the day after death. Lighting the flame on the wood funeral pyre was an obligation of the eldest son. Among the Hindu the body is seen as an instrument for carrying the soul. Thus with death the corpse is not regarded as a person since the soul has left. The reason for the preference of cremation over burial in the ground is to induce a feeling of detachment and to speed up passage of the soul to its ultimate destination. In earlier times, the wives of the deceased engaged in the practice of *suttee* that consisted of the widow throwing her body on the funeral pyre of her husband. The marriage bond was too strong to be broken by death, and through the practice of *suttee* the wife would be able to join the soul of her husband on his journey into the afterlife.

Basically funerals are for the benefit of the living; the dead have no awareness of the proceedings. The deceased are incorporated into the world of the dead, and the survivors are faced with the challenge of getting on with the business of living. Coping with the death of a spouse or close friend is among the more stressful life events. It is perhaps as a way of dealing with the stress of survivors that all cultures have elaborated standardized and normative ways of conducting funeral ceremonies and burial rituals. It may also be that the human tragedy of confronting death has led to a nearly universal set of beliefs in human immortality in some form or another. Accordingly, if life is a one-way street ending in death, then as one door closes another one opens.

Conceptions of Immortality

Survey research consistently indicates that approximately 95 percent of Americans believe in life after death. The belief in life after death stands in sharp contrast to the widespread fear of death and the dread of dying (Dawkins, 2006). Many people believe death to be followed by transmigration of the soul to some beautiful and heavenly place. The specific mechanism by which this shall occur remains unclear. This set of beliefs seems to stand in opposition to the mourning and sadness following the death and dying process. If death were a transition to a more desirable place it would then seem that death should be followed by joyous celebration and congratulations. Since this typically is not the case, there is some degree of ambiguity and uncertainty about the quality and prospects of life after death.

Much of religion is geared toward a denial of the finality of death (Becker, 1973). Experiences with life as a gift, as a journey, and as a mystery are found among men and women everywhere. While the specific content of beliefs about life, death, and the soul are richly varied, some version of these is universal. Within this context, the death crisis is of such a magnitude that men and women cannot remain indifferent. Social creations of the soul and beliefs about what happens to the soul after death are responses of the living to the tragedy of separation and the lack of continuity in valued social relationships. All cultures hold some notion about the soul, how it animates the body, and how it continues its journey after death has occurred.

The many ways of honoring the dead include visiting gravesites, leaving flowers or a gift, and saying a prayer. These are important activities for the living and few would stop and ponder whether or not the deceased have an awareness of what is happening. Instead, the visitors to a gravesite act "as if" there is a consciousness among the dead and an awareness of the homage being paid to them (Warner, 1962).

Throughout most of the human past, the spirits of the dead were presumed to remain in the community of the living. In some cases, the spirits of the dead were believed to be benevolent and protective. In other cases, the spirits of the dead were regarded primarily as malevolent. In yet other cases, the dead remained as guardians within the community, but only as long as they were revered and remembered.

In many cultures, the belief in continuity of the soul is much more prominent than the emphasis on eternity. The continuity is promoted by a ceremonial remembering of the dead. In Madagascar the dead are remembered in their rewrapping ceremony, and in ancient China the dead are remembered by having their names inscribed on ancestral tablets. In several tribal groups in traditional Africa, the humanity of the newborn infant was held to be tentative. By observing the behavior of the child during infancy, it could be determined which characteristics of deceased ancestors were manifested. After surviving the first year of life, the child was accorded human status and given the name of a deceased ancestor he or she resembled. Each of the above forms of remembrance grows out of positive images of both the elderly and the spirits of the dead. Remembrance is also a social obligation that is not to be avoided without serious consequences. In many cultures the spirits of the dead provide guardian spirits as long as traditions are preserved and followed.

Adherents to the customs of the Jewish religion are obligated to light a candle on the death anniversary of a child, a sibling, a spouse, or a parent. The ritual falls annually on the date of the relative's death according to the Hebrew calendar. Among the Orthodox, a prayer is recited three times a day, and many attend synagogue for the evening, morning, and afternoon services. Many synagogues have a special memorial plaque on one of the walls with names of the members who have died. Visiting the gravesite of the deceased on the anniversary of death is another form of remembrance. These forms of commemoration for the loved one are deeply engrained in Jewish life to honor the memory and the souls of the deceased.

In Mexico the Day of the Dead is celebrated on the first two days of November. The tradition involves building private altars to honor the deceased. Sugar skulls are created, favorite foods and beverages are made available, and petals of marigold are strewn to guide the souls from the street to the altar. The first day of November is set aside to honor deceased children, while the second day of November is designated as a time to honor departed adults. The rituals and ceremonies stem from the belief that on these days the soul of the departed will visit the living. The intent of the rituals is to permit departed souls to hear the prayers and comments of the living directed toward them.

A rich folklore has persisted into the 21st century about the coexistence of the spirits of the dead along with the living. Encounters with ghosts are widely reported along the Cumberland and the Southern Appalachian region (Montell, 1975). The variability of the accounts of ghosts include lost souls who roam the earth, those who return to settle a score, and those who are wandering wearily and aimlessly in the search of pure love. Elaborate precautions are frequently taken when a person has died from homicide or suicide. Ghosts make their presence known not only through apparitions but also through dragging chains, dropping a dish, or rapping on the wall or a table. Judith Lewis Herman (1992) noted that the ghosts often have a story to be told before they can rest in their graves. They may be unwilling or unable to leave until their unfinished business has been completed.

At the Civil War battlegrounds, the frequent sighting of ghosts has been taking place recurrently over the past 150 years. As places such as Antietam, Gettysburg, and Chickamauga, thousands of soldiers fell in a single day. The carnage was unprecedented in human warfare. As a result of the troubling and unfinished lives of the military dead, manifestations of ghosts in the forms of apparitions, noises, and eerie feelings have been widespread. Rangers at the parks have reported hearing agonizing groaning sounds and seeing bushes move. Other psychic sounds have included mumbled voices and distant gunfire.

The journey of the soul to a remote place or condition, such as Heaven, Hell, Nirvana, or some other state of existence, provides a way of getting the spirits of the dead out of the community of the living. Those who believe in the malevolence of ghosts are especially benefited by perceptions that they are neither present nor do they intervene into the affair of everyday life. Beliefs in divine judgment generally help to uphold social norms among the living and to offer the promise of a better life that will provide relief from suffering and injustice in this life. For some the promise of a rewarding afterlife may provide some degree of hopefulness and optimism under what otherwise may be intolerable conditions.

The belief in reincarnation is prominent among Eastern religions and among an increasing number of people in the West. According to this belief, the immortal soul of the person who has died will be reincarnated into a new body, this may involve many lifetimes over many centuries. Proponents claim supporting evidence from the thousands of cases of small children reporting detailed information and intricate memories of their past lives (Stevenson, 2000). The growing popularity of the concept in the West has been promoted by therapists who have made extensive use of hypnosis and "regression techniques." These procedures permit individuals under supervision to discover a previous identity and some of the details of a previous life (Wambach, 1978).

The finality of death is psychologically disturbing to many people and there appears to be a desire for something more after life is all over. Biological reproduction makes a contribution to the evolutionary process, but this contributes very little. Further, specific contributions to the social heritage of any given group of people account for very little over long periods of time. Through having a brain and a consciousness, people want more. At the individual level, beliefs in immortality serve as stable anchoring points in a world of increasing complexity, confusion, and skepticism. In the final analysis, beliefs in immortality are matters of faith and wishful thinking.

Conditions of Uncertainty

Uncertainty about the future is one of the defining characteristics of the human condition. This fact is evident in all manifestations of everyday life and action. We are all at the mercy of forces beyond our control. We can control only a small number of the events that shape the contours of our lives. The best we can do is to hope for outcomes that are in our favor. It is perhaps for this reason that the belief in luck is a major sustaining illusion for many people. It is also for this reason that beliefs in the inscrutability of God and the unfathomable decrees of Heaven are basic to many contemporary religions.

We create illusions to avoid a sense of backing into an unknown future. The world has not become more coherent as a result of the vast changes that have been introduced from modern technology and scientific investigations. Levels of uncertainty and perceptions of risk continue to escalate with the unfolding of the twenty-first century. We have not reduced the scope of the unknown but only increased our awareness of the possible. It contrast to many of the arrogant assumptions about mastery and control in the fields of engineering and technology, several books and journal articles have been published in recent years on everyday anxieties, fears, and uncertainties (Furedi, 1997; Glassner, 1999).

According to Mary Douglas and Aaron Wildavsky (1983), all societies operate with some combination of confidence and fear. Some dangers are selected for emphasis while others are relegated to the background. In general, humans are not very good at selecting the relevant things to worry about. This is not a gap between reality and perception, but an inability to know the dangers in any given case until after a calamity has occurred. When bridges collapse, terrorists attack, or the *Titanic* sinks, it is typically experienced as an unexpected and unpredictable event. Under conditions of crisis, individuals become unclear about what to believe, how to act, and what goals are worth pursuing.

It is out of conditions of uncertainty and incomplete information that the mythology surrounding death and immortality has been elaborated. The myths are constructed to fill in the gaps of human knowledge. Such topics as death, reincarnation, and immortality are laden with human emotionality, but the subjects defy our ever finding the ultimate truth. Yet guidelines are provided for specific groups on how to approach the ending of life in a meaningful way. The journey of life is thus accompanied by the eternal mystery of death, and the fear of death is basically a fear of the unknown and an unwillingness to accept a void of nothingness.

9

Humans and
Other Animals

Images of the relationship between humans and other animals take
a variety of forms in a variety of cultures. At one extreme, the anthropomorphic principle dominates: the physical world is endowed with
spiritual qualities, animals and other living things are endowed with
souls, and humans are engaged in a symbiotic relationship with all that
exists. Under these conditions, the natural environment is humanized;
the world is one of enchantment; and the sphere of the sacred encom-
passes a relatively large portion of human activity. Many of the perceived
normal, natural, and inevitable attributes of the human condition are
endowed with sacred qualities.

At the other extreme in human cultures we find a distinctly modern
view of the physical world. According to the modern view, all that exists
in the final analysis can be reduced to physical chemistry. Extensive scientific and technological vocabularies are enlarged to name inanimate
objects and the qualities and attributes of inanimate things. The more
than 800,000 words in the English language have elaborated nouns and
adjectives at the expense of verbs and adverbs. The result is an overall
view of the world that is impersonal, inanimate, and comprised of clash-
ing, mechanical forces. It is a language that is ideally suited for science
and technology, but somewhat limited in its suitability for describing
human hopes, aspirations, and experiences.

The perceived gap between humans and other animals is extensive
in modern cultures. We tend to emphasize qualitative differences
between humans and animals. The native Indian tribes of North America, by way of contrast, emphasized animistic world views. Animism
was reflected not only in their imagery of what exists and what is possible
but also in their language systems. By postulating animistic, spirit-like

qualities to all that exists, humans were required to live harmoniously with their natural environments. For example, if an animal was slain in the hunt, the hunter had to obtain forgiveness from the spirit of that animal. The slain animal had to be appeased to prevent its soul from wreaking havoc on the personal life of the killer. The animistic worldview extended not only to all living things but also to what would be regarded by us as inanimate and inert objects.

In the early days of anthropology, Edward B. Tyler (1873) drew upon animism as a plausible explanation for the origin of religion. He maintained that in both primitive and modern societies, religion is grounded in the soul concept. The soul was postulated as an explanation of dreaming and death. While it is the soul that gives the body its vitality and energy, the two may be separated. While sleeping the body is at rest and this permits the soul in dreaming to leave the body and go on a journey. Interactions may occur with other souls, those of the dead as well as those of the living. According to Tyler, death was seen as a permanent departure of the soul from the body. The soul thus has a continued existence after the destruction of the body. The soul concept was extended in primitive societies to animals, plants, and even inanimate objects.

In Irving Hallowell's (1975) study of the worldview of the Ojibwa, he noted that the animistic components of their language extended to all that exists. His subjects found that our language and worldview were not acceptable. Our language was seen as defining the world primarily in terms of "dead" objects. On the other hand, to the anthropologist it seemed somewhat extreme that the Ojibwa imputed animistic qualities to even dull, mundane, and uninteresting things. Hallowell asked of an old man, "Are you sure that all of these stones we see about us here are alive?" His subject thought for a long time and then replied, "No, but some are." He recalled a time during his youth in which his father was directing an important tribal ceremony. His father's magic became so powerful that a big round boulder started to move, gained momentum and followed him around a tent several times.

The respondent knew that this happened because he was there and saw it happen. Others who were present also saw the movement of the stone. So, while stones usually do not move, sometimes they do. The Ojibwa were less dogmatic and categorical in their views than we are. Usually stones are seen as mundane objects. Hallowell also heard of another incident during a time of trouble when a huge stone opened up a door and made available to the shaman some medicine that was needed for the treatment of illness. So, under unusual and extraordinary circumstances stones, may move or open up doors.

Emile Durkheim (1961) drew heavily on the relationship between humans and animals in developing his theory of religion. His concern with *The Elementary Form of the Religious Life* led to an examination of totemism. From his analyses he concluded that religion is a unified system of beliefs and practices which unite into a moral community all of those who adhere to them. In totemism, the collective consciousness of the clan is manifested in the identification with a specific animal or plant species. Clan solidarity is expressed outwardly in symbols, emblems, rituals, and taboos. In Durkheim's view, religious worship is indirectly a worship of society itself.

A sense of kinship is shared with all members of the same totem, even though blood ties cannot be established. There is a strong taboo against killing the totem animal, and all individuals are required to marry outside their totem. In the subsequent writings of Sigmund Freud (1990), he drew heavily on the morality associated with totemism in developing his theories of the Oedipus complex and the incest taboo. Freud assumed that the Oedipus complex was innate and universal. This perspective held that it is normal for the child to wish to have a sexual relationship with the mother and to wish the death of the father as a rival. Today, neither psychologists nor anthropologists accept Freud's notions about totemism as the grounds for the beginning of both morality and religion.

Echoes of both animism and totemism are found in the modern world. For example, the symbolism of totemic animals is evident in the many choices available for decorating the body with tattooing art. The selection may be one's personal zodiac sign, an animal whose imagined qualities are worthy of emulation, or a chosen animal to serve as a guardian spirit. Whatever the choice and for whatever the reason, the body is being embellished and customized around the subjective meanings attributed to the selected animal.

In the modern world, we draw upon animistic and totemic principles to express basic human concerns. We speak through the animals in children's books, in commercial art, in Disney movies, and in many forms of animated entertainment. Many pet owners claim that they can communicate with their dog or cat by speaking to them in English.

We speak through the animals in expressing our concerns with mastery and control over events, in expressing membership and belonging, and in giving a sense of purpose to what otherwise would be meaningless events. In effect, we create social order and a moral universe by speaking through the animals in a variety of ways.

In the past few hundred years of Western history, animals have been forced off their traditional environmental ranges, and their continued existence is problematic. This disruption continues at an accelerated rate at the same time we have become increasingly aware from biology of the animal roots of human nature. For example, we now know that we share more than ninety-five percent of our genetic material with the other primates, such as apes. Most people, however, see the differences as so great that we are qualitatively different. Few moderns see animals as possessing a soul. While some specific animals are admired by some people, most are objects of negative typifications.

Ambivalence Toward Animals

In modern culture, linguistic usages tend to establish a linkage, rather than to make a sharp separation between humans and animals. One dictionary definition of the term "animal" is that of "a bestial person; a brute," and correspondingly a dictionary definition of the term "beast" is that of "a brutal person." In everyday speech, the term animal is associated with uncivilized and socially disapproved behavior. Criminals, hoodlums, and punks are described as animals who deserve to be treated as such and punished accordingly. In these usages, animal behavior is contemptible behavior, and the term is used to express the view that important social norms have been violated.

Following along these lines, animal vocabularies are used to capture the essence of an insult: "you're a rat," "you're a skunk," "you're a pig," " you're a gorilla," "you're a jackass." Such references are not so much to the objective qualities and attributes of the animals in question as to the connotative meanings that have been imputed to them. Negative typifications of animals are drawn upon for expressing disapproval of human conduct. Standards of conventional morality have not been upheld, something out of the ordinary has happened, and the individual in question is held accountable for his or her behavior (Neal, 1985).

The animal insult asserts a totemic linkage between the person and the animal. Through asserting kinship with an animal, the deviant behavior of the person stems from character defects that are inherent, innate, and biologically based. Animal types of adaptation to the natural environment shape sources of motivation, guiding life principles and orientations toward other people. Knowing that a person is a rat, a snake, or a pig conveys several implications for future relationships. A great deal of trouble could be circumvented by avoiding the person in question, and, if possible, severing social relationships with him or her altogether. If avoidance is not possible, the totemic imputation provides ready-made justifications for punitive and retaliatory action.

In situations where avoidance is not possible, other types of adaptation may occur through the use of animistic vocabularies. For example, clerical workers making up a secretarial pool in a large research office have been known to construct a menagerie of those who stand above them in the power structure. The menagerie, or animal farm, is limited to bosses and authority figures who insist upon precise and detailed compliance to the orders given. In such an office observed by the author, the secretaries came to define one of the bosses as a "weasel," another as a "frog," yet another as a "wolf," and a fourth as a "bear." These totemic symbols were regarded as capturing the essence of implicit personality types. Patterns of work style and order giving were drawn upon to confirm the totemic designations. The secrecy surrounding the totemic typifications became a source of pleasure to the secretaries and served as a psychological mechanism for inverting the power structure. The superiority of the subordinates was confirmed through their withholding of secret knowledge about the bosses from the bosses themselves. The bosses and authority figures were lacking in true or valid knowledge about how they were perceived by subordinates.

Beliefs about the qualities and attributes of animals set limits around what is normal, natural, and inevitable in human affairs. Animals are drawn upon for setting boundaries around the moral universe and reflect the basic human principles of separating the genuine from the spurious, and of separating the authentic from the inauthentic. One of the evident uses of animals in the creation of an orderly universe is to be found in the food taboos of any given society and in the cultural definitions of what forms of animals are suitable for human consumption (Douglas, 1979).

In modern biological classification schemes, humans are neither vegetarians nor carnivores. Instead they appear to be capable of eating and thriving on a wide variety of diets (Pollan, 2006). But there are limits; some substances are toxic and not suitable for human consumption. Yet what are the substances that pollute the body rather than provide nourishment for it? Taken collectively, humans have not been able to definitively answer this question over the past hundred thousand years of cultural evolution. Instead, the nutritional effects of different diets on the human body have remained an unresolved issue.

From a purely dietary standpoint, there may be no inherent reason for excluding grubs, snails, grasshoppers, or snakes from the dinner menu; nor is there any purely objective reason for excluding rats, cats, dogs, or mules. These exclusions are based on conventional notions about the moral universe, notions about moral pollution, and notions about taboos that must be observed to keep the physical universe from becoming disorderly and unpredictable. The creation of a moral universe is arbitrary, selective, and based on conventional definitions. But once created, the realities that were symbolically created become endowed with objective, factual qualities that are binding on the conduct of a normal, rational person (Berger, 1969).

Animism and Totemism in Modern Culture

Animals are like people in that they are of variable qualities. Some are defined as disturbing and deplorable creatures, while others are defined as worthy of admiration, respect, and emulation. The positive typification of animals is oriented toward creating symbols to express group hopes, aspirations, and ideals. The symbol gives visual, tangible, and artistic referents to the desire for group effectiveness. For example, according to legend, the Roman armies made extensive use of the gamecock as a desirable model for the martial arts. Before sending soldiers into battle, a cockfight would be staged as a source of inspiration. The gamecock symbolized courage, dedication, and a willingness to die for a cause. These qualities were set up as ideals for the individual soldier to emulate. The gamecock thus came to symbolize military aspirations for the individual soldier and was depicted on Roman coins and other national symbols (McCaghy and Neal, 1973).

Several types of groups in modern culture draw upon animistic symbols to create visual representations of group hopes, aspirations, and ideals. These include youth organizations, military units, and athletic teams. The symbols selected have clearly identifiable referents in nature and become elaborated to reflect desires for identity, belonging, and membership. They also express collective hopes for effectiveness in goal attainment.

The research of Ralph Linton (1962) indicated the extensive use of totemic symbols among units of the United States Army during World War I. Linton focused on the symbolism of "the rainbow" for members of the 42nd Infantry Division. The symbol of the rainbow had very little meaning for the unit while it was in training in the United States. But the symbol took on sacred qualities in combat situations. The appearance of a rainbow over enemy lines was taken as a sign of guardianship and as an omen of subsequent victory in battle. Several soldiers reported seeing the rainbow over enemy lines after a combat encounter, even when the weather conditions would not ordinarily have permitted such an occurrence.

The use of totemic symbols within military units serves to divide personnel into specific groups that are set apart from others. A type of kinship develops among those authorized to draw upon and to use the symbol as a namesake and as a source of identity. Artistic representations of totemic symbols are used to decorate and embellish such forms of property as the command post, trucks and jeeps owned by the military unit, the shoulder patches worn on military uniforms, and the flags that are carried in formal parades. Within the group a respectful attitude developed toward the group's namesake and its representation, while a strong taboo operates against the use of the symbol by members of any other military unit.

Intercollegiate athletic teams resemble military units in the creation and use of totemic symbols. The menagerie of college teams include the symbolic representations of eagles, falcons, seahawks, tigers, cougars, lions, panthers, bobcats, wildcats, bulldogs, gophers, wolverines, broncos, beavers, ducks, and bears. The qualities of the animal in question are elevated and exaggerated to provide a set of ideals for teams to draw upon and to emulate. The embellished qualities of animals serve as unifying symbols, as sources of inspiration, and as a means for drawing boundaries to separate members from nonmembers.

The selective use of totemic symbols in athletic contests grows out of what Paul Blumberg (1963) described as situations of "structured inherent uncertainty." An element of chance operates in competitive sports, as in many other areas of social life. Athletic skills and abilities are not enough to ensure victory in any given contest. The potential of the chance occurrence is always present. In any given case, an inferior team may stage an extraordinary performance, while a superior team may have an "off day," or for a variety of reasons fail to match their usual level of performance. Under these circumstances, the totemic symbol becomes a magical device for reducing the inherent uncertainty of the outcome. Linking a team with a totemic animal provides a tonic of reassurance, a form of social guardianship, and a buffer against failure.

On college campuses, the use of totemic symbols is restricted and limited. For example, at Bowling Green State University the symbolism of the falcon is prominently displayed in the basketball arena, in the ice arena, and in the football stadium. The symbol has no place, however, in the library or within the classroom, suggesting that the academic and intellectual sides of the campus are separated from the forms of idealism that operate in competitive sports. Similarly, the clowning of Freddy and Freda Falcon at intercollegiate athletic events is humorous and meaningful to fans and to spectators, but would not be tolerated as acceptable in the library, in the math class, or in the scientific laboratory.

The use of animism on Wall Street is reflected in the use of "bulls" and "bears" to designate the positive and the negative typifications that are inherent in market volatility (Neal and Youngelson, 1986). The "bulls of Wall Street" symbolize hopes, aspiration, and greed; while "the bears" give concrete referents to the emotions of fear, to the risk of failure, and to the frustrations of human effort. The folklore of Wall Street holds that if we are in the beginning of a bull market, it is a good time to invest. But if the bull market is topping out, the wise investor sells. If an investor overreacts to a small upturn in the market prior to a precipitous drop, he or she is said to have been caught in a "bear trap." Such symbolic uses of animism are drawn upon to reduce some of the inherent uncertainty of risk-taking behavior.

By giving animistic qualities to impersonal forces, the stock market is assumed to have a life of its own, which operates independently of the decisions of individual investors. Prices on the stock market fluctuate, and through buying and selling investors are making predictions about the future course of events. Errors in prediction frequently occur, and the consequences are enormous. For example, in the last six months of 2008 the market value of all stock sold on the New York Stock Exchange dropped by several hundred billion dollars, suggesting that previous greed had motivated investment sentiment, and errors in judgment were made in designating a "bear" as a "bull."

The ambivalence toward animals in the modern world grows out of the perceived gap between the pyramidal structure called civilization and the collective memories of more primitive times in which humans lived in proximity to "natural" environments. Animals are embellished in some respects with idealized and ennobling qualities that set them apart from the artificiality of advanced civilization. But animals are also designated as lower evolutionary forms that lack the refinements and sensitivities produced in humans through exposure to cultural developments. In either case, the perceived gap between humans and other animals grows out of the overall ambivalence toward the merits and qualities of modern culture. The many forms of uncertainty that are implicit in the human condition reflect the limits of human knowledge in problem-solving efforts.

Endangered Species

Rather than emphasizing the kinship of humans with other animals, the book of Genesis provides reinforcement for the view that humans are qualitatively different from all other animals. Genesis also provides justification for human "dominion over the fish of the sea, over the fowl of the air, and over the cattle, and over every creeping thing that creepeth upon the earth." With humans elevated to a special place and given a position of superiority, they are then free to do whatever they wish with all other animals. They may domesticate them, shoot them, skin them, abuse them, place them in captivity, or make pets out of them.

The very large increase in the number of people in the world over the past 200 years has put a tremendous amount of pressure on habitats that once supported a large number of species (Gleich and Nicoly, 2002). Along with the increasing density of the human population, many species have vanished or are now on the verge of extinction. The term "endangered species" refers to the population of a species that is at the risk of becoming extinct. Some species are threatened as a result of predation; others because the environment required for their survival has been destroyed.

Buffalo, elephants, bengal tigers, leatherback turtles, giant pandas, polar bears, black rhinos, clouded leopards, gazelles, and whales are among the many mammals that are now or have been threatened by extinction. The list of endangered species has increased dramatically over the past ten years. More than 7,700 species that live in Africa and Asia are currently threatened. As a part of the globalization process, meat, fur, skins, and animal parts are sold on an increasingly massive scale throughout the world. As seriously as poaching and subsistence hunting may be, however, the chief threat to the world's wildlife stems from habitat destruction.

At the time of the Lewis and Clark expedition, there were around 30 to 60 million bison (buffalo) roaming the Great Plains. By the 1890s, their population had dwindled to fewer than a thousand. During the 19th century the buffalo were wantonly slaughtered in ever-growing numbers. American Indians as well as travelers over the Oregon Trail had slaughtered the buffalo for subsistence. With the subsequent development of the automatic rifle and building railroads through the Great Plains, the buffalo were often shot from the trains as a sport. For example, the Grand Duke Alexis of Russia included a buffalo hunt on the Great Plains as a part of his grand tour of the United States, and was joined by such frontier notables as Buffalo Bill Cody and Colonel George Custer (Slotkin, 1994). When the value of buffalo hides increased and the tongue of the buffalo came to be regarded as a delicacy, commercial hunters killed buffalo in large numbers, leaving their skinned carcasses on the plains to rot. Subsequently, the plowing of the grasslands and fencing of the plains for farming purposes destroyed the range habitat of the buffalo (Isenberg, 2000). The domestication of the buffalo for food and the protection provided for wild buffalo at Yellowstone National Park has resulted in a numerical increase in the buffalo in recent years.

During the 19th century, the vulnerability of the whales of the world became evident, and they approached extinction as a result of hunting. The commercial use of the byproducts of whales included the valuable whale oil, ambergris for use in making perfumes, and a waxy substance found in the head cavity of the sperm whale that was excellent for making candles. Today we regard whales as remarkable and beautiful animals, and we hold them in affection. Those in the whaling industry thought otherwise. In his book on the history of whaling, Eric Jay Dolin (2007) described commercial whaling as "a bloody, brutal, stinking, dangerous, sometimes lucrative, always high-risk business." The American export of the products of whaling remained a staple ingredient of international trade for more than 250 years. The market for whale oil has now become negligible, but the hunting of whales continues on the part of those nations that have a market for their whale meat–loving consumers.

The whales are the world's largest animals and among the most endangered. Unregulated whaling depleted the whale population, and several whale species became endangered. In contrast to the buffalo, whales are not suitable for domestication. The biggest threats to whales after hunting are accidental entrapment in fishing nets, collisions with ships, and attacks by killer marine organisms. In addition, the hazards to whales include beaching, straying into dangerous and unnatural waters, and the increasing pollution of the world's oceans. As a result of the many environments that are unfriendly to whales, there is a high probability of extinction even without the abusive hunting practices.

The polar bear has become a threatened species as a result of global warming. The rapid melting of sea ice has drastically reduced marine habitats that are necessary for polar bear, ice-inhabiting seals, and seabirds. As the Artic climate gets warmer, the ice melts earlier in the summer and freezes later in the winter. This means that polar bears spend less time on ice and thus have less time to hunt seals and build up fat reserves. With a shortage of food, females have trouble providing milk for the young, and if they do not achieve a minimum weight, they will not give birth at all. If there is a serious shortage of food, the polar bear will eat their young and sometimes each other.

The preservation of the northern spotted owl has been one of the more contentious issues in environmental efforts to preserve endangered species. As a result of heavy logging operations over the past 150 years, only about ten percent of the old growth forests remain. As the forest dwindled, so did the number of spotted owls (Andre and Velasquez, 1991). The spotted owl feeds on the rich plant and invertebrate life created by decaying timber. Along with the environmentalists, animal rights activists maintain that every living creature has a right to life and that we have a duty to protect unique species and especially one with the regal characteristics of the spotted owl.

The timber industry maintains that the benefits of preserving the spotted owl are negligible when compared to the serious economic damage to lumbering operations in the Pacific Northwest. Many of the lumber mills are totally dependent on old growth cuts, and more than 28,000 jobs will be lost in preserving the spotted owl. In contrast, environmentalists maintain that the jobs will vanish anyway in the next thirty years as the old growth forests disappear and the mills are forced to close (Andre and Velasquez, 1991). The spotted owl controversy was a watershed case in the prospects of implementing policies grounded in resource management and the concept of environmental sustainability (Yaffe, 1994).

In an inventory of life on earth, Michael Gleich, Dirk Maxeiner, and Fabian Nicolay (2002) concluded that there have been more species on earth than stars in our galaxy. The diversity of lifestyles ranges from organisms as small as bacteria to as large as whales. There are more than 34 million species of parasites that feed exclusively on human beings. Of the estimated 106 billion human beings who have lived on this planet, only six billion are alive today. In their view, the biological diversity of animal types make up the infrastructure of this planet and provides the underpinnings for human existence. Rather than continuing to promote destructive exploitation, the authors recommend moving toward an era of sustainable utilization.

Animal Rights Activism

Partly drawing upon increased awareness of endangered species and the many forms of cruelty to animals, several organizations have emerged around claims that animals should no longer be regarded as property, used for food or clothing, held in captivity for entertainment, or abused and killed in scientific experiments. Animal rights activists use the term *species terrorism* to describe the many ways animals are terrorized, injured, or killed. In their view, animal terrorism is found in fur farms, animal factories, scientific laboratories, and bio-medical research centers. The true weapons of mass destruction are the rifles, stun guns, cutting blades, knives and forks that are used to dismember, experiment on, kill, or consume animal bodies (Newkirk, 2000).

The animal rights advocates seek to put an end to the rigid conceptual distinction between humans and other animals. Animals have the ability to suffer and their suffering must be taken into account in their relationships with humans. It is true that animals cannot read or write, build bridges, or elaborate a religious system, but they do have the ability to suffer and to experience pain and pleasure. Peter Singer (2001) has drawn upon the philosophical implications of the pain suffered by animals to make a case for the equal rights of animals. From this perspective, there are many ways that animals are tortured and mal-treated in modern society that are morally wrong.

The factory farming of animals is particularly disturbing to animal rights activists. Almost all of the chickens, pigs, and cattle that end up in our supermarkets have been subjected to inhumane conditions. The squalid conditions of confinement in their production can be defined as torture. For example, chickens are often confined to small cages that are stacked on top of each other. Pigs are often produced commercially in such small cages that they cannot even turn around. Vitamins A and D are added to the diet of animals in order to reduce the need for exercise and sunlight. In factory farms, animals are injected with hormones to maximize their growth and pumped full of high doses of antibiotics to control disease. The substances used in the production of animals as food commodities work their way into the human body with potentially negative consequences (Bernstein, 2004).

Through applying the factory model to the production of animals, the concern is with efficiency and profits to the exclusion of a regard for what is being done to animals. For example, pigs are very social animals and their quality of life is greatest when they have freedom of movement in interacting with other pigs. The deplorable conditions of animal pro-duction stand in sharp contrast to the positive images of animals in chil-dren's stories. Through using animals to address human qualities and concerns, children admire and develop a fondness for them. Our society in general is showered with images of happy animals living on farms where cows graze in lush green pastures, where chickens have the run of a barnyard, and free-roaming animals live out their days in sunny fields. Such positive images are far removed from reality. Today, the incredible pain and suffering of animals in systems of mass production is invisible to a large meat-consuming public.

Most people think of chicken, ham, and steak as foods to be obtained from the supermarket without pondering the slaughter of ani-mals and the conditions under which they are produced. A few years ago, a committee planning a spring folk festival at Bowling Green State University proposed having a farmer bring a pig to campus and slaughter it before an audience of students. Since very few students had any aware-ness of the slaughter of animals, it seemed like a good educational idea. The proposal was soundly rejected by the president of the university in asserting, "There will be no slaughter of an animal before an audience of my campus." Because we are shielded from a great deal of what is going on in our society, we lack intelligent insight into the forces shaping the events in which we are engaged (McKibben, 1993).

Many of the animal rights activists who are aware of the procedures in the production and slaughter of animals become vegetarians. In becoming a vegetarian, it is often recognized that there is no way meat can be made available to consumers without the injury and suffering of animals. If animals are accorded equal rights with humans, then it is morally wrong to cause unnecessary suffering to chickens, turkeys, ducks, pigs, cattle, calves, and other animals Further, it is argued that meat production is a wasteful way of feeding people. If more people followed the vegetarian way of life, the need would be reduced for the large-scale clearance of forests and the environmental destruction of habitat. An interrelated argument holds that vegetarianism has a long history of association with religious and spiritual values. The killing of animals "fractures the harmony of nature and puts 'a veil of blood' between the individual and holiness" (Twigg, 1981).

In contrast to those who approach animal rights from only an ethical or philosophical stance, others take a more direct action approach. More than thirty years ago, a youth group in England decided to act on their concern about the cruelty of hunting animals. Under the label Band of Mercy, they attacked hunters' vehicles by slashing their tires and breaking their windows. Afterwards, they left notes explaining what they had done and why. In 1973, the Band of Mercy burned to the ground a new research laboratory that was being built by Hoechst Pharmaceuticals. Their intent was to prevent the abuse of animals in medical experiments before they could start (Newkirk, 2002).

The Animal Liberation Front (ALF) is one of the more militant activist groups and is oriented toward inflicting damage on those who profit from the misery and exploitation of animals. Particular emphasis is placed on "liberating" animals from such places of abuse as scientific laboratories, factory farms, and fur farms. The activists maintain that animals taken from farms or laboratories are not "stolen" because they were never rightfully owned in the first place (Best and Nocella, 2004). The activists see a resemblance between the liberation of animals and the antislavery movement. The ownership of slaves and the restrictions on their freedom of movement is seen as resembling the ownership and confinement of animals.

In recent years, radical environmentalists and animal rights groups have claimed responsibility for hundreds of crimes involving arson, bombings, vandalism, harassment, and the release of animals. Some militant groups have no membership lists and are only loosely organized. For this reason, most of the crimes have remained unsolved. Although there have been no or very few injuries, the damage to property amounts to several hundred million dollars. As with the extremists who bomb abortion clinics, the violence of animal rights activists is oriented toward imposing their own values and lifestyles on everyone else.

Both the FBI and Homeland Security have designated eco-terrorism and animal rights activism as the leading forms of domestic terrorism. By operating through autonomous cells and being unconstrained by geographical location, these groups are difficult to infiltrate and stop. Law enforcement agencies are increasingly baffled and stymied by the increasing violence and sabotage. Since the intent of the activists is to disrupt, very few resources are required and very few clues are left except for the spray paint signs claiming animal rights abuse. The animal rights activists claim that the real terrorism in the United States consists of corporate crimes and the many policies of the government in upholding the abuse of animals and damage to the environment.

The mythology surrounding the relationship between humans and other animals continues to evolve. The modern emphasis on human mastery and control has been geared toward promoting consumer and economic values at the expense of the environment. The emphasis on animal rights and the sustainability of the environment are very recent developments. These conceptual frameworks have arrived a little late for maintaining the habitats that are necessary for the preservation of many species of animals. The biblical notion about humans asserting "dominion" over the environment and other species of animals is increasingly colliding with the emerging ideas about sustainability and the role of humans in serving a custodial function.

Scientific testing in recent years indicates that genetic material is shared by all animal life forms. For example, the chimpanzee, which is our closest animal relative, has a genome sequence that is about 98.8 percent identical to that of our own. The commonalities with primates and mammals suggest that the gap between humans and other animals is not as great as is commonly assumed in the mythology of modern civilization. Learning theorists in psychology, scholarly studies in bionomics, and bio-medical researchers in testing pharmaceuticals have long been aware of the similarities between humans and other animals (Neal, 1976).

The many phases of the emphasis on animal rights are colliding with the use of animals in research to find a cure for human diseases. The opposition to using animals in laboratory research is greatest when animals are used for testing cosmetics and when animals are unnecessarily abused in the process of using them for testing pharmaceuticals. The many benefits from the use of animals in medical research include the development of insulin, antibiotics, and vaccines against hepatitis and polio. Additionally, the use of animals in laboratory research has greatly increased our understanding of the human nervous system. The momentum of the animal rights movement is of such a magnitude that it will not dissipate anytime soon. The debates will continue on whether humans are qualitatively different from other animals or whether the differences are only minimal and of a minor degree.

10

Human Sexuality

And the Lord God formed man of the dust of the ground, and breathed into his nostrils the breath of life; and man became a living soul....

And the Lord God caused a deep sleep to fall upon Adam, and he slept; and he took one of his ribs, and closed up the flesh instead thereof;

And the rib, which the Lord God had taken from man, made he a woman, and brought her unto the man.

And Adam said, This is now bone of my bones, and flesh of my flesh: She shall be called Woman, because she was taken out of Man.

—Genesis 2:7, 21–23

Stories about the creation of man and woman, their relationship with each other, and the reasons for sexual reproduction are but specific instances of the many forms of mythology surround human sexuality in the various cultures of the world.

The Genesis accounts of creation have provided historical justifications for the rule of patriarchy and supported notions about male superiority. Rather than recognizing the mythical underpinnings of religious beliefs, there are many fundamentalists today who strongly believe that the first woman was indeed Eve and that she was literally made out of Adam's rib (Reik, 1973). With the Women's Liberation Movement in modern times, beliefs about male priority and male superiority have receded into the background as an increasing number of women have sought to increase independence and equality (Glazer and Waehrer, 1977).

The research of anthropologists during the 20th century clearly established the variability of human sexual behavior. The modern notion of cultural relativity points toward the conclusion that the qualities that differentiate men and women and that regulate sexual behavior are surrounded by elaborate mythological accounts. Who to have sex with, how, when, and under what conditions are regulated by normative mandates. What is defined as masculine behavior in some societies is defined as feminine in others (Mead, 2001). Premarital sexual intercourse is strictly forbidden in some cultures, but is openly permitted in others (Malinowski, 1962). The prevailing ideologies in some cultures place emphasis on the erotic pleasures of sex, while in others pleasures are subordinated to concerns with sexual reproduction.

Since the sexual impulse is biological as well as social, it can never be completely controlled nor completely up to the individual. The modern cultural apparatus is one that tends to promote materialistic values and to emphasize the pleasure principle. Mass entertainment, for example, is saturated with themes of sexuality, and the grief and pleasures to be derived therefrom. Both soap operas and popular movies dramatize the sexual underpinnings of human conduct. Themes related to libido impulses and animal desires are predominantly emphasized. While a great deal of mass entertainment involves a morality play on how people sin and suffer from it, the appeal to viewing audiences stems to a very large degree from the symbolism of the erotic stimulus to which they are exposed, and the pleasure derivable from observing the misery of others (Nuttall, 2001).

The modern crisis of sexuality grows out of historical traditions, both religious and secular, that elevated sexuality to such a high degree of importance. What was once thought of as normal and natural has very little to do with modern forms of sexual expressiveness. The certainties of the past have crumbled under the modern emphasis on freedom and personal choice (Eisler, 1995). The discovery of a viable set of beliefs and norms about human sexuality does not appear to be on the horizon. Instead of seeking to impose a new morality upon everyone, it becomes increasingly important to recognize the diversity of modern beliefs, desires, and preferences. It is clear that history is not yet done with exploring the many possibilities on female-male relationships.

Gender Borders and Boundaries

A great deal of the problems in male-female relationships derives from the process of social classification by which borders and boundaries are drawn around what are presumed to be biological differences (Neal and Collas, 2000).. From the standpoint of statistical probability, males and females do differ in genitalia, in hormonal balances, in muscle mass, and in several other aspects. But in observing such overall differences, there is a tendency to overlook the fact that a great deal of variability occurs within the categories of male and female. The basic fallacies, however, grow out of cultural embellishments and individual perceptions. Biological characteristics have no relevance for social participation, career development, and freedom of movement.

The data on human variability do not support the conclusion that women are any weaker than men in any regard other than muscle mass. The level of intelligence is just as great or greater than that of men. In recent years, women have demonstrated their ability to master technical skills and vocational endeavors that were once regarded as in the domain of men. In the realm of sexuality, women's overall capacity for performance and potentials for pleasure are superior to those of men. At any given age level, the life expectancy of females is greater than for males. All such data provide evidence that contradict notions about women as the "weaker sex." Thus, whatever the overall statistical differences between women and men, there is no evidence to justify the disadvantaged positions to which women have been historically relegated in most institutions in most societies (Montagu, 1970).

The arbitrary constructions of gender become obvious and clearly evident in the differential definitions of male and female characteristics in various cultures. For example, the American definitions of appropriate male and female behavior produced problems for U.S. military personnel in the Vietnam War. Vietnamese men showed affection for each other by holding hands and sometimes kissing. Such practices in Vietnam are regarded as normal and natural expressions of friendship among men. American soldiers, however, regarded the physical demonstrations of affection among men as disgusting and deplorable behavior. The display of "feminine" characteristics among Vietnamese men led some Americans to conclude that the Vietnamese were "a defective people," and thus not worth the sacrifices Americans were making on their behalf (Lawson, 1989).

Gender categories are perceived to be exclusive in the sense that all human beings belong to one category or the other. Those who fall into one category are believed to share a common set of traits that distinguish them from the members of the other category in significant ways. The notion that "men are men" and "women are women" is a form of circular and tautological thinking. Such a perception fails to recognize the empirical variability of "male-like" characteristics among men and "female-like" characteristics among women. The languages we use in people classifications necessarily involve distortions, omissions, and incompleteness. For example, gendered status at birth is ambiguous in about two percent of the cases (Epstein, 1990). This ambiguity puts into question all of those people who believe gender differences are categorical and absolute. We can see then that our perceptions are sometimes erroneous and misleading as a result of the linguistic distortions implicit in our binary, either-or classification.

The constructions of gender are deeply embedded in the cultural traditions of any given group of people. Yet there is nothing automatic about given individuals having the characteristics that are ascribed to their gender status. A great deal of time and effort is frequently required for becoming a masculine male or a feminine female. For example, muscle building, weight lifting, shoulder development, and steroid use are among the behavior practices by which men seek to become men. Other examples that demonstrate the quest for masculinity include playing war games, working in dangerous occupations, and engaging in such forms of risk-taking as sky diving, motorcycle riding, and auto racing. While women also participate in these forms of edgework (Lyng, 1990), the motives for men are more clearly evident in confronting danger and demonstrating personal control for confirming their masculinity.

According to Lazar, Karlan, and Salter (2006), the Marlboro Man was among the most influential people who never lived. The Marlboro Man was a mythical figure created by advertisers to psychologically link cigarette smoking with the cultural ideal of what a man should be. The myth of the Marlboro Man came into existence as a cowboy to reflect the idea that the right brand of tobacco would give you independence and strength. The cowboy is among the most romantic of the mythical characters in American culture. The cowboy is seen as tall, handsome, adventurous, and courageous. The cowboy worked hard, suffered hardship, was willing to risk death if it was necessary, and was capable of rising to the occasion for dealing with whatever problems developed. These are among the qualities worthy of emulation by the masculine, American male. The masculinity of the cowboy myth resulted in the early death of the Marlboro Man from cigarette smoking.

But if becoming a man is difficult for the typical male, becoming a woman can be even more difficult for the typical female. Cultural standards of physical appearance and female beauty are deeply entrenched. The messages from mass advertising suggest that that if a woman does not measure up to them it is her own fault. Further, it is claimed that if she does not measure up, she will not be valued as attractive and desirable. In response, many resort to dieting, exercising, and having breast implants and other forms of cosmetic surgery in attempts to build self-esteem as a woman (Pitts-Taylor, 2007). Regardless of what women do, however, there still is a sense of sexual inadequacy because of a perceived failure to measure up to what they are socially expected to be. Failure to achieve what constitutes unattainable standards of female attractiveness often results in diminished self-worth (Finkelstein, 1991).

The boundaries drawn around conventional definitions of male and female in classification schemes inherently contain divisiveness and some degree of estrangement. Men and women are perceived to be different kinds of animal creatures; differing in physical capabilities, in impulse tendencies, in levels of emotionality, and in capacities for rational decision-making. The forms of estrangement are likely to reach their highest level of intensity under those conditions in which stereotyped images have been internalized and attempts are made to apply them in male-female relationships. Exaggerated perceptions of biological and psychological differences tend to interfere with the interpersonal dynamics of men and women when they cross gender borders and enter into relationships with each other (Neal and Collas, 2000).

In drawing on the concept of a *stereotype*, Walter Lippmann (1961) emphasized the frequently wide gaps between our subjective perceptions and the objective realities of the world. Such gaps are frequently becoming evident in the typification of men and women. Critical judgment is lacking in the failure to recognize individuality and the variability in qualities of those who are placed in a social category. The folk definitions of the biological and psychological qualities of women that set them apart from men are simply in error and filled with contradictions. For example, if women are weak and gentle, then it does not follow that they will be prepared to meet the challenges of childbirth and child rearing. The capacity to give birth requires a woman to be strong, and if she is to meet the challenges of protecting and socializing the child she must be assertive. Thus, the typical woman could not adequately carry out her role expectations and requirements if, indeed, she possessed the qualities that are imputed to her (Chodorow, 1979).

Women and men are socialized with divergent definitions of identity, and the traits ascribed to each make it difficult for them to comfortably enter into relationships with each other. Appropriate traits for the male role include independence, dominance, assertiveness, strength, power, invulnerability, and an economy of verbal expression (Snell, 1986; Williams, 1985). It is due to societal expectations that men get locked into the box of masculine identity. Incorporating these traits into a self-identity increases the problematic aspects of sharing a lifestyle with an individual who is characterized by a correspondingly opposite set of characteristics (Sattel, 1976; Lewis, 1978).

The divisiveness of boundaries is evident in the predominance of close friendship ties with members of the same sex. Friendships are formed among those who share similar characteristics, who provide reinforcements for one's own understanding of the world, and who offer support for one's own identity. Lillian Rubin (1985: 66) observed, "Women make time for female friendships because they offer a shared intimacy that is quite different from what they experience with a man." Nancy Chodorow (1979) found that women are most emotionally satisfied in relationships with other women and that relationships with men are less satisfying. Apparently, the basic rewards of friendship are much easier to find among those within one's own sexual category than among those whose profiles of personality traits and understandings of the world are different from one's own.

According to Rubin (1985), men's friendships with other men demonstrate less intimacy than friendships that women have with other women. Male socialization tends to promote the avoidance of self-disclosure, especially as it relates to the verbalization of emotions and personal feelings. In adult life, this is expressed in comparatively low levels of mutual self-disclosure, shared feelings, and demonstrations of emotional closeness (Williams, 1985). Among men, expressions of affection and tenderness are inhibited, and the open expression of emotions is restricted. As a result, male conversations are frequently directed toward such impersonal topics as work, cars, sports, and politics, rather than toward disclosing their feelings (Rubin, 1985).

The box of the feminine identity, however, is equally problematic for women. Traits deemed appropriate for the female role include dependence, passivity, weakness, emotionality, supportiveness, and verbal expression (Williams, 1985). Such traits are not genetically determined at birth but are a consequence of the type of socialization that promotes continuity from one generation to the next. Women are put into a box in which they are expected to be gentile, quiet, and flirtatious, to acquiesce, and to turn their anger inwardly (Storm, et al., 1981). Men show assertiveness, and women are expected to accept and to understand. Such prescriptions for the proper relationship between men and women account for a great deal of the perceptual context for hostile interactions in couple relationships.

The cultural boundaries defining the center and the periphery of gender classifications have become blurred as vast changes have occurred. Modern and egalitarian values have replaced traditional ones; the double standard has weakened; and sexual permissiveness has increased for both men and women (Reiss, 1986). Remaining single and the practice of cohabitation have become viable alternatives to marriage (Gwartney-Gibbs, 1986), and voluntary childlessness has become a viable alternative to parenthood (Miall, 1986). The many challenges to the older forms of female-male relationships result in greater uncertainty in the patterns of interactions between men and women. As a result, it becomes difficult for the member of either sex to have an adequate grasp of the moods, motives, intentions, and behavior of the other (Neal and Collas. 2000).

Aphrodite, Venus and Modern Celebrities

Classical mythologies have been perpetuated because of the pleasure they bring from reading them. They have provided excellent raw material for embellishment in drama, literature, and the arts. The gods of the ancient Greeks and Romans were very human-like, only more so. Their normative offenses included murder, rape, adultery, incest, treachery, and even cannibalism (Stapleton, 1986). Because the pantheon of gods had relevance only in the days gone by, they are no longer a direct threat to us.

The Egyptians, Greeks, Romans, and many others had highly developed belief systems that were based on multiple gods. The multiple deities were anthropomorphic in that they were presumed to have human-like characteristics. The gods interacted with each other and sometimes took human form to interact with living human beings. When the Romans conquered ancient Greece, they assimilated much of the polytheistic culture of the Greeks. The Roman gods resembled those of the Greeks in that they had specialized abilities and specialized functions to perform.

From Greek and Roman mythologies, the myths of Aphrodite and Venus have had an enduring effect on modern consciousness. In sculpture, paintings, and even modern thinking, the goddesses of love and beauty have been inspirational for depictions of the perfect woman. As goddesses, Aphrodite and Venus embodied the ultimate in lust and impulse tendencies. They were unrestrained by any conception of right and wrong. Their beauty and desirability precluded a sense of marital fidelity or any other line of action other than what Destiny or Fate had preordained for them. Each had amorous affairs and copulated with mortals, as well as with other deities.

According to one version of the Aphrodite myth, she was the daughter of Zeus and Dione. According to another, she sprang from the sea foam that had been generated when the testicles of Uranus were severed by an angry son and thrown into the sea. Aphrodite was a soft, weak creature who was irritable, yet she stole away the wits of even men of wisdom (Stapleton, 1986). Out of a sense of jealousy, the wife of Zeus forced Aphrodite to marry Hephaestus, the god of fire and the forge. Her husband was both lame and ugly, and Aphrodite soon found a more exciting lover in Ares, the god of war. Her husband was jealous and sought revenge by crafting a magnificent bronze hunting net that was invisible and placed it above the bed. When Aphrodite believed that her husband was away on a journey, she sent a message for Ares to come visit her. Soon after his arrival, he jumped into bed with Aphrodite, and while they were nude and copulating they were caught in the net. Hephaestus invited the other gods to come and embarrass the naked couple.

Hermes allegedly commented to Apollo that he would be glad to change places with Ares even if there were three times as many nets. Zeus eventually convinced Hephaestus to release the embarrassed couple. Afterwards, Aphrodite traveled to many places and engaged in a multitude of affairs. The mythological characters of Cupid, Eros, and Hermaphrodite sprang from her womb. Apparently, the Venus myth among the Romans was a variation on the episodes of Aphrodite (Hamilton, 1956).

While we no longer believe in the myths about Aphrodite and Venus, we do have modern representations of them. The modern goddesses of love, beauty, and vicarious sexuality are found disproportionately among the celebrities of stage and screen. Roland Barthes (1997) noted that the contrived images of Greta Garbo, presented in the cinema of the 1930s, "plunged audiences into the deepest ecstasy." The viewers apparently lost themselves in images that represented an absolute state of flesh and sexuality that "could neither be reached nor renounced" (p. 56). The deification of an image was a forerunner to the multiple sex goddesses that have been created in the entertainment media over the past several decades.

The symbolic meanings of Aphrodite and Venus have been captured in the modern admiration and celebration of well-known and famous people. The modern celebrities of concern have very little in common with each other except for their glorified personalities. The celebrations of famous women are based on what their audiences of admirers presume to be their personal qualities and attributes. The notoriety of a beauty queen, a poster queen, or a sex symbol rests on qualities imputed to them from the images they present and the forms of lust and desire they evoke.

Identification with the celebrities of the mass media serves to divert attention away from stresses and tensions of the immediate environment. The actual social distance between celebrities and their admirers is so great that there is no sanctioning power of one over the other (McEvoy and Erikson, 1981). In the absence of direct interaction, celebrities become identification models that permit individuals to vicariously reflect on their own hopes and aspirations. The imagery is a form of daydreaming in which human emotions intensify and take concrete focus. Such daydreaming humanizes impersonal events and allows the individual to project himself or herself into someone else's world of understanding, meaning, and action. In this process, entertainment and information, fact and fiction, reality and façade, and time and place become blended into inseparable patterns. The public performances and the personal lives of celebrities serve as models of what to do, how to live, and what is possible.

The media's relentless coverage of the deaths of celebrities contributes to their sanctification (Zelizer, 1992). Through modern technological means of preservation, images of the dead become frozen in time, surrounded by manufactured fantasies, and lacking in the reality checks that are associated with the aging process (Dixon, 1999). We will never know, for example, what a seventy-year old Marilyn Monroe, Natalie Wood, Princess Diana, or John F. Kennedy would look like, or be like. As with Aphrodite and Venus, the famous dead have become our new saints by transcending the limits of earthly existence. The sounds and images on film and recordings become repositories of collective dreams by perpetuating the mythologies of celebrities and the excitement surrounding their troubled lives.

As a result of charismatic imputations by their fans, celebrities are seen as invulnerable and immortal. This has been especially evident in the rumors and legends surrounding the life of Elvis Presley (Gregory and Gregory, 1992). Reported sightings of Elvis were frequent occurrences for more than twenty-five years after his death. Today there are hundreds of live impersonators of Elvis who attempt to emulate his style of dress, his voice inflection, and his hip movements. The worldwide elaborations of his life, legend, and cultural symbolism have placed him in history as a figure that transcends the realities of mortal existence (Smit, 2001). As a result of charismatic imputations, his popularity has expanded and he has taken on a larger-than-life status.

With the passing of time, the collective memories of celebrities tend to become endowed with immortality. For example, the sensuous images of Marilyn Monroe continue to endure. As a result of her premature death, her imagery became frozen in time. Like the goddesses Aphrodite and Venus, she will forever remain young. In effect, she has become a mnemonic device for sexuality and sex symbolism. In our prosthetic memories (Landsberg, 2004), the modern celebrities have replaced the heroic and mythological figures of the past as major emblems of hope, aspirations, and wishful thinking.

Commodification of the Body

While goddesses and celebrities are exceptional embodiments of physical beauty, several forces have converged in recent years to promote a standardized model of what every woman should look like and be like. Pressures to conform to a standardized model stem from many different sources in modern society. The creation of the beauty myth was primarily a byproduct of the trend toward the commodification of everything (Song, 2003). Sperm banks, in vitro fertilization, organ transplants, genomic medicine, and surrogate motherhood are among the many marketable products of the modern world. There is a market for whatever is of interest or value.

The term commodification of everything refers to the process by which all things are transformed into objects having marketable value.

Marketplace values are extended to aesthetic embellishments of the human body, to human sexuality, to religion, and to all other aspects of the human condition. All human activity, wants, desires, and life plans have been subjected to the creation of commodities and to evaluations in terms of the market paradigm (Kurtner, 1997).

In the recent past, sexuality was thought of as personal, private, and one of the more intimate aspects of life. In contrast to the older view of sex as a taboo topic, sexuality is blatantly represented in modern music, mass entertainment, adult bookstores, sex manuals, sex magazines and pornographic movies. In the commercial enterprise, the production and distribution of sexual materials found a ready-made market from those wishing to add a greater degree of excitement to their personal lives. Freedom of speech and other civil liberties collided with opposing views on what should or should not be tolerated in the modern community.

Charismatic sexuality was a prominent theme in the development of advertising. The visual displays in advertising for deodorants, toothpaste, perfumes, diets, and hair gels linked the use of commercial products with physical beauty. The promise was to create a gorgeous and charismatic self that would facilitate developing intimate relationships with other beautiful and attractive people. In effect, the message from commercial advertising seemed to be that the human body in its natural form is ugly and in need of a great deal of embellishment. While the desired outcomes are unattainable, such commercial lures continue to be elaborated in order to keep people buying in their quest for the unattainable cultural ideal (Wolf, 1991).

Because personal appearance is such an important part of the social display of the self, an inordinate amount of time and effort go into devising conduct and appearances that are intended to invoke the desired responses in others. Apparently, the self as a meaningful social object requires a great deal of embellishment. Customizing the body takes a variety of forms. These include tattooing, hair implants, seeking solutions to the problems of baldness, attempts to eliminate the wrinkles associated with aging, and exercising to produce the desired body builds and shapes. These efforts at embellishment of the body are efforts to create and sustain images that will have some calculated effect on others (Finkelstein, 1991). More than a million American women have had breast implants to make a favorable impression on others and to enhance self-esteem.

In addition to breast size as a distinguishing characteristic of beauty, there is also an emphasis on slimness. It is the equation of slimness with beauty that has led to serious eating disorders in recent years. Many young adult females suffer from the eating disorders of anorexia and bulimia. The woman suffering from anorexia has an intense fear of gaining weight or becoming fat, even though she may presently be underweight for her age and height. Bulimia, on the other hand, occurs with recurrent episodes of binge eating that are uncontrolled, followed by self-induced vomiting, or misuse of laxatives, diuretics, enemas, or medications.

The relentless pursuit of slimness stems from the images conveyed in advertising, television, the movies, and fashion models. While dieting has become a multi-billion-dollar industry, the general public is saturated with the promotion of a standardized model of beauty that is unattainable for most people and results in self-disrespect and shame for some who fall short of what they think is expected of them.

Sexuality and Its Discontents

The meaning of sexuality is complicated by its commodification in advertising and mass entertainment. Each continuously expands the emphasis on sexual pleasure, desires, and possibilities at the same time that sexuality has come to occupy center stage in the political arena, in right-wing religious groups, and in social movements. The modern crisis of sexuality grows out of the historical traditions, both religious and secular, that elevated sexuality to such a high degree of importance. What was once thought of as normal and natural has very little to do with modern forms of sexual expressiveness. The certainties of the past have crumbled under the modern emphasis upon personal freedom and rational choice (Rosenthal, 2005). The discovery of a viable set of beliefs and norms about human sexuality does not appear to be on the horizon. Instead of seeking to impose a new morality on everyone, it becomes increasingly important to recognize the diversity of modern beliefs, desires, and preferences.

Few topics evoke such intense responses as those related to the erotic possibilities of our bodies. While eroticism has been elevated to a preeminent place in our modern, hedonistic, pleasure-seeking society, sexuality has less to do with our bodies than with words, images, rituals, and fantasy (Weeks, 1985). The place of sex in the lives of individuals has fallen into a moral vacuum, resulting in confusion, bewilderment, and uncertainty. One of the major myths surrounding human sexuality is that it is primarily biologically motivated and driven by impulse tendencies.

The difficulties of individuals in their sex lives are grounded in the cultural forces that lead them to want more and to expect more than can be attained. The quest in people's personal lives often takes the form of escape from the harsh realities of aspects of their lives that are beyond personal control and mastery and are bereft of meaning. The pleasures of sex are presumed by many to serve as compensation for working at a job that lacks intrinsic rewards, to compensate for the impersonality of modern bureaucratic life, and to provide warmth and comfort is a world that appears to be cold and indifferent. The discontent in part stems from the failure of sexual relationships to provide self-actualization and self-esteem. The promises from advertising and mass entertainment are glorified for commercial purposes and have very little to do with real-life experiences.

Conventional norms prohibiting premarital and extramarital sex are colliding with increasing sexual permissiveness. Survey research clearly indicates that today adolescents are having their first sexual intercourse at an earlier age, that they are more sexually active, and that they have a greater variety of partners than did their parents and their grandparents. The sexual revolution may be understood as growing out of the models provided by commercial advertising, MTV, and other forms of mass entertainment. Apparently, young people are doing it more, but enjoying it less. Both males and females have become sex objects in an emerging culture promoting sensation (Hendin, 1975).

The inventories of current practices that are inconsistent with the prevailing forces from the past are well known. These include, for example, premarital sex, unwed motherhood, cohabitation, aborting an unplanned pregnancy, marital infidelity, and terminating rather than continuing an unhappy marriage (Chilman, Nunnally, and Cox, 1988). These changes partially arise out of the quest for social justice on the part of women, and partially out of a growing emphasis upon personal choice in the forms and types of relationships with members of the opposite sex.

Because of the vast changes that have occurred, Georg Simmel's (1950) conception of the stranger seems applicable to modern men and women. They may be physically close together while psychologically feeling miles apart. They have difficulty understanding the moods, motives, and intentions of each other. They have difficulty in openly expressing their emotional states and their fears and aspirations. They often feel trapped in relationships that have turned sour and feel that there is no satisfactory way out (Neal and Collas, 2000).

A crisis of meaning originates from the fact that neither men nor women have a useable past for defining many of the problems that surface in their relationships. When these relationships become troublesome, ordinary men and women frequently sense that they are up against issues they do not understand. They cannot determine what it is that threatens the values they vaguely discern as being their own. The crisis of meaning becomes evident in the decision-making process. How are decisions to be made? Who has the right to decide? How are the available resources to be allocated? When decisions are made, can they be counted on as binding on conduct? If these questions cannot be answered with confidence, gender relationships become chaotic and lacking in coherence. Because men were traditionally the primary holders of power, a crisis of meaning had to develop in order to create more equitable relationships.

Drawing upon her clinical practice, Leonore Tiefer (1995) concluded from her observations on the variety of sexual orientations and practices that *Sex Is Not a Natural Act* (the title of her book). If human sexuality were exclusively a product of impulse tendencies and biological drives, it would be much less complicated than it is today. Many other species have rutting seasons in which males and females come together for mating purposes and then separate. There is no such biological programming among human beings, and as a result, they may mate at any time of the year. While there is a disproportionate emphasis on the biological aspects of sex in popular thinking, we can never adequately understand human sexuality by only looking at its "natural" components. Sexuality today has become much more than a source of intense pleasure; it has also become a source of intense anger, anxiety and hostility.

It is clear is that the sexual revolution did not work out as expected. The older social norms had been restrictive and greatly reduced the options available to men and women. The sexual revolution for women meant freedom from the restraints that had been imposed upon their mothers, grandmothers, and ancestors who preceded them. The new freedoms for women gave men access to a greater range of sexual partners than ever before. However, as the boundaries of sexual options and opportunities expanded, the opportunities for meaningful and committed relationships diminished (Rubin, 1985).

Separation of the wants and desires of individuals from the basic needs of an orderly society has become problematic. All societies need to regulate and control the sexual impulse in some way or another. Sociologists have claimed that a completely promiscuous society is not theoretically possible. Who to have sex with, when, and, how and under what circumstances must be regulated. For example, regulation is necessary to fix responsibility for childbearing and childrearing, to permit stable relationships to develop among men and women, and to reduce the levels of conflict within the social realm. But in making these observations, it is also clear that many of the normative restrictions from the past have lost their hold over conduct in the modern world. The present context is one of uncertainty about the ingredients of authentic sexual identities of men and women, as well as uncertainty about what is normal, natural, and inevitable as men and women cross gender borders and enter into relationships with each other.

11

Alpha and Omega

In the beginning God created the heaven and the earth. The earth was without form, and void, and darkness was upon the face of the deep; and the Spirit of God was moving over the face of the waters. And God said, "Let there be light"; and there was light. And God saw that the light was good; and God separated the light from the darkness.

—Genesis 1:1–4

One of the great mysteries of the human condition is that of how we got here; how it all got started. The cultures and religions of the world, now and in the past, have offered a rich variety of profound answers to these questions. In response to the mysteries of life, humans have been successful in creating innovative sets of meaning to serve as sources of unity and cohesion for the members any given society.

Alpha and omega are the first and last letters of the Greek alphabet. The two are frequently associated with an appellation of God in the Book of Revelation, in which Christ declares, "I am the Alpha and the Omega." In this context, alpha and omega refer to being there in the beginning and at the end, being there at the time of creation and at the time of destruction. In the Hindu mythology of ancient India, the world has been created and destroyed several times.

Many monotheistic religions hold that creation was a product of one God who was self-created, all-powerful, all-knowing, and all-present. While this seems clear and coherent enough, philosophical controversy has persisted over whether God created humans in his own image or whether the existence of God and the qualities imputed to him are human creations. Erich Fromm (1967) maintained that humans created God in pretty much the same way that other forms of culture are created. But after he was created, a process of reification occurred. God was endowed with a factual, objective existence independent of human

161

thought and action. Once this reification occurred, humans then petitioned God to grant favors and to return to them some of the qualities they had projected into God in the first place.

In the 19th century social scientists drew upon the doctrine of progress and were concerned with the evolution of religion along with the evolution of all other social institutions. Basic questions of interest to classical theorists were how did we get to where we are now, where are we now, and where are we headed as we move into the future. Today, we no longer apply the notion of progress to the rapid changes occurring in social institutions, and evolutionary theories of society are no longer of concern. Yet they merit a review in studies of the mythologies ultimately related to origins, development, and destiny. While evolutionary sequences in the development of religion remain as speculation, and can never be discovered, they do permit a review of the many forms that the relativity of mythology takes.

Anthropologists generally regard animism and totemism as the earliest forms of religion in the evolution of human societies. It was from animism that the soul concept emerged and was imputed not only to humans but also to animals and sometimes inanimate objects. However, it was totemism that provided the primary creation myths in primitive society. According to the totemic myths, the origin of a particular clan stemmed from a revered totemic animal. All who were members of a totemic group shared a sense of kinship, although they may not be able to trace their kinship through known relatives. Since kinship prevailed among all members of the same totem, strong norms prohibited the killing of the totemic animal. Killing the totemic animal would be the equivalent of in-group murder (Freud, 1918). In similar fashion, the norm prohibiting incest required marriage outside of one's totemic group. The totem resembled the flag in modern nationalism, although in a much elaborated and embellished form.

In his analysis of religion, Emile Durkheim (1990) drew heavily on totemism for developing his conception of what is central to religion in primitive society as well as in the modern world. He observed that the totemic principle provided the name and symbolized the identity of a clan or tribe, and therefore of a society. It is the collectivity that creates the totem, and totemism in turn serves as the basis for those things regarded as sacred. According to Durkheim, "A religion is a unified system of beliefs and practices relative to sacred things, that is to say things that are set apart and forbidden—beliefs and practices which unites in one single moral community all those who adhere to them." Thus, religion was central to the collective identity of any particular people and the primary social glue for binding people together in a sense of moral community.

Polytheism came into a position of prominence with the emergence of ancient civilizations. The pantheon of gods among the Sumerians, the Babylonians, the Assyrians, and the Greeks shared several characteristics in common. A symbolic deity was constructed to represent the essential functions of a society. For example, Aphrodite, Ishtar, Demeter, Freya, and Venus were created in their separate cultures as the goddess of beauty, sexuality, and fertility. The gods displayed such remarkably human characteristics as anger, envy, resentment, vindictiveness, and jealousy. The Greek gods often took human form and interacted directly with human beings. These interactions sometimes became sexual and resulted in the production of humans who claimed to be of divine origin. The Greek mythological heritage has exercised a powerful influence in Western literature, mass entertainment, scientific technology, and space research (Littleton, 2007). The book by Allan Lazar and his associates (2006), *The 101 Most Influential People Who Never Lived*, lists ten gods and goddesses from Greek mythology. Among others, these include Prometheus, Apollo, Pandora, Odysseus, Midas, Pygmalion, and Icarus.

In contrast to those who saw animism, totemism, and polytheism as emerging first in the evolutionary process, Father Wilhelm Schmidt (1958) maintained that monotheism was the earliest form of religion. In his view, concepts such as spirits and ghosts, the souls of animals and plants and polytheism, were all the result of degenerative speculative thought. He had observed that in many primitive societies, there were accounts of how the world had been created by a High God. But while there were frequent references to the High God in primitive accounts of creation, there was very little ritual or ceremony directed toward him. It was generally believed that he had lost interest in the objects of his creation and removed himself to a remote part of the sky. Offering prayers or petitions to him would be acts of futility, since he was no longer there to listen to them.

The universality of the High God served important functions in the development of the ancient city (de Coulanges, 1965). With its emergence, the ancient city became a confederation of a diverse array of families, clans, and tribes. Separate gods and deities were obstacles to the creation of a shared sense of trust and community. The strangers who came to the city for an exchange of goods also brought with them deities that were specific to their own particular group. The introduction of monotheism provided the city with a God that was unique, immense, and universal. In sharing a God that was applicable to all of mankind, new sources of unity, morality, and rules of conduct were provided and facilitated the growth of government and the regulation of trade relationships. Anthropologists generally agree that the emergence of a fully-developed monotheism was relatively late in the historical process.

The many forms of mythology about creation and the ultimate human destiny have their origin in long traditions and are the products of many minds and many generations over long periods of time. The validity of religious beliefs is not at issue here, but only the many creative ways that men and women confront the conditions of their existence. Such collective beliefs have a reality of their own, serve therapeutic functions, and provide sources of understanding and action among their adherents.

The Creation Myth

In the 17th century, Bishop James Ussher maintained from his analysis of the scriptures "The beginning of time fell on the beginning of the night which preceded the 23rd day of October in the year 4004 BC" His analysis had focused on the "begats" and the generational levels in the Bible. While we now recognize the absurdity of his claims, his analysis was widely accepted for more than 200 years. Archeology and paleontology had not yet been developed as sciences to indicate that the planet Earth had been around for several billion years. Bishop Ussher failed to recognize the inappropriateness of applying the modern conceptions of time to the remote and inaccessible past. Yet notions about "when time began" and "when time shall be no more" have been of interest to many religious groups.

Essentially, Bishop Ussher's analysis consisted of a mixture of mythical time with historical time. Mythical time frequently involves the Australian aborigines' notion of "everywhen": there were certain events that happened in the past, that could still happen today, and will happen again in the future. In contrast, historical time involves organizing time into a linear framework of before and after. Most creation mythologies were transmitted through an oral tradition and modified in the transmission from one generation to another. The sacred texts we have today were transmitted by scribes during historical time and have only been around for a few thousand years.

The cultures of the world have varied myths about the creation of the world. But whatever the belief, the shared content of the mythology helps to establish a collective identity. Some variations on the myths of creation hold that the world and everything in it sprang from a cosmic egg; others that the earth was created out of chaos; yet others maintain that the world was created out of a void or out of nothing. The Jainist religion of India claimed that the earth was never created, but instead that it has always existed. Some of the myths of the Pacific Islanders deemed that their particular island was carried there and set in place by a giant sea turtle.

Examples of the belief in creation emerging from chaos are found in the ancient civilizations of Babylonia and Egypt. Many of the stories held that an orderly universe developed out of such forms of chaos as confusion, darkness, and water. The dual themes of indeterminacy and potentiality were emphasized. The Chinese version of the myth held that in the beginning there was chaos and out of it emerged light from which the sky was built. The principle of yin and yang, male and female, had their origin in the primal duality of sky and earth.

A corollary myth focused on the emergence of a cosmic egg that represented the beginning of all things orderly. There was a time in which all was darkness over water. The cosmic egg, as a symbol of fecundity and fertility, became a source of life and rebirth as well as the basis for the duality of male and female. Frequent references are made to the mother earth and to the father sky. While two parents are necessarily related in the myth, they are also capable of independence and separate determinism (Long, 1963). These myths suggest that the power of creativity was present in the beginning. The Polynesian version of the myth held that the breaking of the shell of the cosmic egg gave rise to the evolution of all life forms.

One of the basic functions of religious mythology is to provide sacred grounds for a sense of order in a social system. Guiding principles are thus established for what is normal, natural, and inevitable in human relationships, particularly those of intimacy. The rules and regulations of a normative order serve as a buffer against conditions of incoherence and meaninglessness. It is for this reason that the shared myth of how order and predictability were created out of chaos becomes one of the sustaining sources of identity among given groups of people.

While humans occasionally have an interest in excitement and risk-taking, there is generally a low degree of tolerance for uncertainty and chaos. It is perhaps for this reason that the creation of order out of chaos occupies such a prominent place in the creation mythology of so many of the world's religions (Berger, 1969). The accounts are not so much geared toward an explanation of how the physical earth was created as toward the basis for predictability in an orderly society.

According to the book of Genesis, an all-powerful God with human-like characteristics created the world out of a "void." As noted in the opening quote to this chapter, "God said, Let there be light; and there was light." This implies that God existed prior to the creation and that God himself was self-created. It also implies that there was nothing, or no material reality, prior to his act of creation. This myth suggests that the mode and the content of creating the cosmos were conscious and intentional as well as based on a deliberate plan of action.

Charles Darwin's book *The Origins of the Species by Means of Natural Selection* (published in 1859) laid out one of the most important scientific theories of modern times. Darwin had collected a vast amount of evidence on the diversity of biological characteristics within species, as well as similarities and variations between species. He hypothesized that a process of natural selection was operative over long periods of time to promote differentiation. As a result of variations in adaptability to environmental conditions, some organisms survived, reproduced, and increased numerically, while others faded away. Over hundreds or even thousands of generations, differences accumulate through a process of genetic drift to ultimately produce new species.

Darwin's theories generally have been supported and enhanced by developments in the fields of genetics, archeology, and paleontology. Most men and women in the sciences, and virtually all modern biologists, accept the theories of evolution as being a valid set of explanations. A slow gradual process of change has contributed to the increased complexity and diversity of life forms.

In contrast to the near consensus in the scientific community, some Christian fundamentalists have rejected Darwin's theories and sparked a great deal of controversy over the years. The constitutional separation of church and state precludes the teaching of religion in the public schools. However, in attempts to circumvent court rulings, a group of American creationists reformulated their arguments by detailing notions about "intelligent design." Without specifying the designer, or making reference to the God of Christianity, assertions are made that a conscious intelligent process best explains the essential features of the universe and of living things, not evolution or natural selection.

Many in the scientific community hold that intelligent design is not science but a disguised claim for supernatural intervention in the origin of life. They believe that because the principles of intelligent design are not verifiable by scientific methods, they should not be taught as science in the public schools. The controversy reflects the multiple realities of the modern world. While advances of science have changed the modern world, such developments have not precluded the expansion and elaboration of religious institutions (Berger, 1999). Through the separation of institutions in a pluralistic society, all institutional areas have been developed and enhanced.

The Destroyer Myth

Nothing lasts forever. The edifices that humans create in the development of cultures and civilizations are so fragile that they cannot endure for very long. People seem to be unable to create societies that are compatible with human proclivities as well as with their own guidelines to morality. Greed and avarice, along with sexual deviancy and abnormality, seem to be especially disappointing to gods that are judgmental and wrathful. In effect, the gods who were the creators of all that exists become dissatisfied with the objects of their creation and decide to destroy them. The destroyer myth in the religions of the world are sufficiently prominent that a great deal of anxiety persists about how and when life as we know it will vanish. Reasoning by analogy from the life cycle, our experiences with birth and death provide a miniature model of the creation and destruction of the world.

In the Hebrew tradition, evidence for the possibility of the destruction of the world was presented in the account of the Great Flood and the story of Noah and his family. According to the legend, when Adam and Eve ate the forbidden fruit from the Tree of Knowledge, they had disobeyed the command of God, while at the same time they acquired the ability to make choices. An important corollary of the ability to make choices was an awareness of the difference between right and wrong, good and evil. The accumulation of wrong choices over time led to God's displeasure with the objects of his creation. After intending to destroy the world by sending forth a Great Deluge, God made the decision to save a righteous man and his family.

Noah was instructed by God to build a huge ark that would be large enough for his family and a mating pair of all the animals God had created. After Noah and his family and all of the animals had entered the ark, the Great Deluge started, and the heavy rains continued for forty days and nights. The highest mountains were covered to the depth of at least twenty feet and all remaining humans and other creatures died. At the end of 150 days, the ark landed on the mountains of Ararat. Noah then faced the responsibility of building a new world that included the development of agriculture and all other viable aspects of culture.

Several major accounts of flood stories predated that of Noah in the ancient Greek mythology, in the ancient writings of Mesopotamia, and in accounts from the Sumerians. The flooding of the great rivers at the cradle of civilization provided the raw material for a great deal of elaboration on the role of the sacred in human affairs. The stories sent a message to future generations about human vulnerability and about the potential consequences of disobedience to a wrathful god.

Following the Cuban Missile Crisis, a great deal of concern was expressed in the United States about the possibility of the destruction of the world from an all-out nuclear war. Opinion was divided over whether or not there would be any survivors if such a war were to take place. Some turned to the scriptures and maintained that not all would perish. It was noted that a great flood once destroyed the world and there were survivors. Noah and his family had been chosen to perpetuate the species. This view held that a merciful God would provide humanity with an opportunity for a fresh start. The survivors, it was argued, would have an opportunity to build a new social order that would be a substantial improvement over the old one.

The destroyer myth again surfaced in the Biblical account of the destruction of Sodom and Gomorrah. Because of the wickedness of their inhabitants, divine fire and brimstone were sent down from heaven to obliterate the two cities. Prior to the destruction, angels were sent down to search for righteous people. Only four were found. These included Lot, his wife, and their two daughters. As they were led out of the city, the four were commanded not to look back under any circumstances. As the two cities were being destroyed, Lot's wife looked back and was instantly turned into a pillar of salt. Accounts of Sodom and Gomorrah subsequently have become metaphors for excessive vice and sexual deviancy.

The recurrence of the destroyer myth occupies a prominent place in the New Testament. Specifically, the prophecies of the book of Revelation hold a dim view of the human condition (Kirsch, 2006). According to the prophecies, signs of the impending last days include such disturbing events as a darkening of the sun, the moon turning blood red in color, stars falling to earth, and the emergence of false prophets. The tribulations that will follow consist of the suffering and sorrow from plagues, pestilence, and famine. After an epic battle at Armageddon between the forces of good and evil, Jesus Christ will descend from heaven in the guise of a warrior-king to lead the army of the righteous to victory. After the battle, Satan will be bound in chains and confined to a bottomless pit. With the defeat of evil, Christ will then reign over an earthly kingdom for one thousand years.

At the end of the millennium, Satan will break out of his bonds, and Jesus Christ will find it necessary to fight a second and final battle. Afterwards, the world as we know it will be destroyed once and for all. The book of Revelation holds that "a new heaven and a new earth" will be created. The dead will be resurrected and subjected to the final judgment along with the living. The Christian saints, martyrs, and true believers will spend eternity in a state of perfect bliss. Everyone else will join Satan in a lake of fire and brimstone.

The notion of the Rapture is included in the Christian eschatology of some religious groups. It is a doctrine of hope for those who are born again. Rather than being required to endure the suffering and sorrow of the Tribulation, dedicated Christians will be taken up from this earth. This notion was expressed on a bumper sticker in Portland, Oregon, which read, "When the Rapture comes, this vehicle will be empty." Thus, there are wide variations among Christians on how and when the end will come and what will be required of them.

One of the major uncertainties in Christian eschatology surrounds the question of when the Second Coming will occur. Some note that the Tribulation is now occurring in a turbulent world and that currently disturbing events are advanced indicators that the end time is near. Others observe that the timing of the return of Christ to the world is not knowable. It is out of this uncertainty that the Bible has been carefully searched for hundred of years in the search for coded information about when that momentous event will occur.

Millenarianism

Millenarian movements are religious groups that predict the occurrence of an apocalypse, the end of the world, "when time shall be no more," the Second Coming, the arrival of the Messiah, or some other supernatural event that will radically transform social life as it is presently known and understood. Whatever the predicted event, the righteous are believed to constitute a select group that will be saved; all others will suffer or be destroyed. The acceptance of knowledge revealed from biblical scriptures or from supernatural contact has led several messianic groups to set specific dates for the destruction of the world.

Leon Festinger and his associates (1956) made a study of one such group to determine how they cope when a prophecy fails to be fulfilled. The group had set a specific date for the end of the world, and the members had made special preparations for the occasion. An outside observer might think that the failure of such a prophecy would have unequivocally refuted the accuracy of such a belief. Surely such a specific prediction as the world ending on a particular day had been subjected to a clear, definitive, and crucial test.

Festinger's research indicated that instead of being rejected because of the failure of prophecy, the initial beliefs became even stronger than before. The group members now felt the world had been saved by their devotion and commitment. For a short period of time following the disconfirmation, the movement increased its fervor and directed efforts toward winning additional converts. Strongly held beliefs thus depend on social supports for confirmation, rather than on objective verifiable evidence.

One of the noteworthy prophecies about the Second Coming was foretold in upstate New York by a Baptist layman named William Miller (1782–1849). After long biblical study, he concluded that the world as we know it would come to an end sometime in the year 1843. His subsequent followers numbered around a million people in New England and the American Midwest, and they came to be known as the Millerites. When 1843 came and went, his followers insisted that Miller redo his calculations and come up with a more specific date. Miller settled for October 22, 1844, as the day the end would come. The excitement of his followers continued to build as the date approached, but they were disappointed when the predicted event and the expected ecstasy did not occur (Boyer, 1992). But instead of falling apart, the movement became reorganized into new variations on the original ideology. The Millerites were faced with the problem of deciding what to do with the rest of their lives while waiting for the end of the world, convinced that the end was near, but not knowing when the event would occur.

Millenarianism has a special appeal to those who have intense feelings of alienation and estrangement. This takes the form of seeing the present world as evil and unjust, as a world they are unable to change through their own efforts (Hobsbawm, 1959). It is out of a passionate longing for a better world that the alienated become susceptible to the persuasive appeals of a charismatic leader. A special relationship develops between a leader and his or her followers. The special qualities imputed to the charismatic leader include forcefulness, perceived morality, and valid knowledge. In symbolizing the hopes and aspirations of a constituency, a charismatic leader becomes emblematic of group solidarity, effectiveness, and aspirations.

A wave of messianic optimism emerged in the 1890s among the Plains Indians after an intense sense of despair arising from governmental policies forcing them to reservations. From their lifestyle of poverty, hunger, and dependency, conditions were ripe for the emergence of a social movement to offer some degree of hope. Wovoka, a Piute Indian and a charismatic leader, emerged to offer a divinely inspired doctrine of hope and to prophesy a radical transformation of the world. The Indians were taught Ghost Dance songs and dances that were to be performed in anticipation of the return to earth of the Great Spirit or his emissary.

The prophecy held that when the grass turned green the following spring, the great herds of buffalo and wild horses would return. The earth would be covered with a new soil and all of the white men would disappear. At the time of divine intervention, all who had danced the Ghost Dance would be taken up in the air and suspended until a new earth was created. Upon their return to the new earth, the Indian dead ancestors would be resurrected to join the living. Once the new earth was created, only Indians would live there.

The conditions faced by the Plains Indians in the last part of the 19th century were intolerable. Their cultures had not been able to sustain them; they had been forced from tribal lands and relocated in reservations; their children had been taken from them and placed in assimilation schools, and encroaching settlers had confiscated their tribal lands. Diseases had been imported by settlers and soldiers to which they had no immunity. There seemed to be no solution to the demands that had been placed on them. It was within this context that the Ghost Dance as a messianic movement offered the promise of a solution to the dire circumstances they confronted. Turning to supernatural solutions frequently occurs in human affairs when all other approaches have turned out to be inadequate or disastrous.

The Ghost Dance movement served to revitalize parts of the native cultures that had been lost (Wallace, 1966). It offered the promise of a return to an aboriginal way of life. The chain reaction of the excitement associated with the spread of the movement was alarming both to Indian agents and to the military. A major uncertainty growing out of the movement stemmed from the manner in which the white men were to disappear. In some cases, it was believed that the oppressors would disappear with the arrival of the messiah. In other cases, it was maintained that the Great Spirit would bring with him the necessary weapons and that the Indians must be trained and prepared to use them.

The growing tensions and fear on the part of the military resulted in the Indian massacre at Wounded Knee in South Dakota. An assembly of tribal groups for a Ghost Dance ceremony was very disturbing to the remnants of Custer's regiment, the 7th Cavalry. The uneasiness was in part based on the perception that the Ghost Dance movement would result in an uprising among the Indians to reclaim their tribal lands. In December 1890, the 7th Cavalry surrounded the natives and started firing indiscriminately. Most of the Indians had already been disarmed and had no way to defend themselves. Before the firing stopped, the soldiers tracked down and killed every living Indian they could find, including old men, women, and children. Instead of the Indians bringing back their ancestors, the hope for any way of returning to their traditional culture and heritage was extinguished. The Medal of Honor was awarded to several of the soldiers who enthusiastically carried out the massacre.

Under conditions of crisis, myths evolve to make sense out of a chaotic world and fill in the gaps in what is accepted as factual information. This may be illustrated, for example, in the emergence of the cargo cults of Melanesia and New Guinea (Worsley, 1957). As European colonialism spread to the islands of the Pacific, the natives pondered the mysterious arrival of ships on the horizon that were loaded with manufactured goods. They never saw the Europeans do any work to produce the goods they used. The tight controls Europeans maintained over access to the manufactured goods suggested that they might be magical or supernatural in origin. Several attempts were made to discover the secrets to the cargos, including intensely listening to the messages of missionaries and attempting to show a magical type of reverence for flags and flagpoles.

It was within this context that the natives developed the notion that access to the cargoes could be achieved only through divine intervention. Several forms of the cargo cults developed in the 19th and 20th centuries around the belief that through the coming of a messiah, or the return of a legendary folk hero, the natives of Melanesia would have unlimited access to manufactured goods. Airstrips and warehouses were constructed out of coconut, straw, and other jungle material to be prepared for receiving the manufactured goods when they arrived. With the coming of a messiah, the Europeans would vanish, never to return, the native dead would be resurrected, old people would regain their youth, sickness would vanish, peace and harmony would prevail, and inexhaustible supplies of the cargo would arrive for the exclusive benefit of the natives.

Indigenous people had been in contact with thriving European communities but were not able to share the abundance of their modern lifestyles. They became envious of Europeans but had no direct means for achieving their standard of living. The millennial movements in the South Pacific were attempts to use magic to achieve parallel lives for themselves without being controlled and dominated by the Europeans. Millennial movements thus promise the blending of the spiritual with the terrestrial in a world that will be inhabited by a humanity freed from the pain and limitations of human existence.

Through making a distinction between insiders and outsiders, members and non-members, believers and non-believers, the apocalyptic myth serves to create meaning and solidarity. Beliefs in the Rapture, eventually participating in a divine paradise, and achieving eternal life represent the ultimate in religious faith and hope. Such beliefs serve as a source of endurance in an unjust world and provide a basis for believing that current hardships are but a steppingstone to a better future.

12

The Secular Apocalypse

The promise of the Enlightenment did not work out as expected. Through the use of human rationality it was believed that we would be able to collectively build a better world. Through empirical observation we would be able to attain truth and objectivity and thus free societies from the prejudices of subjectivity (Harvey, 1991). The conditions of late modernity, however, suggest that the historical promise of the Enlightenment failed to deliver the expected outcomes. Social science research over the past 80 years suggests that our knowledge (ideas we carry around in our heads) is characterized by relativity, incompleteness, and uncertainty.

Secular mythology in the scientific community is evident in perspectives on the fate of the world. Those addressing our ultimate destiny, from their limited vantage points, are engaged in myth making. Plausible explanations serve as a substitute for empirical fact. Our empirical knowledge has its limits. As a result we develop mythologies to fill in the missing gaps of information. As social life has become more highly secularized, it has not reduced the need for myth-making. In the final analysis, truth claims in the scientific community rest on consensus among the experts. Scientific agreement on facts occurs within an historical context and thus becomes relative.

The secular approach requires us to recognize that our knowledge is always incomplete and that our information is only partial and fragmentary (McKibben, 1993). What we see in the world around us is knowable only from a particular vantage point. We have not reduced the scope of the unknown, but only increased our awareness of the possible. In contrast to the many arrogant assumptions about mastery and control in the fields of engineering and technology, several books and journal articles have been published in recent years on everyday anxieties, fears, and uncertainties (Ferudi, 1997; Glassner, 1999; Bourke, 2005).

According to Johanna Bourke (2005). "fear has become the emotion through which public life is administered." An endless range of terrifying possibilities face people in the early part of the twenty-first century. Included among them are fear of another terrorist attack, fear of criminal victimization, fear of a cataclysmic ecological crisis, fear of a celestial collision, fear of nuclear war, and fear of uncontrollable diseases and pandemics. As a result of the many forms of fear, dim views are held on the prospects for the continuity of social life as it is known and understood.

It is ironic that fear holds such a prominent place in modern culture at the very time in which control over so many areas of life are without historical precedent. This irony may stem from feelings among individuals that there is very little control that resides in their own hands and that they must depend on experts or professionals for solutions to the problems that concern them. The psychological basis for fear may stem from the loss of a sense of community, having to rely only on one's own resources in times of trouble (Putnam, 2000), and from the difficulty in finding a sense of meaning, purpose, or coherence within the increasing complexity of modern social life. Collectively, fear may also be promoted by the use of traumatic scripts in the news media that are devoid of coherent explanations.

The catastrophes of concern to the scientific community include collisions, dramatic volcanic eruptions, and pandemics. Any of these occurrences in an extreme form could have disastrous consequences for life on this planet. From an inventory of the many craters produced by the collision of asteroids, "shooting stars" and "falling stars" have lost their romantic connotations. While the fear of a nuclear holocaust has receded into the background of public consciousness, it returns to the forefront during times of crisis. This occurs, for example, with news reports of "rogue nations" moving toward developing a nuclear capability. And the fear of a worldwide pandemic from which a medical response cannot be developed fast enough has become a chronic form of stress in the human condition.

Celestial Collisions

There is a great deal of debris from the formation of stars and planets, and for billions of years they have bombarded the earth. Scientists have identified only about 120 of the terrestrial impact craters. Most of them have been filled in by erosion and even more have not been identified because they are located beneath the ocean. There are still thousands of chunks of rock orbiting the sun that, if they collided with the earth, could cause terrible destruction that would dwarf the more familiar natural disasters.

Had it not been for the extraordinary distances and vast reaches of empty spaces within the universe, violent collisions between the stars would have rendered life forms impossible. Without the immense space, the frequent near misses of celestial objects would have pulled the planets from orbits around their suns and flung them off into interstellar space. Under such conditions, they would have quickly cooled to hundreds of degrees below zero. If our sun had collided with a passing star a few billion years ago, none of us would have been born. Life as we know it would never have existed (Greenstein, 1988).

While we cannot know with certainty the age of our planet, the latest thinking among scientists is that the earth was created out of a collection of celestial materials about four to five billion years ago. The earth was formed the same way the sun, planets, and stars were formed. Initially, the earth was a hot glowing ball of gases with temperatures perhaps reaching millions of degrees Fahrenheit. The ball of gases diminished in size from spinning and the surface of the earth gradually cooled down. As the earth got smaller, the gases changed to liquids, and the heavier materials settled to the middle of the earth. A solid crust eventually formed over the liquid materials with the cooling process. Over time, cracks developed in the earth's crust, oceans and lakes were formed, and the vapors collecting above the earth led to cloud formations. Pressure and heat in the center of the earth was pushed up through the cracks to create landforms.

The crust of the earth is not a solid shell (Ulin, 2004). Instead, it is made up of huge tectonic plates that drift on top of the soft, underlying mantle. Over long periods of time, these plates change their size as they move both horizontally and vertically. These plates, which range in size from 50 to 250 miles thick, sometimes crash into each other and sometimes separate. It is the movement of these plates that causes earthquakes and volcanoes; that produce ocean trenches and mountain ranges; and that cause continents to drift.

The earth is not now, nor has it ever been, a solid, static entity. It is always in the process of change and modification. In the early years of the earth's formation, there was an enormous range of volcanic activity, as the molten lava in the center of the earth was forced up through cracks and weak spots in the outer crust. It was from this process that the volcanic mountains of the world were formed. And it was because of this constant upheaval in the earth's crust that fossils of ancient marine life may be found at the top of the Rocky Mountains.

Within this dynamic, living planet conditions developed that were favorable to the emergence of life forms. Among the many chemical combinations that are necessary for the creation and maintenance of life, water is clearly the most important one. Water is predominant in all living things, and among humans about 60 percent of their bodies is water. Further, water is a component in the process of photosynthesis that is essential for the production of plant food upon which life depends. Water is the source of oxygen in the atmosphere, provides the sweat that keeps us cool on a hot day, and keeps the climate of the earth from becoming bitterly severe (Greenstein, 1988).

The sun has been called "the light of the world." This is indeed the case. Along with water, the heat from the sun is critical for sustaining both human and nonhuman life. If the sun had been more luminous, the earth would have been intolerably hot, and if the sun had been much cooler, the planet would have been too cold for sustaining human life (Greenstein, 1988). If the furnace of the sun were to go out, or if there were prolonged and significant blockage of the sunlight from reaching the earth, life on this planet would vanish.

The fossil evidence indicates that the earliest life forms appeared about three to four billion years ago. Between the earliest one-celled organisms that were capable of reproduction to the more complex mammals that exist today, there have been many more species than there are stars in the galaxy (Gleich, Maxeinere, and Nicolay, 2002). The fossilized remains suggest an enormous diversity of life forms that existed over the past billion years. The emergence of *Homo sapiens* as a separate and distinct species was a very long and complex process. From the hominids that emerged on the plains of Africa a few million years ago, an evolutionary process resulted in the modern species of *Homo sapiens*. It was perhaps the biological capacity to develop a language, to create cultures, and to form social groups for engaging in problem solving that accelerated the dominance of humans within the animal kingdom. Our species has been around for only about a hundred thousand years. In cosmic time, this brief interval is little more than the blink of an eye.

More than 99 percent of the species that ever lived are now extinct. Since the beginning of life on this planet, there have been several mass extinction events. The most recent occurred about 65 million years ago and has been noteworthy because of an ongoing interest in the extinction of the dinosaurs. But over the past 540 million years, there have been five major extinction events in which 50 percent or more of the existing species became extinct. The fossil evidence suggests that the largest mass extinction took place about 250 million years ago, eliminating 70 percent of the land animals and 95 percent of the marine life.

Because these extinctions occurred in the remote past, it becomes difficult to identify the underlying causal conditions in any given case. It may be that over the past 540 million years, the pathways to species extinction were highly varied. It seems that the major extinctions were produced by sudden and dramatic changes in environmental conditions. The many explanations include violent volcanic eruptions, relatively sudden global warming, cosmic rays, and epidemics. Of these explanations, cosmic collision theory has been one of the more prominent ones in recent years. According to E.O. Wilson (2002), humanity's destruction of the biosphere could cause the extinction of half of all existing species over the next 100 years.

The vulnerability of the planet to cosmic collisions was dramatically displayed by the Tunguska incident of Siberia in 1908. Firsthand observers witnessed a large fireball moving through the sky at an extremely fast speed before it crashed and exploded. The blast could be heard 500 miles away. It took scientists 20 years to identify the major clues to the explosion and its consequences. The epicenter of the crash was located to the north of the Tunguska River. The destruction of the crash covered hundreds of square miles and included thousands of scorched trees pointing outwardly from the center of the crash. The asteroid was 164 feet wide and exploded with a force estimated to be equivalent to a 15-megaton H-bomb (Matthews, 2009).

The discovery of the meteorite impact crater at Chicxulub, Yucatan Peninsula, in Mexico provides confirming evidence of the disappearance of the dinosaurs about 65 million years ago. The impact basin of the crater is about 200 to 300 kilometers wide and is buried beneath 1100 meters of sediment, blocking it from view. Scientists believe that an asteroid about six to twelve miles in diameter produced the impact crater. The consequences were sufficiently severe to produce at least six months of darkness after the collision. This caused a severe drop in global temperatures and about 50 to 70 percent of the world's species disappeared along with the dinosaurs (Sharpton, 1995).

Astronomers have identified an asteroid more than a mile wide that is currently on a course that will likely come within 30,000 miles of the Earth in the year 2028. The chances are that it will be a "close miss," but the margin of error is conceded to be more than 180,000 miles. Within this margin of error, a collision is clearly within the realm of possibility. The collision of an asteroid of this size traveling at a speed of about 17,000 miles an hour would have an impact equivalent to two million atomic bombs of the size dropped on Japan in World War II. If such an asteroid hit one of the oceans, it would create a tidal wave several hundred feet high, and the tsunami would have devastating consequences for the large cities and residential areas located along the coastline. If it struck land, it would blast a crater about 20 miles across and clog the atmosphere with dust and vapor that would darken the sky for several months.

Awareness of the catastrophic effects of celestial collisions has been facilitated by the development and deployment of the Hubble Telescope into outer space. For example, in 1994 astronomers observed the debris from a comet smashing into Jupiter. The largest impact released as much energy as six million H-bombs and left a dark area approximately 7,000 miles across (Matthews, 2009). Many astronomers are of the opinion that it is just a matter of time until another sizable asteroid will collide with the earth. Some are concerned with the importance of research on how to deflect the path of an asteroid headed toward the Earth at 17,000 miles an hour or more.

Mass extinctions permit changes to occur in the dominant species. For example, the extinction of dinosaurs permitted the mammals and birds to become the dominant land animals. According to evolutionary theory, the extinction of a dominant species allows previously secondary life forms to flourish. Their previous predators are no longer around to feed on them. If mammals did coexist with the dinosaurs, they were very small creatures, and nothing like contemporary human beings. Claims by creationists that humans and dinosaurs coexisted lacks credibility within the scientific community. Primates with human-like characteristics emerged only recently, while the last of the dinosaurs disappeared 65 million years ago. If humans and other land-based animals were to become extinct, they would be replaced in a slow evolutionary process by which other species would become dominant.

However, if all life forms were to become extinguished, organic evolution would no longer be continued.

The Nuclear Winter

Daily activities around the world were disrupted by the news bulletin on August 6, 1945, that the city of Hiroshima had been destroyed by an atomic bomb, a new weapon of historically unprecedented proportions. The city of Hiroshima was demolished and the fatalities far exceeded the number that had been expected. Three days later, a second bomb was dropped on the city of Nagasaki. Approximately 200,000 lives were lost from the aerial assaults using nuclear weapons. The bombing of Hiroshima and Nagasaki had provided Americans with the opportunity to avenge the Japanese attack on Pearl Harbor and to bring about a decisive end to World War II. The survivors at Hiroshima and Nagasaki were faced with serious psychological problems from seeing their social worlds instantly vaporized by a weapon about which they had no prior knowledge (Seldon and Seldon, 1989).

The symbolism of the atomic bombing of the Japanese cities goes far beyond the event itself. Nuclear war became endowed with nuances of meaning that include visions of destruction, slow death from radiation sickness, and unexpected disruptions of everyday life. Visions of the mushroom cloud over Hiroshima have become deeply etched into modern consciousness as an indication of the potential consequence of total warfare. Some saw the development of the atomic bomb as unlocking secrets of the universe and its use as resembling the opening of "Pandora's Box." The world could never again be the same (Glynn, 1992).

Some Americans were glad that we were the ones that had developed the bomb, but many wished that it had not been possible for anyone to develop such a weapon. To the military, Hiroshima verified the proposition that a technologically advanced war machine could quickly defeat a less sophisticated and primitive one (Gibson, 1988). Yet to others, Hiroshima provides a model of what can be accomplished through the mobilization of personnel and resources for achieving some specified task.

Levels of anxiety intensified in the early 1950s when President Truman announced the initiation of a crash program to develop the hydrogen bomb. He saw this as necessary for keeping ahead of the Russians in the Cold War. Instead of generating an increased sense of national security, the announcement only intensified awareness of the possibilities of new forms of destruction. Some of the scientists who worked on the Manhattan Project for developing the atomic bomb had second thoughts about their contributions. J. Robert Oppenheimer, the father of the atomic bomb, was strongly opposed to the development of any weapon with an even greater explosive capability (Bird and Sherwin, 2005).

Many of the scientists who worked on developing the atomic bomb suffered intense levels of guilt from their contribution to a research project that resulted in the civilian deaths at Hiroshima and Nagasaki. It had become clear that the scientists who developed the bomb were totally disconnected from the government officials who decided what to do with it. Out of their concerns, the Bulletin of Atomic Scientists created the "Doomsday Clock" to inform the world of the time remaining prior to destruction (McCrea and Markle, 1989). When the Soviet Union exploded their first atomic bomb, the hands on the clock were moved to "three minutes to midnight." When the United States and the Soviet Union tested new nuclear devices within six months of each other in 1953, the doomsday clock was moved to "two minutes to midnight."

Military strategies were devised on each side of the Iron Curtain to assure that neither side could launch a preemptive strike on the other without provoking a retaliatory response with comparable consequences. Retrospective judgments hold that it was a balance of terror that provided the primary source of political stability over the subsequent four decades (Gladdis, 2005). But it was a form of stability that was promoted at the risk of a major catastrophe through a quick and inappropriate launch of a retaliatory response on the basis of an accident or some other form of false information.

The doctrine of "mutually assured destruction" was a deterrence theory maintaining that the threat of annihilation from a retaliatory response would keep each side from launching a nuclear attack (Grinspoon, 1986). Mutual adherence to this doctrine resulted in the escalation of an arms race in which neither side could rest assured that their military capability was adequate. Each adversary was required to invest vast resources in the development of nuclear weapons and increasingly efficient delivery systems. As a result of the threat of nuclear war, men and women throughout the modern world became primarily spectators to a drama that could result in a war being fought and over before they hardly realized that it had started.

By the time of the Cuban Missile Crisis in October 1962, both the United States and the Soviet Union had developed single nuclear weapons with a capacity that exceeded all of the explosives used during World War II. With the face-off over the placement of Soviet missiles in Cuba, the stakes were high and the fate of the world had never before been in so few hands. If the worst possible scenario had been enacted, all traditions, lifestyles and personal relationships would have been irretrievably altered and perhaps ended.

While thousands of people were engaged in the construction of bunker-like fallout shelters in their back yards, several scientists were elaborating on the concept of a "nuclear winter." The debris released into the atmosphere from the explosions of a nuclear war would alter the earth's climate by blocking out the rays of the sun. A rapid drop in temperature would soon result in heavy snowfall covering the millions of burned bodies in metropolitan areas. Drastic environmental changes would occur as temperatures dropped to severely low levels. The plant and animal life upon which humans depend for food would be extinguished (Ehrlich, et al., 1984). If this scenario were to play out, there would be no survivors of an all-out nuclear war.

Appraisals of the aftermath of nuclear war suggested that the planet would become engulfed in "a long darkness," devoid of life forms (Grinspoon, 1986). If this ever occurred, the result would be a human absurdity. The designs and imperatives of the technology to increase national security only resulted in the ultimate insecurity and vulnerability. Since it would be our own end, perceptions of a nuclear holocaust came to be regarded as a form of self-destruction (Lifton and Markusen, 1990).

With the breakup of the Soviet Union and the end of the Cold War, there was a sigh of relief around the world. Americans and Soviets had frightened themselves, each others, and perhaps everyone else by the weapons that had been developed. Controls over the stockpiles of nuclear weapons became a significant problem for both Russia and the United States. While the United States and Russia were engaged in discussions over dismantling nuclear weapons, other nations of the world geared up for the development of their own nuclear weapon capability. From this proliferation, the prospects for an all-out nuclear war again became a probability for some time in the future. The lessons from history indicate that as more sophisticated weapons of war have been developed, they were used sooner or later.

The United States lost out on its major opportunity for the control of nuclear weapons at the end of World War II. At that time, we could have gone to the United Nations and proposed the banning of nuclear weapons in all future wars. The international ban on chemical warfare after World War I had provided a precedent. However, the United States did not want to do this, because at that time, we were the only nation that had nuclear weapons, and we wanted to use them as a threat to the Soviet Union in the event there were any plans for over-running Western Europe. Nevertheless, the Soviet Union developed the capacity for producing nuclear weapons much sooner than we thought possible.

An increasing number of nations are developing nuclear capability, and there is no reason to believe they would not be willing to use them in future warfare. We know from Nazi Germany and the Soviet Union that fanatical leaders are not guided by a concern for basic human values or for the consequences of their policies or actions. Retaliatory responses of the type developed in the ideology of the Cold War could readily set in motion forces leading to the nuclear winter about which many scientists have been concerned.

Catastrophic Pandemic

Of the many potential disasters in the modern world, the dangers and risks in the field of health are foremost. Recent examples of collective fear include the anthrax scare, the fear of mad cow disease, and a potential pandemic from an avian flu outbreak. Rather than focusing on the many positive benefits of modern medicine, there is a tendency to concentrate on the worst-case scenario and to ponder the question of "what if."

Rather than taking pride in the increases in life expectancy or the eradication of smallpox on a worldwide basis, contemplation is frequently directed toward the full range of modern disasters and catastrophes. And rather than thinking in terms of the probability of a particular health disaster, there is a focus in public discourse, especially in the news media, on emphasizing the worst-case scenario (Clarke, 2005).

The combination of urbanization and globalization has greatly increased the probabilities for the evolution and rapid dissemination of deadly viruses and bacteria for which immunities cannot be developed fast enough. The increased density of population in the modern metropolitan areas permits the rapid spread of communicable diseases. The speed of commercial airplanes permits humans to carry disease from one part of the world to all others within a relatively short period of time. The many benefits of international travel for business and pleasure generates a special risk for the rapid spread of communicable diseases.

At the time of the American Revolution, Philadelphia was the second largest English-speaking city in the world, and it had a population of only about 25,000 people. Today most of us think of a community with only 25,000 people as a small town. In contrast, on a typical workday in downtown Manhattan, more than 24 million people occupy an area within a ten-mile radius. In 1800, there were only four cities in the entire world with a population of one or more million people. There are now 24 metropolitan areas of the world with ten million or more people (Neal, 2007). Although the vast improvements in public health have made cities safer places to live, they are especially vulnerable to new and deadly diseases. But in the final analysis, modern societies are so interconnected that regardless of where people live, their lives are deeply affected by the events transpiring in urban areas.

The Malthusian prediction in 1798 held that human population tends to increase until it is held in check by disease, war, disaster, and famine. The Malthusian prediction has taken on a special urgency with the modern fear of a pandemic that would decimate or eliminate the human population. The plagues of earlier times are now drawn upon for insights into what may lie ahead (Kiple, 2005). The influenza virus that emerged in 1918 spread around the world and produced fatalities whose numbers exceeded those of the First World War. The many other plagues of interest to historians include the pandemic centered in Constantinople in the sixth century, the Black Death in 14th-century Europe, the fatal impact on indigenous peoples of the diseases spread through European colonization, and the more recent fatalities from HIV, the AIDs virus.

The Great Plague of London in 1665–66 killed an estimated 70,000 to 100,000 people, or about one-quarter of the population. The dock areas outside of London were the first to be struck by the bubonic plague, which was believed to have been carried to London from Amsterdam by Dutch trading ships infested with rats. The city of London was traumatized, and the royal family as well as wealthy merchants and professionals fled the city (Bell, 1924). The residents of London were further traumatized by the Great Fire, which destroyed the capital city in the year following the plague (Lessor, 1961).

In the sixth century, unidentified microorganisms decimated the most powerful empire in the world. It was the first of several devastating plagues that was to strike Europe. The commercial trade routes from Asia brought more than commodities. They also included microorganisms for breeding deadly diseases for which the indigenous population had no natural immunity. In an historical analysis of the plague, William Rosen (2008) attributed the plague to *Justinian's Flea*. At the time of Justinian's rule, the Roman Empire extended from Italy to North Africa, and the center of its power had shifted to Constantinople. By the time the plague ended, 25 million people had died, and the classical world of Emperor Justinian had plummeted into chaos. The effects of the plague for ending the Roman Empire and initiating the Middle Ages has left an indelible imprint on the history of Europe.

The catastrophe of the Black Death in 14th-century Europe was one of the most calamitous epidemiological events in human history (Dobson, 2007). The bubonic plague was carried over trade routes from central Asia and was disseminated to major ports along the coastal areas of Europe. Within the space of only a few years (1347 to 1352), about a third of the population of Europe died. In some communities the death rate soared to about 80 percent of the population, while in other communities the fatalities were much lower (Kelly, 2005). Plagues over the next 400 years were recurrent and calamitous as they moved from east to west.

Since the germ theory of disease had not yet been established, speculation ran rampant in the causal explanations of the Black Death. Many believed that the plague was the vengeance of a wrathful God who was disappointed with the sins of the world. Others drew upon earthquakes and unusual weather patterns. Yet others attributed the plague to the rot and decay of the rubbish accumulating in the streets or by the foul odors emitted by dung heaps to poison the air. During the plague, another explanation emphasized the intensifying effects of the large number of corpses that accumulated before they could be buried.

While we do not have accurate data on the total fatalities from the flu pandemic of 1918, reasonable estimates place the number of dead somewhere between 50 and 100 million people. The massive scientific investigation undertaken to deal with this problem was the largest ever up until that time. The statistics indicated that young adults had died at extraordinary and alarming rates (Barry, 2005). The greater immunity of older adults stemmed from prior exposure to some form of influenza.

The epidemic spread more rapidly in densely settled populations and among those living in crowded conditions. While the epidemiological aspects of the disease were clarified, many questions about the disease itself remained unsettled.

We now know that the more serious of the epidemics stem from the transmission of disease from animals to humans. Contaminated meat, eggs, and dairy products are indirect sources of infectious diseases. Wild animals, farm animals, and pets are all potential sources of communicable diseases. The infections can be transmitted directly through bites, scratches, or through contact with animal droppings. Bird flu, Ebola, Lyme disease, cholera, sleeping sickness, and yellow fever are among the many infectious diseases transmitted by ticks, mosquitoes, and other animals.

The diseases the Europeans brought with them facilitated the colonization and conquest of the world. For hundreds of years, the Europeans had been exposed to diseases transmitted from such domestic animals as cows, horses, pigs, sheep, and goats. By contrast, the civilizations of the Americas were supported primarily by the domestication of plants rather than animals (Diamond, 1997). The high levels of mortality from contact with Europeans weakened local populations to such an extent that conquest of them was relatively easy. Europeans regarded the voyage of Captain Cook in the late 1700s as a remarkable achievement, yet its spread of disease had disastrous consequences for native populations (Moorehead, 2000).

New strains of swine flu were detected in several countries of the world in the spring of 2009. In response, schools were closed, sports and recreational events were canceled, and several retail establishments closed their doors. The overreaction turned out to be what Marc Siegel (2005) has called a "false alarm." Beliefs about an impending flu pandemic are promoted by the Centers for Disease Control, by the World Health Organization, by the news media, and by the pharmaceutical industries. Promoting a deadly and traumatic script is a way of securing additional funding by drawing on the justification that it is prudent to take protective measures to deal with what might occur. Spreading fear is an effective way of enhancing potential profit and power.

The overuse of antibiotics in the modern world is leading to the emergence of infectious diseases we may not be able to cure. The more often bacteria are exposed to antibiotics, the greater the likelihood that resistant strains will evolve. A large percentage of the antibiotics prescribed by physicians over the past sixty years have been prescribed inappropriately. In agriculture, antibiotics are fed to healthy animals in order to promote their growth and to compensate for unsanitary conditions. Drug-resistant bacteria may be transmitted from animals to humans from eating contaminated meat and from the farm waste runoff that enters our rivers, lakes, and ground water.

The risk of a catastrophic pandemic is greatly intensified by the many forms of globalization which have produced a highly interdependent world. Throughout most of human history, societies were more nearly self-centered and highly isolated from the rest of the world. Today, sophisticated technologies that extend human capabilities bind all of the people of the world together in ways that were not possible a hundred years ago. International travel for business, pleasure, and commerce permits the rapid dissemination of infectious diseases from one part of the world to all others. In this transmission, biotic agents are likely to evolve drug-resistant characteristics.

The Route of the Dinosaurs

Dinosaurs have come to occupy a prominent place in modern consciousness. Schoolchildren are fascinated with the number and variety of dinosaurs that once existed on this planet. We know of them through the limited number of fossilized remains that have been recovered in modern times. The available evidence suggests that the dinosaurs were killed off about 65 million years ago, long before the species of *Homo sapiens* developed on this planet. Along with their disappearance, more than two-thirds of the world animal and plant species joined them in becoming extinct.

The giant lizards in their multiple forms were the earth's dominant species for more than 160 million years. Only a limited number of their fossilized bones remain as vestiges of their times. While scientists are not able to provide definitive explanations of why they disappeared, it appears fairly clear that something deadly and disastrous had occurred. Some believe that a huge meteorite or comet or both hit the earth with sufficient impact that the planet's climate was drastically altered in a short period of time. Others suggest that the dinosaurs may have become victims of the evolution of a deadly virus or microbe to which they had no natural immunity. Yet others maintain that it was intense volcano activity over several years that resulted in blocking out the rays of sunlight. The bulk of the dinosaurs may have turned out to be a lethal characteristic when their food supply became highly limited. If so, they may have died of hunger.

The reign of the dinosaurs provides lessons for the human condition. Our continued existence on this planet depends upon our adaptability to the natural environment. If there are drastic changes in the world's climate, or if the natural environment becomes overly toxic, or if we are unable to develop immunity fast enough to deadly microorganisms that may evolve, or if our food supply becomes drastically limited, we may be destined to travel the route of the dinosaurs. If humans become unwilling or unable to reproduce themselves, we would vanish from this earth in a single generation.

We have a basic desire as humans to use our intelligence in order to assert control and mastery over our own fate. However, in the long-run scheme of things, it may be the greatest of ironies that the human intelligence we value so highly, and that places us in a dominant position within the animal kingdom, may turn out to be a maladaptive characteristic. The brain that permitted us to drastically alter the physical environment, that permitted us to have automobiles and airplanes, that permitted us to develop affluent lifestyles, was also the intelligence that resulted in altering the global environment of the planet earth so drastically that we could no longer live here. If so, we became the primary architects of our own demise. The arrogant assumption that there is a technological fix for any identifiable problem may not be verified during the most drastic of human catastrophes. If so, we will have been active participants in the earth's "sixth extinction" (Kolbert, 2014).

References

Adorno, Theodore W., et al. 1950. *The Totalitarian Personality*. New York: Harper.

Alexander, Jaffrey C. 2004. "On the Social Construction of Moral Universals: The Holocaust from War Crimes to Trauma Dramas." In *Matters of Culture: Cultural Sociology in Practice*, edited by R. Friedland and J. Mohr. New York: Cambridge University Press.

Allen, James. 2000. *Without Sanctuary: Lynching Photography in America*. Santa Fe, NM: Twin Palms.

Alpert, Harry. 1939. *Emile Durkheim and His Sociology*. New York: Columbia University Press.

Alter, Robert. 2005. *Imagined Cities: Urban Experiences and the Language of the Novel*. New Haven, CT: Yale University Press.

Anderson, Benedict. 2001. *Imagined Communities: Reflections on the Origin and Spread of Nationalism*. London: Verso.

Anderson, Walter Truett. 2004. *All Connected Now: Life in the First Global Civilization*. Boulder, CO: Westview Press.

Andre, Claire, and Manuel Velasquez. 1991. "Ethics and the Spotted Owl Controversy." *Issues in Ethics* 4, No 1.

Aneshensel, Carol S. 1992. "Social Stress: Theory and Research." *Annual Review of Sociology* 18: 15–38.

Aneshensel, Carol S., Ralph R. Frerichs, and George J. Huba. 1984. "Depression and Physical Illness." *Journal of Health and Social Behavior* 25: 350–371.

Arendt, Hannah. 1963. *Eichmann in Jerusalem: A Report on the Banality of Evil*. New York: Penguin.

Aron, Raymond. 1955. *The Century of Totalitarian Personality*. New York: Harper.

Aronson, Marc, and John W. Glenn. 2007. *The World Made New: Why the Age of Exploration Happened and How It Changed the World*. Boston: National Geographic.

Barkan, Elazar. 2000. *The Guilt of Nations*. New York: W.W. Norton.

Barry, John N. 2005. *The Great Influenza: The Story of the Deadliest Pandemic in History*. New York: Penguin.

Barthes, Roland. 1997. *Mythologies*. New York: Hill and Wang.

Bauman, Zygmunt. 2010. *Liquid Love*. Malden, MA: Polity Press.

Beck, Aaron T. 1999. *Prisoners of Hate: The Cognitive Basis of Anger, Hostility, and Violence*. New York: HarperCollins.

Becker, Ernest. 1973. *The Denial of Death*. New York: Free Press.

Becker, Howard S. 1960. "Notes on the Concept of Commitment." *American Journal of Sociology* 66: 32–40.

Bell, Walter George. 1924. *The Great Plague in London in 1665*. London: John Lane.

Bellah, Robert N. 1975. "Civil Religion in America." In *Life Style Diversity in American Society*, edited by Saul D. Feldman and George W. Thielbar, 16–34. Boston: Little, Brown.

Ben-Yehuda, Nachman. 1980. "The European Witch Craze of the 14th Century." *American Journal of Sociology* 86: 1–31.

Bengston, Vern L. 1970. "The Generation Gap: A Review and Typology of Social Psychological Perspectives." *Youth and Society* 2: 7–32.

Berger, Peter L. 1969. *The Sacred Canopy.* Garden City, NY: Anchor Books.

_____, ed. 1999. *The Desecularization of the World: Resurgent Religion and World Politics.* Grand Rapids, MI: William B. Eerdmans.

Berger, Peter L., and Anton Zijderveld. 2009. *In Praise of Doubt: How to Have Convictions Without Becoming a Fanatic.* New York: HarperCollins.

Berkowitz, Bruce. 2003. *The New Face of War: How War Will Be Fought in the 21st Century.* New York: Free Press.

Bernikow, Louise. 1986. *Alone in America: The Search for Companionship.* New York: Harper and Row.

Bernstein, Mark H. 2004. *Without a Tear: Our Tragic Relationship with Animals.* Champaign: University of Illinois.

Best, Steven, and Anthony J. Nocella. 2004. *Terrorists or Freedom Fighters? Reflections on the Liberation of Animals.* Brooklyn, NY: Lantern Books.

Bird, Kai, and Martin J. Sherwin. 2005. *American Prometheus: The Triumph and Tragedy of J. Robert Oppenheimer.* New York: Alfred Knopf.

Blackman, Douglas A. 2008. *Slavery by Another Name: The Re-Enslavement of African Americans from the Civil War to World War II.* New York: Anchor Books.

Blumberg, Paul. 1963. "Magic in the Modern World." *Sociology and Social Research* 47: 147–160.

Bock, Allan W. 1996. *Ambush at Ruby Ridge.* Berkeley, CA: Berkeley Publishing Group.

Bourke, Joanna. 2005. *Fear: A Cultural History.* Emeryville, CA: Avalon.

Bowman. Charles K. 1971. "The Anti-Pornography Campaign: A Symbolic Crusade." *Social Problems* 19: 217–237.

Boyer, Paul. 1992. *When Time Shall Be No More: Prophecy Belief in Modern American Culture.* Cambridge, MA: Belknap Press.

Brokaw, Tom. 1998. *The Greatest Generation.* New York: Random House.

Brown, Roger, and James Kulik. 1977. "Flashbulb Memories." *Cognition* 5: 73–99.

Browne, Ray B., and Arthur G. Neal. 2001. *Ordinary Reactions to Extraordinary Events.* Bowling Green, OH: Popular Press.

Campbell, Angus. 1981. *The Sense of Well-Being in America.* New York: McGraw-Hill.

Campbell, Joseph. 1986. *The Power of Myth.* New York: Anchor Doubleday.

Cannon, Walter V. 1972. "Voodoo Death." In *Reader in Comparative Religion,* edited by W.A. Lessa and E.Z. Vogt, 433–439. New York: Harper and Row.

Casland, S. Vernon, Grace E. Cairns, and David C. Yu. 1969. *Religions of the World.* New York: Random House.

Castells, Manuel. 1997. *The Power of Identity.* New York: Blackwell.

Cesarani, David. 2004. *Becoming Eichmann.* Cambridge, MA: Da Capo Press.

Chambers, Whittaker. 1952. *Witness.* New York: Random House.

Chang, Iris. 1997. *The Rape of Nanking: The Forgotten Holocaust of World War II.* New York: Basic Books.

Chaplin, Ralph. 1948. *Rough and Tumble Story of an American Radical.* Chicago: University of Chicago Press.

Chilman, Catherine S., Elam W. Nunnally, and Fred M. Cox, eds. 1988. *Variant Family Forms.* Nuberry Park, CA: Sage.

Chodorow, Nancy. 1979. *The Reproduction of Parenting.* Berkeley: University of California Press.

Clarke, James W. 1998. *The Literature of Wrath: Race, Violent Crime, and American Culture.* New Brunswick, NJ: Transaction.

Clarke, Lee. 2005. *Worst Cases: Terror and Catastrophe in the Popular Imagination.* Chicago: University of Chicago Press.

Crossman, Richard, ed. 2001. *The God That Failed*. New York: Columbia University Press.

Darwin, Charles. 1859. *On the Origin of the Species by Means of Natural Selection*. London: John Murray.

Dawkins, Richard. 2006. *The God Delusion*. Boston: Houghton Mifflin.

DeBoer, Connie. 1978. "The Polls: Abortion." *Public Opinion Quarterly* 41: 553–564.

De Coulanges, Numa-Denys Fustel. 1965. "The Ancient City." In *Reader in Comparative Religion*, edited by W.A. Lessa and E.Z. Vogt, 89–102. New York: Harper and Row.

Dershowitz, Alan M. 2002. *Why Terrorism Works: Understanding the Threat, Responding to the Challenge*. New Haven, CT: Yale University Press.

Diamond, Jared. 1997. *Guns, Germs, and Steel: The Fates of Human Societies*. New York: W.W. Norton.

Dixon, Wheeler Winston. 1999. *Disaster and Memory*. New York: Columbia University Press.

Dobson, Mary. 2007. *Disease: The Extraordinary Stories Behind History's Deadliest Killers*. London: Quercus.

Doering, Susan G., Doris R. Entwisle, and Daniel Quanlan. 1980. "Modeling the Quality of Women's Birth Experiences." *Journal of Health and Social Behavior* 21: 12–21.

Dolin, Eric Jay. 2007. *Leviathan: The History of Whaling in America*. New York: W.W. Norton.

Donnely, Jack. 1989. *Universal Human Rights in Theory and Practice*. Ithaca, NY: Cornell University Press.

Douglas, Mary. 1979. "The Abominations of Leviticus." In *Reader in Comparative Religion*, edited by W.A. Lessa and E.Z. Vogt, 241–244. New York: Harper and Row.

Douglas, Mary, and Aaron Wildavsky. 1983. *Risk and Culture*. Berkeley: University of California Press.

Downton, James V., Jr. 1980. "An Evolutionary Theory of Spiritual Conversion and Commitment." *Journal for the Scientific Study of Religion* 19: 381–396.

Duncan, Hugh Daniel. 1968. *Symbols in Society*. New York: Oxford University Press.

Durkheim, Emile. 1951. *Suicide*. Glencoe, IL: Free Press.

_____. 1961. *The Elementary Forms of the Religious Life*. New York: Collier Books.

Dyer, Joel. 1998. *Harvest of Rage: Why Oklahoma City Is Only the Beginning*. Boulder, CO: Westview.

Edkins, Jenny. 2003. *Trauma and the Memory of Politics*. New York: Cambridge University Press.

Ehrlich, Paul R., Carl Sagan, Donald Kennedy, and Walter Orr Roberts. 1984. *The Cold and the Dark: The World After Nuclear War*. New York: W.W. Norton.

Eisler, Riane. 1995. *Sacred Pleasure: Sex, Myth, and the Politics of the Body*. New York: HarperCollins.

Elder, Glen H. 1974. *Children of the Great Depression*. Chicago: University of Chicago Press.

Eliade, Mircea. 1963. *Myth and Reality*. New York: Harper Torchbooks.

Elliott, Gil. 1972. *The 20th Century Book of the Dead*. New York: Ballantine.

Epstein, Julia. 1990. "Either/Or-Neither/Both: Sexual Ambiguity and the Ideology of Gender." *Gender* 7: 99–142.

Erikson, Kai T. 1966. *Wayward Puritans: A Study in the Sociology of Deviance*. New York: John Wiley.

Farr, Kathryn Ann. 2001. "Women on Death Row: Media Representation of Female Evil." In *Memory and Representation*, edited by D.E. Eber and A.G. Neal. Bowling Green, OH: Popular Press.

Faust, Drew Gilpin. 2008. *The Republic of Suffering: Death and the American Civil War*. New York: Alfred A. Knopf.

Fein, Helen. 1993. *Genocide: A Sociological Perspective*. Newbury Park, CA: Sage.

Ferudi, Frank. 1997. *The Culture of Fear*. Washington, D.C.: Cassell.

Festinger, Leon, Henry W. Rieckens, Jr., and Stanley Schachter. 1956. *When Prophecy Fails*. Minneapolis: University of Minnesota Press.

Feurer, Lewis S. 1969. *The Conflict of Generations*. New York: Basic Books.

Finkelstein, Joanne. 1991. *The Fashioned Self*. Philadelphia: Temple University Press.

Fischer, Claude S. 1981. "The Public and Private Worlds of City Life." *American Sociological Review* 46: 306–318.

Fox, Renee C. 1980. "Evolution of Medical Uncertainty." *The Milbank Memorial Fund Quarterly Health and Society* 58, No. 1:1–49.

Frank, Jerome D. 1964. *Persuasion and Healing*. New York: Shocken Books.

Frankfurter, David. 2006. *Evil Incarnate: Rumors of Demonic Conspiracy and Satanic Abuse in History*. Princeton, NJ: Princeton University Press.

Frankl, Victor E. 1965. *Man's Search for Meaning*. New York: Washington Square Press.

Freud, Sigmund. 1990. *Totem and Taboo*. New York: W.W. Norton.

Fromm, Erich. 1967. *Escape from Freedom*. New York: Avalon Books.

Furedi, Frank. 1997. *Culture of Fear*. Washington, D.C.: Cassell.

Galanter, Marc. 1989. *Cults, Faith Healing, and Coercion*. New York: Oxford University Press.

Gallagher, Richard F. 1961. *Nuremberg: The Third Reich on Trial*. New York: Avon Books.

Gibson, James William. 1988. *The Perfect War: The War We Couldn't Lose and How We Did*. New York: Vintage Books.

Gillin, John. 1958. "Magical Fright." *Psychiatry* 11: 387–400.

Gladdis, John Lewis. 2005. *The Cold War: A New History*. New York: Penguin.

Glassner, Barry. 1989. "Fitness and the Post-Modern Self." *Journal of Health and Social Behavior* 30: 180–191.

_____. 1999. *The Culture of Fear*. New York: Basic Books.

Glazer, Nona, and Helen L. Waehrer. 1977. *Woman in a Man-Made World*. Chicago: Rand McNally.

Gleich, Michael, Dirk Maxeinere, and Fabian Nicolay. 2002. *Life Counts: Cataloguing Life on Earth*. New York: Atlantic Monthly Press.

Glendon, Mary Ann. 2001. *The World Made New: Eleanor Roosevelt and the Universal Declaration of Human Rights*. New York: Random House.

Glynn, Patrick. 1992. *Closing Pandora's Box*. New York: Basic Books.

Goffman, Erving. 1953. *Behavior in Public Places*. New York: Free Press.

Goldhagen, Daniel Jonah. 1996. *Hitler's Willing Executioners: Ordinary Germans and the Holocaust*. New York: Knopf.

Gorer, Geoffrey. 1967. *Death, Grief, and Mourning*. Garden City, NY: Anchor Books.

Grainge, Paul, ed. 2003. *Memory and Popular Film*. New York: Manchester University Press.

Green, Rebecca L. 2000. "Re-Living the Past: Re-Creating the Future." In *Memory and Representation*, edited by D.E. Eber and A.G. Neal, 21–54. Bowling Green, OH: Popular Press.

Greenstein, George. 1988. *Symbolic Universe: Life and the Mind in the Cosmos*. New York: William Morrow.

Gregor, A. James. 1974. *Interpretations of Fascism*. Morrison, NJ: General Learning Press.

Gregory, Neal, and Janice Gregory. 1992. *When Elvis Died*. New York: Pharos.

Grier, William H., and Price M. Cobb. 1969. *Black Rage*. New York: Bantam.

Griffin, David. 2004. *The New Pearl Harbor*. Northhampton, MA: Olive Branch Press.

Grinspoon, Lester, ed. 1986. *The Long Darkness: Psychological and Moral Perspectives on Nuclear Winter*. New Haven, CT: Yale University Press.

Groat, H. Theodore, Evelyn C. Knisely, and Arthur G. Neal. 1975. "Contraceptive Nonconformity Among Catholics."

Journal for the Scientific Study of Religion 14: 367–377.

Gusfield, Joseph R. 1963. *Symbolic Crusades.* Urbana: University of Illinois Press.

Gwartney-Gibbs, Patricia. 1986. "The Institutionalization of Premarital Cohabitation." *Journal of Marriage and the Family* 48: 423–434.

Hallowell, A. Irving. 1975. "Ojibwa Ontology, Behavior, and World View." In *Teachings from the Mother Earth,* edited by Dennis Tedlock and Barbara Tedlock. New York: Liveright.

Hamilton, Edith. 1956. *Mythology: Timeless Tales of Gods and Heroes.* New York: Mentor Books.

Harmer, Ruth Mulvey. 1963. *The High Cost of Dying.* New York: Collier Books.

Harrington, Anne. 2008. *The Cure Within: A History of Mind-Body Medicine.* New York: W.W. Norton.

Hart, William. 2004. *Evil: A History of a Bad Idea from Beelzebub to Bin Laden.* New York: MJF Books.

Harvey, David. 1991. *The Condition of Postmodernity: An Inquiry into the Origins of Cultural Change.* Madden, MA: Blackwell.

Hayes, Diane, and Catherine E. Ross. 1986. "Body and Mind: The Effects of Exercise, Overweight, and Physical Health on Psychological Well-Being." *Journal of Health and Social Behavior* 27: 387–400.

Hendin, Herbert. 1975. *The Age of Sensation.* New York: McGraw-Hill.

Herman, Judith Lewis. 1992. *Trauma and Recovery.* New York: Basic Books.

Hervieu-Leger, Daniele. 2006. "In Search of Certainties: The Paradoxes of Religiosity in Societies of High Modernity." *The Hedgehog Review* 8: 59–68.

Hewitt, Christopher. 2003. *Understanding Terrorism in America from the Klan to Al Qaeda.* New York: Routledge.

Hicks, George. 1994. *The Comfort Women: Japan's Brutal Regime of Enforced Prostitution in the Second World War.* New York: W.W. Norton.

Hillary, George A., Charles J. Dudley, and Paula C. Morrow. 1977. "Toward a Sociology of Freedom." *Social Forces* 565: 685–700.

Hillary, George A., Charles J. Dudley, and Thomas P. Thompson. 1979. "A Theory of Integration and Freedom." *Sociological Quarterly* 20: 551–564.

Hobsbawm, Eric J. 1959. *Primitive Rebels.* Manchester, UK: Manchester University Press.

Hoffer, Eric. 1951. *The True Believer.* New York: Harper & Brothers.

Hoffman, Bill, and Cathy Burke. 1997. *Heaven's Gate: Cult Suicide in San Diego.* New York: Harper Paperbacks.

Horowitz, Tony. 2011. *Midnight Rising: John Brown and the Raid that Spearheaded the Civil War.* New York: Henry Holt.

Hughes, Pinnethorne. 1965. *Witchcraft.* Baltimore, MD: Pelican.

Huntington, Samuel P. 1997. *The Clash of Civilizations and the Remaking of the World.* New York: Touchstone.

Isenberg, Andrew C. 2000. *The Destruction of the Bison: 1750–1920.* New York: Cambridge University Press.

Israel, Joachim. 1971. *Alienation from Marx to Modern Sociology.* Boston: Allyn and Bacon.

Jackson, Kathy Merlock. 1984. "Images of Children in American Film." Ph.D. diss., Bowling Green State University.

Jones, Elsie F., and Charles Westoff. 1978. "How Attitudes Toward Abortion Are Changing." *Journal of Population* 1: 5–21.

Kanter, Rosabeth Moss. 1972. *Commitment and Community: Communes and Utopias in Sociological Perspective.* Cambridge, MA: Harvard University Press.

Kelly, John. 2005. *The Great Mortality: An Intimate History of the Most Devastating Plague of All Times.* New York: HarperCollins.

Kelman, Herbert C., and Lee H. Lawrence. 1972. "An Assessment of Responsibility in the Case of Lt. Calley." *Journal of Social Issues* 28: 177–212.

Kertzer, David L. 1983. "Generation as a Social Problem." *Annual Review of Sociology* 9: 125–149.

Kilduff, Marshall, and Ron Javers. 1978. *Suicide Cults: The Inside Story of the People's Temple Sect and the Massacre in Guyana.* New York: Bantam.

Kimball, Charles. 2002. *When Religion Becomes Evil.* San Francisco: HarperCollins.

King, Gilbert. 2004. *Dirty Bomb: Weapon of Mass Destruction.* New York: Penguin.

Kiple, Kenneth F. 2005. *The Cambridge World History of Human Disease.* New York: Cambridge University Press.

Kirsch, Jonathan. 2006. *A History of the End of the World: How the Most Controversial Book in the Bible Changed the Course of Western Civilization.* San Francisco: HarperCollins.

Knell, Hermann. 2003. *To Destroy a City: Strategic Bombing and Its Consequences in World War II.* Cambridge, MA: Da Capo Press.

Knowles, John H. 1977. *Doing Better but Feeling Worse.* New York: W.W. Norton.

Kolbert, Elizabeth. 2014. *The Sixth Extinction.* New York: Henry Holt.

Koppelman, Susan. 2001. "The Oklahoma City Bombing: Our Responses, Our Memories." In *Ordinary Reactions to Extraordinary Events*, edited by Ray Browne and Arthur G. Neal, 102–121. Bowling Green, OH: Popular Press.

Kurtner, Robert. 1997. *Everything for Sale: The Virtues and Limits of Markets.* New York: Knopf.

Kushner, Harold S. 1983. *When Bad Things Happen to Good People.* New York: Avon.

Lacqueur, Walter. 1987. *The Age of Terrorism.* Boston: Little, Brown.

Landsberg, Allison. 2004. *Prosthetic Memory: The Transformation of American Remembrance in the Age of Mass Culture.* New York: Columbia University Press.

Laufer, Roberta F., and Maxine Wolfe. 1977. "Privacy as a Concept and as a Social Issue." *Journal of Social Issues* 33: 22–42.

Lawson, Jacqueline E. 1989. "She's a Pretty Woman for a Gook: The Misogyny of the Vietnam War." *Journal of American Culture* 12: 55–66.

Lazar, Allan, Dan Karlan, and Jeremy Salter. 2006. *The 101 Most Influential People Who Never Lived.* New York: Harper.

Leach, Edmund R. 1975. "Two Essays Concerning the Symbolic Representation of Time." In *Reader in Comparative Religion*, 4th ed., edited by W.A. Lessa and E.Z. Vogt. New York: Harper and Row.

Lessa, William A., and E.Z. Vogt. 1979. *Reuder in Comparative Religion.* Evanston, IL: Row Peterson.

Lessor, James. 1961. *The Plague and the Fire.* New York: McGraw-Hill.

Lewis, Robert A. 1978. "Emotional Intimacy Among Men." *Journal of Social Issues* 34: 109–121.

Lifton, Robert Jay. 1986. *The Nazi Doctors: Medical Killings and the Psychology of Genocide.* New York: Basic Books.

Lifton, Robert Jay, and Eric Markusen. 1990. *The Genocidal Mentality: Nazi Holocaust and Nuclear Threat.* New York: Basic Books.

Linedecker, Clifford L. 1993. *Massacre at Waco, Texas: The Shocking Story of Cult Leader David Koresh and the Branch Davidians.* New York: St. Martin's.

Linton, Ralph. 1962. "Totemism and the A.E.F." In *Reader in Comparative Religion*, edited by W.A. Lessa and E.Z. Vogt. Evanston, IL: Row Peterson.

Lippmann, Walter. 1961. *Public Opinion.* New York: Macmillan.

Lipset, Seymour Martin. 1963. *The First New Nation.* New York: Basic Books.

Lipstadt, Deborah E. 1993. *Denial of the Holocaust: The Growing Assault on Truth and Memory*. New York: Free Press.

Littleton, C. Scott, ed. 2007. *Mythology: The Illustrated Anthology of World Myth and Story Telling*. New York: Barnes and Noble.

Lowenthal, David. 1985. *The Past Is a Foreign Country*. New York: Cambridge University Press.

Lyng, Stephen. 1990. "Edgework: A Sociological Analysis of Voluntary Risk Taking." *American Journal of Sociology* 95: 851–866.

Mair, Lucy. 1969. *Witchcraft*. New York: World University Library.

Malinowski, Bronislaw. 1954. *Magic, Science, and Religion*. Garden City, NY: Doubleday Anchor.

_____. 1962. *Sex, Culture, and Myth*. New York: Harcourt, Brace & World.

Mannheim, Karl. 1952. "The Problem of Generations." In *Essays in the Sociology of Knowledge*. London: Routledge and Kegan Paul.

Matthews, Robert. 2009. "Catastrophism." *Knowledge* (April): 75–79.

May, Rollo. 1991. *The Cry for Myth*. New York: Delta Books.

McCaghy, Charles H., and Arthur G. Neal. 1973. "The Fraternity of Cockfighters: Ethical Embellishments of a Deviant Sport." *Journal of Popular Culture* 8: 557–569.

McCrea, Francis B., and Gerald E. Markle. 1989. *Minutes to Midnight: Nuclear Weapons Protest in America*. Newbury Park, CA: Sage.

McEvoy, Alan, and Edsel L. Erikson. 1981. "Heroes and Villains." *Sociological Focus* 14: 111–122.

McKibben, Bill. 1993. *The Age of Missing Information*. New York: Plume.

McLuhan, Marshall. 1962. *The Gutenberg Galaxy*. Toronto: Toronto University Press.

Mead, Margaret. 2001. *Sex and Temperament in Three Primitive Societies*. New York: Harpers.

Meadows, Marlo. 1990. "God Loves the Sinner." In *The Search for Meaning*, edited by P.L. Berman. New York: Ballantine.

Miall, Charlene E. 1986. "The Stigma of Voluntary Childlessness." *Social Problems* 33: 268–282.

Milgram, Stanley. 1969. *Obedience to Authority*. New York: Harper.

Millot, Bernard. 1972. *Divine Thunder: The Life and Death of the Kamikaze*. New York: Pinnacle Books.

Mills, C. Wright. 1963. "The Cultural Apparatus." In *Power, People and Politics*. New York: Ballantine.

Mitford, Jessica. 1963. *The American Way of Death*. New York: Simon & Schuster.

Montagu, Ashley. 1970. *The Natural Superiority of Women*. New York: Collier Books.

_____. 1998. *Man's Most Dangerous Myth: The Fallacy of Race*. Lanham, MD: Altamira Press.

Montell, William Lynwood. 1975. *Ghosts Along the Cumberland*. Knoxville: University of Tennessee Press.

Moorehead, Alan. 2000. *The Fatal Impact*. New York: Penguin.

Morrison, Samuel Elliott. 1974. *The European Discovery of America*. New York: Oxford University Press.

Morrow, Lance. 2003. *Evil: An Investigation*. New York: Basic Books.

Mosse, George L. 1990. *Fallen Soldiers: Reshaping the Memory of the World Wars*. New York: Oxford University Press.

Naito, Natsuho. 1990. *Thunder Gods: The Kamikaze Pilots Tell Their Story*. New York: Dell.

Naveh, Eyal. 1993. "He Belongs to the Ages: Lincoln's Image in the American Historical Consciousness." *Journal of American Culture* 16: 49.

Neal, Arthur G. 1970. "Conflict and the Functional Equivalence of Social Movements." *Sociological Focus* 3: 3–12.

_____, ed. 1976. *Violence in Animal and Human Society*. Chicago: Nelson Hall.

_____. 1983. *Social Psychology: A Sociological Perspective*. Reading, MA: Addison-Wesley.

_____. 1985. "Animism and Totemism in Popular Culture." *Journal of Popular Culture* 19: 15–23.

_____. 1998. *National Trauma and Collective Memory: Major Events in the American Century*. Armonk, NY: M.E. Sharpe.

_____. 2005. *National Trauma and Collective Memory*, 2nd ed. Armonk, NY: M.E. Sharpe.

_____. 2007. *Sociological Perspectives on Modernity*. New York: Peter Lang.

Neal, Arthur G., and Sarah F. Collas. 2000. *Intimacy and Alienation: Forms of Estrangement in Female/Male Relationships*. New York: Garland.

Neal, Arthur G., and H. Theodore Groat. 1980. "Fertility Decision Making: Unintended Pregnancies and the Social Drift Hypothesis." *Population and Environment* 3: 221–236.

Neal, Arthur G., H. Theodore Groat, and Jerry W. Wicks. 1989. "Attitudes About Having Children: A Study of Couples in the Early Years of Marriage." *Journal of Marriage and the Family* 51: 313–328.

Neal, Arthur G., and Helen Youngelson-Neal. 1988. "The Folklore of Wall Street: Gamesmanship, Gurus, and the Myth-Making Process." *Journal of American Culture* 11: 52–62.

Newkirk, Ingrid. 2000. *Free the Animals: The Story of the Animal Liberation Front*. Brooklyn, NY: Lantern Books.

The 9/11 Commission Report. 2004. *Final Report of the National Commission on Terrorist Attacks on the United States*. New York: W.W. Norton.

Nuttall, A.D. 2001. *Why Does Tragedy Give Pleasure?* New York: Oxford University Press.

Nytagodien, Ridwan Laher, and Arthur G. Neal. 2004. "Confronting an Ugly Past." *The Journal of American Culture* 27: 375–383.

Opler, Morris E. 1958. "An Interpretation of Ambivalence of Two American Indian Tribes." In *Reader in Comparative Religion*, edited by W.A. Lessa and E.Z. Vogt, 374–389. Evanston, IL: Row, Peterson.

Parsons, Talcott. 1954. *Essays in Sociological Theory*. New York: Free Press.

Payne, Stanley G. 1980. *Fascism*. Madison: University of Wisconsin Press.

Pearlin, Leonard I., and Carmi Schooler. 1978 "The Structure of Coping." *Journal of Health and Social Behavior* 19: 2–21.

Peck, M. Scott. 1998. *People of the Lie: The Hope for Healing Human Evil*. New York: Touchstone.

Perry, Michael J. 1998. *The Idea of Human Rights*. New York: Oxford University Press.

Picart, Caroline J.S., and David A. Frank. 2006. *Frames of Evil: The Holocaust as Horror in American Film*. Carbondale: Southern Illinois University Press.

Pickett, Lynn. 2005. *The Secret History of Lucifer*. New York: Carroll and Graf.

Pinch, Geraldine. 2004. *Egyptian Myth*. New York: Oxford University Press.

Pitts-Taylor, Victoria. 2007. *Surgery Junkies: Wellness and the Pathology in Cosmetic Culture*. New Brunswick, NJ: Rutgers University Press.

Pollan, Michael. 2006. *Omnivore's Dilemma: A Natural History of Four Meals*. New York: Penguin.

Poole, W. Scott. 2004. *Never Surrender: Confederate Memory and Conservatism in the South Carolina Upcountry*. Athens: University of Georgia Press.

Power, Samantha. 2002. *"A Problem from Hell": America and the Age of Genocide*. New York: Basic Books.

Putnam, Robert D. 2000. *Bowling Alone: The Collapse and Revival of American Community*. New York: Simon & Schuster.

Rasmussen, Daniel. 2012. *American Uprisings: The Untold Story of America's Largest Slave Revolt*. New York: Harper Perennial.

Rasmussen, Knud. 1979. "A Shaman's Journey to the Sea Spirit." In *Reader in Comparative Religion*, 4th ed., edited by W.A. Lessa and E.Z. Vogt, 308–311. New York: Harper and Row.

Reaves, Dick J. 1995. *The Ashes of Waco: An Investigation*. New York: Simon & Schuster.

Reik, Theodor. 1973. *The Creation of Eve: A Psychoanalytic Inquiry into the Myth of Eve*. New York: McGraw-Hill.

Reiss, Ira L. 1986. "A Sociological Journey into Sexuality." *Journal of Marriage and the Family* 48: 233–242.

Robinson, Wendy Gale. 1997. "Heaven's Gate: The End." *Journal of Computer-Mediated Communication* 3, No. 3.

Rosen, William. 2008. *Justinian's Flea: The First Great Plague and the End of the Roman Empire*. New York: Penguin.

Rosenthal, Edward C. 2005. *The Era of Choice: The Ability to Choose and Its Transformation of Contemporary Life*. Cambridge, MA: The MIT Press.

Rubin, Lillian B. 1985. *Just Friends*. New York: Harper and Row.

Rummel, R.J. 1994. *Death by Government*. New Brunswick, NJ: Transaction.

_____. 1999. *Statistics of Democide and Mass Murder Since 1900*. London: Lit Verlag.

Rutter, Michael. 2005. *Myths and Mysteries of the Old West*. New York: MJF Books.

Sattel, Jack W. 1976. "The Inexpressive Male: Tragedy or Sexual Politics." *Social Problems* 23: 469–478.

Schmidt, Wilhelm. 1958. "The Nature, Attributes, and Worship of the Primitive High God." In *Reader in Comparative Religion*, edited by W.A. Lessa and E.Z. Vogt, 24–40. Evanston, IL: Row, Peterson.

Schuman, Howard, and Jacqueline Scott. 1989. "Generations and Collective Memories." *American Sociological Review* 54: 359–381.

Schwartz, Barry. 1982. "The Social Context of Commemoration: A Study of

Collective Memory." *Social Forces* 61: 374–402.

_____. 2004. *The Paradox of Choice: Why More Is Less*. New York: Harper Perennial.

Seeman, Melvin. 1975. "Alienation Studies." *Annual Review of Sociology* I: 91–124.

Segall, Alexander. 1976. "The Sick Roll Concept: Understanding Illness Behavior." *Journal of Health and Social Behavior* 17: 162–168.

Seldon, Kykoto, and Mark Seldon, eds. 1989. *The Atomic Bomb: Voices from Hiroshima and Nagasaki*. Armonk, NY: M.E. Sharp.

Shapiro, A.K. 1959. "The Placebo Effect in the History of Medical Treatment." *American Journal of Psychiatry* 116: 298–304.

Sharpton, Virgil L. 1995. "Chicxulub Impact Crater Provides Clues to Earth's History." *Earth in Space* 8, No. 4 (December). Houston, TX: Lunar and Planetary Institute.

Shay, Jonathan. 1994. *Achilles in Vietnam: Combat Trauma and the Undoing of Character*. New York: Atheneum.

Sheler, Jeffrey. 2007. *Believers: A Journey into Evangelical America*. New York: Penguin.

Shibutani, Tomatsu. 1966. *Improvised News*. Indianapolis: Bobbs-Merrill.

Shils, Edward. 1988. *Tradition*. Chicago: University of Chicago Press.

Siegel, Marc. 2005. *False Alarm: The Truth about the Epidemic of Fear*. Hoboken, NJ: Wiley.

Simmel, Georg. 1950. *The Sociology of Georg Simmel*. Ed. and trans. by Kurt Wolff. Glencoe, IL: Free Press.

Singer, Peter. 2001. *Animal Liberation*. New York: Harper Perennial.

Slotkin, Richard. 1994. *Gunfighter Nation: The Myth of the Frontier in Twentieth-Century America*. Norman: University of Oklahoma Press.

Smit, Christopher R. 2001. "Reconstructing the King: Death Narratives of Elvis Presley in the 1980s." In *Ordinary Reactions to Extraordinary Events*, edited by R.B. Brown and A.G. Neal, 73–83. Bowling Green, OH: Popular Press.

Smith, Henry Nash. 2005. *Virgin Land: The American West as Symbol and Myth.* Cambridge, MA: Harvard University Press.

Snell, William E., Jr. 1986. "The Masculine Role Inventory." *Sex Roles* 15: 443–454.

Song, Edward. 2003. "Commodification and Consumer Society." *The Hedgehog Review* 5: 109–121.

Stack, Steven, and Jim Gunlach. 1992. "The Effects of Country Music on Suicide." *Social Forces* 71: 211–218.

Stapelton, Michael. 1986. *Illustrated Dictionary of Greek and Roman Mythology.* New York: Peter Bendrick Books.

Starr, Kevin. 2005. *California: A History.* New York: Modern Library.

Stern, Jessica. 2003. *Terror in the Name of God: Why Religious Militants Kill.* New York: HarperCollins.

Stevenson, Ian. 2000. *Children Who Remember: A Question of Reincarnation.* Jefferson, NC: McFarland.

Stockwell, Edward G., and Arthur G. Neal. 1991. "A Critique of the ZPG Urban Stress Test: On the Uses and Misuses of Social Indicators." *Social Indicators Research* 24: 393–402.

Storm, Michael D., Margaret L. Stivers, Scott M. Lamberts, and Craig Hill. 1981. "Sexual Scripts for Women." *Sex Roles* 7: 699–707.

Taylor, Telford. 1992. *The Anatomy of the Nuremberg Trials.* Boston: Little, Brown.

Tiefer, Leonore. 1995. *Sex Is Not a Natural Act.* Boulder, CO: Westview Press.

Time. "A Nation of Health Worrywarts?" (July 25, 1988): 66.

Turner, R. Jay, and Donald A. Lloyd. 1995. "Lifetime Traumas and Mental Health: The Significance of Cumulative Density." *Journal of Health and Social Behavior* 36: 360–376.

Turner, Ronney E., and Charles Edgley. 1976. "Death as Theater." *Sociology and Social Research* 60: 377–392.

Tuveson, Ernest Lee. 1968. *Redeemer Nation: The Idea of America's Millennial Role.* Chicago: University of Chicago Press.

Twig, Julia. 1981. *The Vegetarian Movement in England, 1847–1981.* Ph.D. diss., London School of Economics.

Tyler, Sir Edward B. (1873) 1924. *Primitive Culture.* London: John Murray.

Ulin, David L. 2004. *The Myth of Solid Ground: Earthquakes, Prediction, and the Fault Line Between Reason and Faith.* New York: Penguin.

Vetter, Harold L., and Gary R. Pearlstein. 1991. *Perspectives on Terrorism.* Pacific Grove, CA: Brooks/Cole.

Wagner-Pacifici, Robin, and Barry Schwartz. 1991 "The Vietnam Veteran's Memorial: Commemorating a Difficult Past." *American Journal of Sociology* 97: 376–420.

Wallace, Anthony F.C. 1966. *Religion: An Anthropological Perspective.* New York: Random House.

Wambach, Helen. 1978. *Life Before Life.* New York: Bantam Paperbacks.

Warner, W. Lloyd. 1962. *American Life: Dream and Reality.* Chicago: University of Chicago Press.

Warren, Rick. 2002. *The Purpose Driven Life.* Grand Rapids, MI: Zondervan.

Weber, Max. 1958. *Essays in Sociology.* Trans. by H.H. Gerth and C. Wright Mills. New York: Oxford University Press.

Weeks, Jeffrey. 1985. *Sexuality and Its Discontents.* New York: Routledge.

Williams, Charles. 1959. *Witchcraft.* New York: Meridian Books.

Williams, Dorie Giles. 1985. "Gender, Masculinity-Femininity and Emotional Intimacy in Same-Sex Relationships." *Sex Roles* 12: 587–600.

Wilson, E.O. 2002. *The Future of Life.* New York: Vintage Books.

Wilson, Eric G. 2008. *Against Happiness: In Praise of Melancholy.* New York: Sarah Crichton Books.

Wolf, Naomi. 1991. *The Beauty Myth: How Images of Beauty Are Used Against Women.* New York: Vintage Books.

Worsley, Peter. 1957. *The Trumpet Shall Sound: A Study of Cargo Cults in Melanesia.* London: McGibbon & Kee.
_____. 1997. *Knowledge, Culture, Counterculture, Subculture.* New York: The New Press.

Yaffe, Steven Lewis. 1994. *The Wisdom of the Spotted Owl.* Washington, D.C.: Island Press.

Zelizer, Barbie. 1992. *Covering the Body: The Kennedy Assassination, the Media, and the Shaping of Collective Memory.* Chicago: University of Chicago Press.

Zurcher, Louis A., Jr., R. George Kirkpatrick, Robert G. Cushing, and Charles K. Bowman. 1971. "The Anti Pornography Campaign: A Symbolic Crusade." *Social Problems* 19: 217–237.

Index